Roman forgeries, or, A true account of false records discovering the impostures and counterfeit antiquities of the Church of Rome / by a faithful son of the Church of England. (1673)

Thomas Traherne

Roman forgeries, or, A true account of false records discovering the impostures and counterfeit antiquities of the Church of Rome / by a faithful son of the Church of England.
Traherne, Thomas, d. 1674.
Written by T. Traherne. Cf. Halkett & Laing (2nd ed.).
First ed. Cf. BM.
Errata: p. [15].
[35], 316 p.
London : Printed by S. and B. Griffin, for Jonathan Edwin ..., 1673.
Wing / T2021
English
Reproduction of the original in the Union Theological Seminary (New York, N. Y.) Library

Early English Books Online (EEBO) Editions

Imagine holding history in your hands.

Now you can. Digitally preserved and previously accessible only through libraries as Early English Books Online, this rare material is now available in single print editions. Thousands of books written between 1475 and 1700 and ranging from religion to astronomy, medicine to music, can be delivered to your doorstep in individual volumes of high-quality historical reproductions.

We have been compiling these historic treasures for more than 70 years. Long before such a thing as "digital" even existed, ProQuest founder Eugene Power began the noble task of preserving the British Museum's collection on microfilm. He then sought out other rare and endangered titles, providing unparalleled access to these works and collaborating with the world's top academic institutions to make them widely available for the first time. This project furthers that original vision.

These texts have now made the full journey -- from their original printing-press versions available only in rare-book rooms to online library access to new single volumes made possible by the partnership between artifact preservation and modern printing technology. A portion of the proceeds from every book sold supports the libraries and institutions that made this collection possible, and that still work to preserve these invaluable treasures passed down through time.

This is history, traveling through time since the dawn of printing to your own personal library.

Initial Proquest EEBO Print Editions collections include:

Early Literature

This comprehensive collection begins with the famous Elizabethan Era that saw such literary giants as Chaucer, Shakespeare and Marlowe, as well as the introduction of the sonnet. Traveling through Jacobean and Restoration literature, the highlight of this series is the Pollard and Redgrave 1475-1640 selection of the rarest works from the English Renaissance.

Early Documents of World History

This collection combines early English perspectives on world history with documentation of Parliament records, royal decrees and military documents that reveal the delicate balance of Church and State in early English government. For social historians, almanacs and calendars offer insight into daily life of common citizens. This exhaustively complete series presents a thorough picture of history through the English Civil War.

Historical Almanacs

Historically, almanacs served a variety of purposes from the more practical, such as planting and harvesting crops and plotting nautical routes, to predicting the future through the movements of the stars. This collection provides a wide range of consecutive years of "almanacks" and calendars that depict a vast array of everyday life as it was several hundred years ago.

Early History of Astronomy & Space

Humankind has studied the skies for centuries, seeking to find our place in the universe. Some of the most important discoveries in the field of astronomy were made in these texts recorded by ancient stargazers, but almost as impactful were the perspectives of those who considered their discoveries to be heresy. Any independent astronomer will find this an invaluable collection of titles arguing the truth of the cosmic system.

Early History of Industry & Science

Acting as a kind of historical Wall Street, this collection of industry manuals and records explores the thriving industries of construction; textile, especially wool and linen; salt; livestock; and many more.

Early English Wit, Poetry & Satire

The power of literary device was never more in its prime than during this period of history, where a wide array of political and religious satire mocked the status quo and poetry called humankind to transcend the rigors of daily life through love, God or principle. This series comments on historical patterns of the human condition that are still visible today.

Early English Drama & Theatre

This collection needs no introduction, combining the works of some of the greatest canonical writers of all time, including many plays composed for royalty such as Queen Elizabeth I and King Edward VI. In addition, this series includes history and criticism of drama, as well as examinations of technique.

Early History of Travel & Geography

Offering a fascinating view into the perception of the world during the sixteenth and seventeenth centuries, this collection includes accounts of Columbus's discovery of the Americas and encompasses most of the Age of Discovery, during which Europeans and their descendants intensively explored and mapped the world. This series is a wealth of information from some the most groundbreaking explorers.

Early Fables & Fairy Tales

This series includes many translations, some illustrated, of some of the most well-known mythologies of today, including Aesop's Fables and English fairy tales, as well as many Greek, Latin and even Oriental parables and criticism and interpretation on the subject.

Early Documents of Language & Linguistics

The evolution of English and foreign languages is documented in these original texts studying and recording early philology from the study of a variety of languages including Greek, Latin and Chinese, as well as multilingual volumes, to current slang and obscure words. Translations from Latin, Hebrew and Aramaic, grammar treatises and even dictionaries and guides to translation make this collection rich in cultures from around the world.

Early History of the Law

With extensive collections of land tenure and business law "forms" in Great Britain, this is a comprehensive resource for all kinds of early English legal precedents from feudal to constitutional law, Jewish and Jesuit law, laws about public finance to food supply and forestry, and even "immoral conditions." An abundance of law dictionaries, philosophy and history and criticism completes this series.

Early History of Kings, Queens and Royalty

This collection includes debates on the divine right of kings, royal statutes and proclamations, and political ballads and songs as related to a number of English kings and queens, with notable concentrations on foreign rulers King Louis IX and King Louis XIV of France, and King Philip II of Spain. Writings on ancient rulers and royal tradition focus on Scottish and Roman kings, Cleopatra and the Biblical kings Nebuchadnezzar and Solomon.

Early History of Love, Marriage & Sex

Human relationships intrigued and baffled thinkers and writers well before the postmodern age of psychology and self-help. Now readers can access the insights and intricacies of Anglo-Saxon interactions in sex and love, marriage and politics, and the truth that lies somewhere in between action and thought.

Early History of Medicine, Health & Disease

This series includes fascinating studies on the human brain from as early as the 16th century, as well as early studies on the physiological effects of tobacco use. Anatomy texts, medical treatises and wound treatment are also discussed, revealing the exponential development of medical theory and practice over more than two hundred years.

Early History of Logic, Science and Math

The "hard sciences" developed exponentially during the 16th and 17th centuries, both relying upon centuries of tradition and adding to the foundation of modern application, as is evidenced by this extensive collection. This is a rich collection of practical mathematics as applied to business, carpentry and geography as well as explorations of mathematical instruments and arithmetic; logic and logicians such as Aristotle and Socrates; and a number of scientific disciplines from natural history to physics.

Early History of Military, War and Weaponry

Any professional or amateur student of war will thrill at the untold riches in this collection of war theory and practice in the early Western World. The Age of Discovery and Enlightenment was also a time of great political and religious unrest, revealed in accounts of conflicts such as the Wars of the Roses.

Early History of Food

This collection combines the commercial aspects of food handling, preservation and supply to the more specific aspects of canning and preserving, meat carving, brewing beer and even candy-making with fruits and flowers, with a large resource of cookery and recipe books. Not to be forgotten is a "the great eater of Kent," a study in food habits.

Early History of Religion

From the beginning of recorded history we have looked to the heavens for inspiration and guidance. In these early religious documents, sermons, and pamphlets, we see the spiritual impact on the lives of both royalty and the commoner. We also get insights into a clergy that was growing ever more powerful as a political force. This is one of the world's largest collections of religious works of this type, revealing much about our interpretation of the modern church and spirituality.

Early Social Customs

Social customs, human interaction and leisure are the driving force of any culture. These unique and quirky works give us a glimpse of interesting aspects of day-to-day life as it existed in an earlier time. With books on games, sports, traditions, festivals, and hobbies it is one of the most fascinating collections in the series.

The BiblioLife Network

This project was made possible in part by the BiblioLife Network (BLN), a project aimed at addressing some of the huge challenges facing book preservationists around the world. The BLN includes libraries, library networks, archives, subject matter experts, online communities and library service providers. We believe every book ever published should be available as a high-quality print reproduction; printed on-demand anywhere in the world. This insures the ongoing accessibility of the content and helps generate sustainable revenue for the libraries and organizations that work to preserve these important materials.

The following book is in the "public domain" and represents an authentic reproduction of the text as printed by the original publisher. While we have attempted to accurately maintain the integrity of the original work, there are sometimes problems with the original work or the micro-film from which the books were digitized. This can result in minor errors in reproduction. Possible imperfections include missing and blurred pages, poor pictures, markings and other reproduction issues beyond our control. Because this work is culturally important, we have made it available as part of our commitment to protecting, preserving, and promoting the world's literature.

GUIDE TO FOLD-OUTS MAPS and OVERSIZED IMAGES

The book you are reading was digitized from microfilm captured over the past thirty to forty years. Years after the creation of the original microfilm, the book was converted to digital files and made available in an online database.

In an online database, page images do not need to conform to the size restrictions found in a printed book. When converting these images back into a printed bound book, the page sizes are standardized in ways that maintain the detail of the original. For large images, such as fold-out maps, the original page image is split into two or more pages

Guidelines used to determine how to split the page image follows:

• Some images are split vertically; large images require vertical and horizontal splits.
• For horizontal splits, the content is split left to right.
• For vertical splits, the content is split from top to bottom.
• For both vertical and horizontal splits, the image is processed from top left to bottom right.

Roman Forgeries

Or a TRUE

ACCOUNT

OF

FALSE RECORDS

Difcovering the

IMPOSTURES

AND

Counterfeit Antiquities

OF THE

CHURCH

OF

ROME.

By a Faithful son of the Church of ENGLAND. 1704

LONDON,
Printed by *S.* and *B. Griffin,* for *Jonathan Edwin* at
the three Rofes in *Ludgate-Street,*

1 Tim. 4. 2.

Speaking lies in Hypocrisie, having their Conscience seared with an hot iron.

2 Tim. 3. 8, 9.

Now as Jannes and Jambres withstood Moses, so do these also resist the truth: men of corrupt minds, reprobate concerning the Faith.

But they shall proceed no further: for their folly shall be manifest unto all men, as theirs also was.

TO THE
RIGHT HONORABLE
Sr *ORLANDO BRIDGEMAN*
K<small>NIGHT</small> and B<small>ARONET</small>

One of

HIS MAJESTIES

Moſt Honourable Privy Council ;

The AUTHOR

Devoteth his beſt Services

AND

DEDICATETH

The VSE and BENEFIT of his
Enſuing Labors.

A Premonition.

THe Bishops of Rome, *in the persons of* Zozimus, Boniface, and Celestine, *Successively* opposed the Sixth Council of Carthage, *consisting of* 217 *Fathers (among whom the great* S. Augustine *is acknowledged to be one* :) *in the matter of* * Appeals : *which was the first step made by that irregular Chair, to the* Exorbitant Supremacy *which they afterward claimed.* In *vindicating that* Claim *before the* Council, *they produced two counterfeit* Canons, *fathered upon the* Occumenical Synod *at* Nice; *which were by the Records of* Carthage, Alexandria *and* Constantinople, *in the presence of all those* Fathers, *in the fixth Council of Carthage, detected to be forgeries, as well as by the Tenor of the undoubted Canons of the* Nicene Council *it self.*

A 3 *which*

* *viz* From all the world to the *Rom* Chair.

which are contrary to those by the
Roman Church *pretended*; and so
they were esteemed by the Fathers in
that sixth Council, who were start-
led at the sight of those New unheard
of Monsters, at their first Publication,
above 1200 years ago.

Upon this Passage, I redoubled in
the Book an observation (to make it
more remarkable,) which you will
find cap. 2. pag. 9. to this purpose,
That in the first General Council
of *Nice* it was ordered, that the
chief in every Province should confirm the Acts of his inferior Bishops; And if any Trouble did
arise which could not be decided
by the Metropolitan, Provision
was made Can. 5. (in words so
clear and forcible, that none more
plain can be put into their places)
that the last Appeal should be made
to Councils, and that the *Person*
condemned in any Province should
not

not be received, if he fled to others. *That Parenthefis (In words fo clear and forcible, that none more plain can be put in their places)* *relates to the* CANON *it felf: which here follows that you may fee how forcible it is, and how much plainer then the very Words into which I had contracted it. It is worthy your Confideration, as one of the moft Important Records in Antiquity, confented to by all the Popifh Compilers of the Councils themfelves.*

Can. 5. Concerning thofe that are Excommunicated, whether in the order of the Clergy or the Laitie, by the Bifhops in every feveral province, let the Sentence prevail according to the Canon, that they who are caft out by fome, be not received by others ; But let it be required that no man be excluded the Congregation, by the Pufillanimitie, or contention, or any

This is the Canon oppofed by the Forgeries.

A 4   fuch

such vice of the Bishop. That this therefore might more decently be inquired into, we think it fit, that Councils should every year throughout every Province twice be celebrated, that such Questions may be discussed by the Common Authority of all the Bishops assembled together. And so they that have evidently offended against their Bishop, shall be accounted Excommunicated according to reason, by all; till it pleaseth the Community of Bishops to pronounce a milder Sentence on such But let the Councils be held, the one before the *Quadragesima* before Easter, that all dissention being taken away, we might offer a most pure Gift unto God: and the second about the middle of Autumn.

Had the Canon said, The last Appeal shall be made to Councils; *they that are accustomed to such shifts without blushing*

A PREMONITION.

blushing, might easily have evaded the Words, by affirming the Bishop of Rome to be particularly excepted, without any need of expressing the exception; because by the general and Tacit Consent of all, he is above the Limits of such Laws, and above the Authority of that, and all other Councils. Thus they might still render the matter doubtful by their Subterfuges and Pretences; as indeed they do, in evading one expression of the Canon it self. For whereas the Fathers say, Let the Sentence prevail according to the Canon, that they, who are cast out by some, be not received by others: Those Popish Hirelings make an exception of the Bishop of Rome, where the Oecumenical Synod maketh none: and might as well except him here, though the Council had said in terms, The last Appeal shall be made to Councils. For the last Appeal to any subordinate Authority, over which the Council had any Legislative Power, was ordered, they
                                             might

might *fay to be made to Councils:* But *the* Bifhop *of* Rome *being the Head of the Church, and having the fupreme Authority over all Councils,* was not *thought of in this Canon:* nor was it fit *he fhould be at all mentioned,becaufe that would imply he* was under *their authority.* The Prodigious Height of *their* ufurped Claim *being their fole Defence ,and their incredible* Boldnef *the amazement of ignorant People,which is their chief fecurity.*

But the Council *adding to the former expreffion this claufe,* That Councils fhould every year, throughout every Province, twice be celebrated, (*for this very end*)that fuchQueftions may be difcuffed by the common authority of all the Bifhops affembled together : *it puts an end to the bufinefs : efpecially when they add,* That they who have evidently offended their Bifhop, fhall be accounted excommunicated according to reafon,

till

till it pleaseth the community of Bishops to pronounce a milder Sentence. *But that which renders it most plain and forcible, is this,* Let the Councils be held, the one before the *Quadragesima* before Easter, that all Dissention being taken away, we might offer a most pure Gift unto God. And the second about the middle of *Autumn, All the wit in the world could not have invented a more clear and apparent* provision, *against* the Roman Bishops *absurd and impudent* Pretences. *No Evasion (I think) can possibly be made there from; when it is once noted and understood.* For the Bar put in against the Pope, *is not here in* Words, *but* Things. *It implies that the Controversie must before* Easter *be fully determined: The very end of calling such a Council, and holding it* then, *being* the taking away of all dissention, that we might offer up a most pure Gift *or Sacrifice* to God:

A PREMONITION.

God : *that is, That Unity being resto-*
red to the Church at that time, we might
receive the Sacrament *in Peace and*
Charity. *Whereas, if after the Sentence*
of the Council, *the businesse were to be*
carried to the Court of Rome ; *Suits and*
Quarrels *could not be ended against* Easter, *but would be lengthened in many*
Provinces, *beyond* Easter; *both by rea-*
son of the Seas *and* Regions, *to be pas-*
sed over by old and Crazy Persons, such
as the venerable Bishops were, before
they could come from their own Coun-
tries to the Roman Chair ; *and by*
those Prolatory delays they might find
there, the matter being wholy referred
to the Popes pleasure.

The Variation *of the* Letter *in the*
Book, *made my* Note *on this place look*
too like the Text *of the* Council *it self;*
which for as much as it happened in a
most weighty Place, *I could not with a*
good Conscience *let it pass, without ac-*
quainting the Pious Reader *with the*
same

A PREMONITION.

same. Though the Letter *of the* Canon *it self (to prevent mistakes) is faithfully translated afterwards* page 26, *and* 27. *Yet without giving this* Glofs *upon the* Canon ; *which was the occasion of this* Præmonition, *because so necessary to a clear and full understanding of all the procedure.*

This Note *is the more* weighty, *because the* Nicene Council *is confessed on* both sides, *(by us for its own sake and its conformity to the* Scriptures, *by the* Papists, *for the* Popes, *that have ratified it,) to be of* great Authority ; *next to the* Holy Bible, *the very first, and most indisputable that is. Yet this* Canon *laid in the foundation, utterly overthrowes all the following* Pretences *and* Forgeries *of the* Roman Bishops. *Which I beseech the* Reader *to examine more perfectly. For though by many* Arts *and long* Succeffes, *the* Bishop of Rome *has ascended to an* Ecclesiastical Supremacy ; *and a subtile* Train *of* Doctrines, *is laid, to make him the* Uni-

A PREMONITION.

verſal Monarch of the World, *as much higher then the Emperour*, as the Sun is greater than the Moon, *as they expreſſe it : Yet the Sentence of an* Eminent ✳ Divine *well* acquainted *with theſe* Affairs *in a late Sermon preached before the* Lord Mayor *and* Court of Aldermen *in the City of* London, *and now publiſhed, is very true*, ✳ The Supremacy of the Roman Church was a meer Uſurpation, begun by Ambition, advanced by Forgery, and defended by Cruelty.

✳ Dr. Still.
Sermon on
Acts 24. 17.
pag. 46.

ERRATA.

THe Reader before he enters upon the Book is deſired to correct theſe, as the principal Errata's, with his Pen. Page 35 line 15 dele *now* p. 43 l. 21 r. *love of the world that.* p. 55 for *Councils* r. *Stateſmen* p. 66 l. 16 aſt. *Magdenburg* r. *and.* p. 82 l. 21 for 1635 r. 1535. p. 104 l. 16 for *fit* r. *fift.* p. 107 l. 1 for 1618 r. 1658. p. 109 adde in the Margin 11. p. 137 l. 7 r *Right uſe of the Fathers.* p. 157 l. ult. r. *Tranſeunt.* p. 172 Cap. 15. Contents : for *Falſity* r. *Falſely.*

AN

ADVERTISEMENT

TO THE

READER.

Irenæus, one of the most Ancient Fathers, Scholar to S. *Polycarp*, S. *John's* Disciple, in his Book against Heresies, giveth us four notable marks of their Authors: First, he sheweth how they disguize their Opinions; *Errour never shews It Self,* Iren. P *saith he, left it should be taken naked; but* em. *is artificially adorned in a splendid Mantle, that it may appear truer than Truth it self, to the more unskilful.* 2. That *having* Lib. 1. *Doctrines which the Prophets never preach-* cap. 1. *ed, nor God taught, nor the Apostles delivered, they pretend unwritten Traditions: Ex non Scriptis legentes, as he phraseth it.* 3. *They make a Rope of Sand, that* III. *they may not seem to want Witnesses; passing over the Order and Series of Writings, and as much as in them lies, loosing the Members of the Truth, and dividing them*

B   *from*

*from each other : for they chop and change,
and making one thing of another, deceive
many,* &c. But that which I chiefly intend is the fourth ; *They bring forth a vast
multitude of Apocryphal and Spurious Writings, which themselves have feigned, to
the amazement of Fools ; and that those
may admire them, that know not the Letters (or Records) of the Truth.* How far
the Papists have trodden the foregoing
Paths, it is not my purpose to unfold, only the last, the Heretical pravity of *Apocryphal and Spurious Books* ; how much
they have been guilty of imposing on the
World by *feigned Records,* I leave to the
evidence of the ensuing Pages ; which I
heartily desire may be answerable to the
Merit of so great a Cause.

Vincentius Lirinensis, another eminent
Father, praised by *Gennadius,* died in the
time of *Theodosius* and *Valentinian.* He
wrote a Book *against Heresies* in like manner ; wherein preparing Furniture and
Instructions against their Wiles, he at first
telleth us, that *the Canon of the Scripture
is alone sufficient :* Then, that *the concur-
rence of the Fathers is to be taken in, for
the more clear certainty of their sense and
meaning.* Upon this latter point he saith
afterwards, *But neither are all Heresies to
be*

be *aſſaulted this way, nor at all times, but* Vin. Lir
only ſuch as are New and Green: to wit, ^{cap} 39.
*when they firſt ſpring up, before they have
falſified the Rules of the Ancient Faith,
while they are hindered by ſtraitneſs of
time, and before (the Poyſon ſpreading a-
broad) they have endeavoured to corrupt
the Writings of the Fathers.* So that Hereticks have inclination enough, where
they are not *hindered by ſtraitneſs of time,*
to *corrupt* the moſt Ancient *Writings* of
the Church *:* For which cauſe he further
ſaith in the ſame place, *But Hereſies that* ibid.
*are ſpread abroad, and waxen old, muſt not
be ſet upon in this ſort, becauſe by long
continuance they have had opportunity to
ſteal away the Truth. Whatſoever Profane-
neſſes there be therefore, either of Schiſmes
or Hereſies that are grown Ancient, we
ought in no caſe otherwiſe to deal with
them than either to convince them, if it
be needful, by the Authority of the Scriptures only; or at leaſt to avoid them, as
convicted of old, and condemned by Univerſal Councils.*

In this Admonition the Father informs
us of two things *:* Firſt, that it is poſſible for *Errour to prevail and ſpread a-
broad;* to *continue long,* and *wax old :* Secondly, that having gotten poſſeſſion of

Books

Books and Libraries, it may *falsifie th*
Rules of the Ancient Faith and steal away
the Truth, by corrupting the Writings o
the Fathers. In which case, he will not
have the Controversie decided by the
Fathers, but by the *Scriptures only,* or by
old *Universal Councils.*

But if *Errour* proceed so far, as to corrupt the *Councils* too, then of necessity
we must have recourse to some other re-
medy; either to the *Scriptures alone,* as
he directeth; or else we must detect the
frauds, whereby the *Councils* themselves
are *falsified:* For that they are liable to
the same inconvenience, is evident, both
by the paucity of Ancient Records, and
the many Revolutions that have been in
the World: especially since Nature teach-
eth men to strike at the Root, attempts
are more apt to be made upon *them,* because Hereticks are prone to be most busie in undermining the *Foundation.*

That it is possible for men so far to act
against their Consciences, as to *corrupt*
the Ancient Records of Truth, you see by
the premises: and that it is an easie thing
for them to effect it, that have gotten all
kind of Books and Libraries into their
hands, is apparent; because they that
keep them, order them as they please:

So that if Hereticks be the Lords and Masters of them, for many Ages together, we may not rashly adventure our Salvation upon their *own* Records: All the World knows, that the Church of *Rome* had all the Libraries of these *Western parts*, for many Ages, in her power; & that the *Eastern parts* are swallowed up by the Deluge of *Mahumetanism:* All that can seem harsh, is, that she that pretendeth her self the *Catholick Church*, should be guilty of *Heresie*. But if the property of *falsifying the Fathers and Councils* may pass for a Badge of *Heresie*, there will no greater *Hereticks* be found in the world, than those who stile themselves falsly *Catholicks*. For as the sight of the possibility of such a thing made *Vincentius* talk more like a *Prophet* than a *Father*, the Church of *Rome* hath so behaved her self since his departure, as if she intended eminently to fulfil his Predictions: which will in the process of our Discourse be made evident to the pious and Christian Reader.

S. *Bernard* lived to see the accomplishment of that which *Lirinensis* feared; for he flourished in the Eleventh Age of the Church, when the Pope and his Chair were mounted up to the top of their

B 3   Height

Height and Grandeur; and bearing a
impartial Testimony, he wrote man
things against their Enormities: The V
ces of their Popes, with those of all c
ther Orders and Degrees of men in th
Church of *Rome*, he inveyeth against a
large, in his 33. Sermon upon the *Canti*
cles; smartly touching their *Vain-glory*
Pomp, Luxury, Avarice, Simony, Usurpa
tion, and *Incorrigibleness*: so that for an
Piety or *Conscience* in them, such *fraud*
might easily be digested. He distinguishe
the State of the Church into four severa
periods, or four different times; to eac.
of which he annexeth one peculiar temp
tation: *Terrour* in the *Night* of Persecu
tion, *Errour* in the *Morning* of her Peace
the heat of Lust, and the glaring splen
dour of Riot and Excess, beautified witl
Riches, and varnished over with *Hypocri*
sie in the *Noon* of her prosperity, and th
Guile of Deception in the *Evening*; wher
with great vehemence, and impatien
z , he speaketh *thrice* in little room, o
a certain *business walking in the dark*. Nov
a little before his time, and not long af
ter the second *Nicene* Council, that *Far*
del of Forgeries came forth under th
Name of *Isidore*, which seduced all th
late *Collectors* of the Decrees and Coun
cils,

cils, which have rifen up among the Papifts (at leaft if they have not been wil-
ful *corrupters* of the Records themfelves,
which is much to be feared) and difcovered a defign (probably) to S. *Bernard*
alfo, that was then on foot in the Court
of *Rome*, to alter and deface the *Monuments of Antiquity:* For *Riculphus*, the
Archbifhop of *Mentz*, who firft fcattered
thofe Forgeries abroad, and *Benedictus
Levita*, who firft put them into the *Capitular* Books of the Kings of the *Franks*,
and *being confcious of their weaknefs, got
them confirmed by the Avthority of the*
Roman Chair. *Hincmarus Laudunenfis*
alfo, whom *Baronius* calleth *Noviffimum
ufque ad hæc Tempora Collectorem, The laft
Collector of the Councils, till his own Age.*
All thefe lived before S. *Bernards* time:
So did *Hincmarus*, Archbifhop of *Rhemes*,
who *having a more fagacious Nafiril than
ordinary, as Baronius* obferves, did firft attempt the detection of the fraud, and was
accufed for the fame, and that fo rough-
ly, that as *Baronius* further notes out of
Frodoardus his Hiftory of *Rhemes*, he was
forced to recant; and though he did it,
he was marked with Infamy, for having
attemqted to reprove them. S. *Bernard*
therefore having fuch a Mirrour before

B 4   his

his eyes, speaking covertly for his own *preservation*, yet plainly enough for the Authors *Conviction*, among other notorious and open Abominations, seemeth to strike at this in particular: For shewing the State of the Church to be more miserable under the Pompous Hypocrisie of the *Popes*, than either in the night of persecution under *Heathen* Tyrants, or in the conflicts of *Hereticks* that sprang up in the morning, in the midst of the brightness of that *Glaring Noon*, he talks of, *a work going on in the dark*, a design privily carried on by the instigation and procurement of the *Noon-day Devil, that should shortly after appear to seduce the rest, if there be any in Christ,* (saith he,) *abiding yet in their simplicity: For he hath swallowed up the Floods of the Wise, and the Rivers of the Mighty, and trusteth in himself: that he can take* Jordan *into his mouth, that is, the simple and the lowly that are in the Church.* Which immediately following that *business walking in the dark,* makes me to believe, that he looked upon that *business* as the *Engine* of their *Deception*; which gave him the Hint, to speak by way of Prophesie, concerning the *fourth Temptation* that was yet to come, in the Churches Declension;

on ; and which he exprefly noteth to be
the immediate means of opening the way
for Antichrift to appear. His words are
very Poinant and Emphatical : *It was*
bitter at firft in the Death of Martyrs , Ibid,
more bitter in the conflict of Hereticks ,
but now moft bitter in the manners of Do-
mefticks : She cannot put them to flight,
fhe cannot fly them, they are fo multiplied
upon her : The Plague of the Church is in
the Entrails, and incurable ; therefore its
bitternefs is moft bitter in its peace. But
in what peace ? It is peace , and it is not
peace ; peace from Pagans, *and peace from*
Hereticks, *but truly none from her* Children : *The voice of weeping is in that*
time ! I have nourifhed children, and ex-
alted them , but they have defpifed me !
They have defpifed and defiled me with
their filthy life, their filthy gain, their filthy
commerce ; and finally, with that bufinefs
walking in darknefs. *It remains now that*
the Noon-day Devil fhould appear to feduce
the reft , if there be any in Chrift abiding
yet in their fimplicity.

That S. *Bernard* intended this, is only
my conjecture ; becaufe whatfoever he
fpake againft, under that Title of *Dark-*
nefs , he chofe *obfcure terms,* as it fhould
feem on purpofe : for that *bufinefs* is *Ar-*
canum

canum Imperii, the Great *Myftery of the Roman Chair*, the Popes *Palladium*, not to be feen with profane eyes; nay, the very *Ark* of his *Moft Holy Place*, to be lookt into by none but his own *faithful* Priefts : It was Death to look into it with *fufpitious eyes*, or to expofe it to thofe of the people   Where we may further obferve, that as a Serpent hideth her head, and expofeth any of her members, for the prefervation of that, to the ftroaks of her Enemy ; fo doth the Church of *Rome* defire more to conceal this *Grand Art of counterfeiting Ecclefiaftical Antiquities*, than any other points lefs *Radical* and *Vital* : All other Controverfies are but fuperficial blinds, more freely expofed to her Enemies debates, that mens eyes may be turned another way from this *Arcanum*, which is with all endeavour hidden from the people : And for this caufe they find it better to buy up the *Editions*, than anfwer the *Difcoveries*; which makes Dr. *James* his Treatife, and *Blondels Pfeudo-Ifidorus*, fo rare among the people.

Matters of Fact may be manifeft enough, where the means of contriving them remain unknown : a conjecture in a circumftance therefore deftroys not the Foundation.

Foundation. You will find other kinds of Arguments in the subsequent *Epitome*, than bare conjectures. In the mean time, be pleased to remember, that the Papists have had all kind of Books, nay, and Libraries in their hands; that the Roman Clergy (especially those that attend the Chair) have Glory, Wealth, and Pleasure enough to tempt them to such endeavours; that the Pope hath Power enough to reward his *Creatures*, and that they have actually endeavoured to corrupt such Books by their *Indices Expurgatorii*, as also to put forth Apocryphal and Spurious Pieces; which Dr. *Reynolds*, Dr. *James*, Bishop *Jewel*, and the Learned *Crashaw*, as well as the *Indices* themselves, do evidently declare. It shall here appear more clearly, that they have adulterated all by *Counterfeit Records*; the very places and things corrupted, being themselves produced, detected, and reproved.

I shall not descend into the latter Ages, but keep within the compass of the first 420 years, and lay open so many of their *frauds*, as disguize and cover the face of *Primitive Antiquities*, which ought to be preserved most sacred and pure. It is sufficient to prove, that all
the

the *Streams* are infected by the *Poyson* that is thrown into the *Fountain-head*; and to expatiate downwards, would over-swell the *Book*, which is intended to be little, for the use and benefit of all. Neither shall I talk of the Fathers at large: I will not meddle with their *Amphilochius, Abdias, S. Denis, &c.* but keep close to *Records*, and *publick instruments of Antiquity*, which have the force of *Laws*: Such as *Apostles Canons, Decretal Epistles*, and *Ancient Councils*; which they have either depraved by altering the Text, or falsified, as it were, by Whole-sale, in the intire Lump: And I shall concern my self in the latter, more than the former.

I desire the Reader to note, that I do not trust other mens information, but mine own eyes; having my self seen the *Collectors of the Councils*, and searched into all their *Compilers* for the purpose: Neither do I use our own, but their most affectionate and Authentick Writers, the circumstances of the things themselves (in their most approved Authors) detecting the Forgeries.

Before I stir further, I shall add one passage which befel me in the *Schools*, as I was studying these things, and search-
ing

ing the moſt Old and Authentick Records in purſuance of them. One Evening, as I came out of the *Bodleian Library*, which is the Glory of *Oxford*, and this
Nation, at the Stairs-foot I was ſaluted
by a Perſon that has deſerved well both
of Scholars and Learning, who being an
intimate Friend of mine, told me there
was a Gentleman his Coſen, pointing to a
Grave Perſon, in the *Quadrangle*, a man
that had ſpent many thouſand pounds in
promoting Popery, and that he had a
deſire to ſpeak with me. The Gentleman
came up to us of his own accord: We
agreed, for the greater liberty and pri-
vacy, to walk abroad into the *New-
Parks*. He was a notable man, of an Elo-
quent Tongue, and competent Reading,
bold, forward, talkative enough: He
told me, that the Church of *Rome* had
Eleven Millions of *Martyrs*, Seventeen
Oecumenical Coun ils, above an Hundred
Provincial Councils, all the *Doctors*, all
the *Fathers*, *Unity*, *Antiquity*, *Conſent*, &c.
I deſired him to name me *One* of his *Eleven Millions of Martyrs*, excepting thoſe
that died for Treaſon in Queen *Eliza-
beths*, and King *James* his days: For the
Martyrs of the Primitive times, were Martyrs of the *Catholick*, but not of the *Ro-*

man Church: They only being Martyrs of the *Roman Church*, that die for *Transubstantiation*, the *Popes Supremacy*, the Doctrine of *Merits*, *Purgatory*, and the like. So many he told me they had, but I could not get him to name one. As for his *Councils*, *Antiquities*, and *Fathers*, I asked him what he would say, if I could clearly prove, that the Church of *Rome* was guilty of *forging* them, so far, that they had published *Canons* in the *Apostles* names, and invented *Councils* that never were; forged *Letters* of Fathers, and *Decretal Epistles*, in the name of the first Bishops and Martyrs of *Rome*, made 5, 6, 700 years after they were dead, to the utter disguizing and defacing of Antiquity, for the first 400 years next after our Saviour? *Tush, these are nothing but lyes*, quoth he, *whereby the Protestants endeavour to disgrace the Papists.* Sir, answered I, you are a Scholar, and have heard of *Isidore*, *Mercator*, *James Merlin*, *Peter Crabbe*, *Laurentius Surius*, *Severinus Binius*, *Labbè*, *Coffartius*, and the *Collectio Regia*, Books of vast Bulk and Price, as well as of great Majesty and Magnificence: You met me this Evening at the *Library door*; if you please to meet me there to morrow morning at eight of

the

the Clock, I will take you in; and we will go from Clafs to Clafs, from Book to Book, and there I will firft fhew in *your own Authors*, that you publifh fuch In-ftruments for good *Records*; and then prove, that thofe *Inftruments* are down-right frauds and *forgeries*, though cited by you upon all occafions. He would not come; but made this ftrange reply; *What if they be Forgeries? what hurt is that to the Church of* Rome? No! (cryed I, amazed) Is it no hurt to the *Church of Rome*, to be found guilty of *forging Canons* in the *Apoftles* names, and *Epiftles* in the *Fathers* names, which they never made? Is it nothing in *Rome* to be guilty of *counterfeiting Decrees* and *Councils*, and *Records* of *Antiquity? I have done with you!* whereupon I turned from him as an obdurate perfon. And with this I thought it meet to acquaint the Reader.

A N

AN

ABRIDGMENT

OF THE

CHAPTERS.

Cap. 6. *A further account of* Merlins *design. How some would have* Isidore *to be a* Bishop, *others a* Merchant, *others a* Sinner; *no man knowing well what to make of him.*

Cap. 7. *Of* Francis Turrian, *the famous* Jesuite, *with what Art and boldness he defendeth the Forgeries.*

Cap. 8. *Of* Peter Crabbe, *his Tomes of the Councils. Wherein he agrees with, and wherein he differs from* Isidore *and* Merlin.

Cap. 9. *Of* Carranza *his* Epitome: *He owneth, and useth the Forgeries for good Records.*

Cap. 10. *Of* Surius *his four Tomes, and how the Forgeries are by him confirmed. He hath the Rescripts of* Atticus *and* Cyril, *by which Pope* Zozimus *was convicted of Forgery, in the sixth Council of* Carthage.

Cap. 11. *Of* Nicolinus *his Tomes, and their Contents for the first* 420 *years. How full of Forgeries. His Testimony concerning the sixth Council of* Carthage; *with his way of defending the Popes Forgery therein.*

Cap. 12. Nicolinus *his Epistle to Pope* Sixtus V. *His contempt of the Fathers. He beginneth to confess the Epistle of* Mel-

C   chiades

chiades *to be naught. He overthroweth the Legend about* Constantines *Donation.*

Cap. 13. *The Epistle of Pope* Damasus *to* Aurelius, *Archbishop of* Carthage, *commanding the* Decretals *of the* Roman Bishops *to be preached and published, and Fathering those Forgeries on the H. Ghost.*

Cap. 14. *Counterfeit* Canons *made in the* Apostles *names, defended by* Binius. *A Glympse of his Pretences, Sophistries, and Contradictions. A forged* Council *of the* Apostles *concerning Images, defended by* Binius, *and* Turrian.

Cap. 15. *A Book called the* Pontifical, *falsly fathered upon* Damasus, *an Ancient Bishop of* Rome. *How the most Learned of the Popish* Collectors *use it as the* Text *on which they Comment in their voluminous Books, yet confess it to be a* Forgery *full of lyes and contradictions.*

Cap. 16 *Of the Decretal Epistles, forged in the Names of Holy Martyrs and Bishops of* Rome, *for many hundred years together: The first was sent from* S. Clement, *by* S. Peters Order, *to* S. James (*as they pretend*) *Bishop of* Jerusalem, *seven years at least; and by the truest account, more than seven and twenty years after he was in his Grave.* S. Clements Recognitions, *a confessed* Forgery; *which detecteth*
eth

proved

proved to be a Forgery by Binius *himself.*
He confesseth the Acts of Pope Sylvester
(which he before had cited for good) to
be Forged.

Cap. 23. *Pope* Melchiades *Epistle coun-*
terfeited. Isidore Mercator, *the Great*
Seducer of all the Roman Collectors, *con-*
fessed to be a Forger. The Council of Laodicea *corrupted by the fraud of the Pa-*
pists.

Cap. 21. *Threescore Canons put into*
the Nicene *Council after* Finis, *by the*
care and Learning of Alphonsus Pisanus.
Epistles counterfeited in the name of Sylvester, *and that Council.* A Roman Council, *under* Pope Sylvester, *wholly counter-*
feited. Spurious Letters Father'd on Pope
Mark, Athanasius, *and the Bishops of* E-
gypt, *to defend the Forgeries that were*
lately added to the Nicene Council.

Appendix. *Cardinal* Baronius *his Grave*
Censure and Reproof of the Forgeries. His
fear that they will prove destructive and
pernicious to the See of Rome.

A

A

TRUE ACCOUNT

OF

FALSE RECORDS;

Difcovering

THE FORGERIES

OR

Counterfeit-Antiquities

OF THE

CHURCH of *ROME*.

CAP. I.

Of the Nature, Degrees, and Kinds of Forgery.

THE Sin of *Forgery* is fitter to be ranked with Adultery, Theft, Perjury, and Murder, than to be committed by *Priefts* and *Prelates*: One *Act* of it is a Crime to be punifhed by the *Judges*; what then is a whole *Life* fpent in many various and enormous Offences of that nature?

If

Roman Forgeries.

If a *Beggar* forge but a Pass, or a Petition, putting the Hands and Seals of two *Juſtices of the Peace* to it, he is whipt, or clapt into the Pillory, or marked for a *Rogue*, though he doth it only to satisfie his Hunger

If a Leaſe, a Bond, a Will, or a Deed of Gift be razed, or interlined by Craft, it paſſeth for a Cheat; but if the whole be counterfeited, the Crime is the greater.

If an Inſtrument be forged in the *Kings* Name, or his Seal counterfeited, and put to any *Patent*, without his privity and conſent, it is High Treaſon.

If any Records of Antiquity be defaced, or wilfully corrupted, relating to the benefit of men, it is like the Crying Sin of *removing thy Neighbours Landmark*, which *Solomon* cenſures in the *Proverbs*. But if thoſe Records appertain to the Right of Nations, the Peace of Mankind, or the Publick Welfare of the World, the Sin is of more myſterious and deeper nature.

If Counterfeits be ſhuffled in among good Records, to the diſorder and confuſion of the Authentick, and a *Plea* maintained by them, which without thoſe Counterfeits would fall to the ground, upon

upon the depofition of Falfe Witneffes; *Theft* and *Perjury* are effectually couched, together with *Lying*, in the Cheat.

If the Records fo counterfeited concern the Church, either in her Cuftoms or Laws, her Lands, or the limits of her Jurifdiction, the Order of her Priefts, or any other Spiritual or Ecclefiaftical Affair, befides other fins contained in it, there is fuperadded the Sin of *Sacriledge*.

The higheft degree of Forgery is that of altering the *Holy Scriptures*; becaufe the Majefty offended being Infinite, as well as the Concernment, the Crime is the more heinous.

The higheft, next under that, is to counterfeit *Rules* in the Names of the *Apoftles*, *Oecumenical Councils*, moft glorious *Martyrs*, and Primitive *Fathers*, that is, to make *Canons*, *Letters*, *Books*, and *Decrees* in their Names, of which they were not the Authors.

If the Church of *Rome* be guilty of this Crime, her *Antiquity* and *Tradition*, the two great *Pillars* upon which fhe ftandeth, are very *rotten*, and will moulder into nothing.

If *Money* be fpent in promoting the Forgery, or any thing given, directly or indirectly, to its Fautors and Abettors,

in

in order to the Usurpation of any *Spiritual* Priviledge or Power ; he that doth it , is guilty of *Simony*: And in many cases , Simony , Lying , and Sacriledge; are blended together.

Finally , If they that make the Forgeries rather them upon GOD, or upon the *Holy Ghost*, the Sin of *Blasphemy* is added to Forgery ; for it maketh God the Father of Lies ; and being done *maliciously*, it draweth near to the unpardonable sin.

That some *Popes* have been guilty of *Simony*, cannot be doubted by them that are any thing versed in Church-Antiquity. *Hart*, in his Conference with *Reynolds*, noteth out of Dr. *Genebrard*, that the Popes, for the space of seven score years and ten almost, from *John* VIII. to *Leo* IX. about fifty Popes did revolt wholly from the vertue of their Ancestors, and were *Apostatical*, rather than *Apostolical:* and that some of them came not in by the *Door*, but were *Thieves* and *Robbers*.

That it is not impossible to *forge* Records for the Bolstering up of *Heresies*, those counterfeit *Gospels, Acts, Epistles, Revelations,* &c. that were put forth by Hereticks in the Names of the *Apostles*, do sufficiently evidence ; which being

extant

extant a little after the Apostles decease, are pointed to by *Irenæus*, condemned in a *Roman Council* by *Gelasius*, and some of them recorded by *Ivo Cartonensis*, in a Catalogue *lib.* 2. *cap.* 2 . The *Itinerary* of *Clement*, and the Book called *Pastor*, being two of the number.

I note the two last, because S. *Clement* in his first Epistle to S. *James*, is *made* to approve the one, and Pope *Pius* in his Decretal magnifieth the other. Which giveth us a little glympse of the Knavery by which those Ancient Bishops and Martyrs of *Rome* were both abused, having Spurious Writings fathered upon themselves; for had those *Instruments* been their *own*, they would never have owned such abominable *Forgeries*. But of this you may expect more hereafter, *Cap.* 16. and *Cap.* 17.

These aggravations and degrees of Forgery we have not mentioned in vain, or by accident. In the process of our discourse, the Church of *Rome* will be found guilty of them all, except the first, which is beneath her Grandeur; and in so doing, she is very strangely secured by the height of her impiety. For because it does not easily enter into the heart of man to conceive, that men, especially Christians,

Chriſtians, ſhould *voluntarily* commit ſo tranſcendent a Crime, the greatneſs of it makes it incredible to inexperienced people, and renders them prone to *excuſe* the Malefactors, while they *condemn* the Accuſers.

But that the Church of *Rome* is guilty in all theſe reſpects, we ſhall prove not by remote Authorities, that are weak and feeble, but by demonſtrations derived from the Root and Fountain. I will not be *poſitive* in making *compariſons*; but if my *reading* and *judgment* do not both deceive me, ſhe is guilty of more Forgeries than all the Hereticks in the world beſide : Their greatneſs and their number countenance the *Charge*, and ſeem to promiſe that one day it ſhall paſs into a *Sentence* of *condemnation* againſt her.

CHAP.

Roman Forgeries.

CAP. II.

Of the Primitive Order and Government of the Church. The first Popish Encroachment upon it, backed with Forgery. The Detection of the Fraud in the Sixth Council of Carthage.

IT is S. *Cyprian's* observation, that our Saviour, in the first Foundation of the Church, *gave his Apostles equal honour and power, saying unto them, Whose soever sins ye remit, they are remitted unto them; and whose soever sins ye retain, they are retained,* Cyprian. *Tract .de Simpl. Prælator.* The place has been tampered with, but unsuccessfully: For though they have thrust in other words into the Fathers Text, in some Editions of their own; yet in others they are left sincere: As Dr. *James* in his *corruption of the Fathers, Part. 2. Cap. 1.* does well observe. But the most remarkable attempt of the Papists is, that whereas they have set *a Tract concerning the Primacy of the Roman Church* before the Councils, containing many Quotations out of the *Bastard Decretals,* which they pretend to be extracted, *ex Codice antiquo, que, out of an Old Book*, without naming any Author ; clofing it with this paffage of S. *Cyprian*, they leave out thefe words of Scripture , *Whofe foever fins ye remit, &c.* as rendring the Fathers Teftimony unfit for their purpofe. You may fee it in *Binius* his Collection of the Councils, *&c.*

Bin. *Tom.* 1.
Tractat de
Primat.
&c.

When the Apoftles had converted Nations, they conftituted *Bifhops*, *Priefts*, and *Deacons*, for the Government of the Church ; and left thofe Orders among us, when they departed from the world.

It was found convenient alfo for the better Regiment of the Church , when it was much inlarged, to erect the Orders of *Archbifhops*, and *Patriarchs*.

The *Patriarchs* being Supreme in their feveral Jurifdictions , had each of them many Primates and Archbifhops under him, with many Nations and Kingdoms allotted to their feveral *Provinces* ; every of which was limited in it felf, and diftinct from the refidue : as appeareth in that firft *Oecumenical Council* affem. bled at *Nice*, *An. Dom.* 327. where it was ordained, *Can.* 6 that *the ancient cuftom fhould be kept*; the Jurifdiction of the Bifhop of *Rome* being exprefly noted to be equal to that of the other Patriarchs.

It

In the two preceding Canons they or-
dain: 1. *That in every Province Bishops* Concil.
should be consecrated by all the Bishops Nicen. I.
thereof, (might it consist with their con- Can. 4.
venience to meet together; if not) at least
by three being present, the rest consenting;
but the confirmation of their Acts is in e-
very Province reserved to the Metropolitan.
2. *That the last Appeal should be made to* Concil.
Councils; and that the person condemned Nic. I.
in any Province, should not be received, if Can. 5.
he fled to others. Can. 4. and 5.

In the first of these Canons it was ordered, that the chief in every Province
should confirm the Acts of his Inferiour
Bishops, the Patriarch of *Rome* in his,
and every other Patriarch in his own
Jurisdiction. In the last, if any trouble
did arise that could not be decided by
the Metropolitan, provision was made
(in words so clear and forcible, that
none more *plain* can be put into their
places) *that the last Appeal should be made*
to Councils, ~~and that the person condem-~~
~~ned in any Province, should not be recei-~~
~~ved, if he fled to others.~~

But the City of *Rome* being in those
days Queen of the World, and lifted up
above all other Cities, as the Seat of the
Empire, the *Bishop* thereof began to wax

proud

proud in after-times, and being discontented with the former *Bounds*, invaded the Jurisdictions of his *Fellow-Patriarchs*.

For though the Foundation upon which the Government was laid was against it, yet when persons were *Immorigerous*, if any Bishop were censured by his Metropolitan, or Priest excommunicated by his Bishop, or Deacon offended with his Superiour, who chastised him for his guilt; though the Canon of the Church was trampled under foot thereby (which forbad such irregular and disorderly flights) the manner was, for those turbulent persons to flee to *Rome*, because it was a great and powerful City; and the Roman Bishop trampling the Rule under foot, as well as others, did (as is confessed) frequently receive them. Nay, their ambition being kindled by the greatness of the place, it tempted them so far, as to favour the Delinquents, and oftentimes to clear them, for the incouragement of others, invited by that means, to *fly* thither for relief, till at last the Cause of Malefactors was *openly* Espoused; and while they were excommunicated in other Churches, they were received to the Communion in the Church of *Rome*.   Here-

Hereupon there were great murmurings and heart-burnings at the firſt in the *Eaſtern Churches*, becauſe *Rome* became an *Aſylum*, or City of *Refuge*, for diſcontented perſons; diſturbing the Order of the Church, ſpoiling the Diſcipline of other Provinces, and hindering the Courſe of Juſtice; while her Biſhop uſurped an Authority, which neither *Scripture* nor *Canon* gave unto him.

It is recorded alſo, that they ſometimes acquitted Malefactors without hearing Witneſſes, and ſent Orders for the Reſtauration of thoſe, who made ſuch irregular flights, into the Provinces of other Patriarchs that were Subject indeed to the Roman *Empire*, but not within the *Province* of the Roman *Patriarch* *Concil. Carth. 6. Epiſt. ad Celeſtin.*

Nay, when thoſe Orders were rejected, (if ſome of their own *Collectors* may be believed) the Roman Biſhops, through favour of the Empire, got Magiſtrates and Souldiers to ſee them executed by *plain force*: which grew chiefly ſcandalous in the times of *Zozimus*, and *Boniface*; of which you may read the three laſt and beſt *Collections* of the *Councils*, ſet forth by the Papiſts, *Binius*, *Labbè*, and the *Collectio Regia*, unanimouſly conſenting in their Notes on the *ſixth Council of the of Carthage.* And that this was the cause of calling that Council, they confess in like manner.

For to stop these intolerable Incroachments, and to suppress the growth of an Aspiring Tyranny, this seasonable Council was called at *Carthage*, confisting of 2 7 Bishops, among whom S. *Augustine* was one present in particular.

To this Council *Zozimus* the Roman Patriarch sent three persons, one of which was *Faustinus*, an Italian Bishop, to plead his Cause, with two *Canons* fathered upon the *Nicene* Council; designing thereby to justifie his Power *of receiving Appeals* both from *Bishops* and *Priests*, but by the care and wisdom of that *Council* they were detected and confounded, the Fraud being made a Spectacle to the whole world.

For first, the Copy which *Cæcilianus,* Archbishop of *Carthage*, brought from *Nice,* (he being himself one of the Fathers in that Council) was orderly produced, and the two Canons which the Roman Bishop sent were not there. Next, because it might be pleaded upon the difference of the Copies, that the Copy of *Carthage* must give place to that of *Rome, Rome* being the greater *See;* they

sent

sent Messengers to the Patriarch of *Alexandria*, to the Patriarch of *Antioch*, and to the Patriarch of *Constantinople*, (and admonished the Bishop of *Rome* to do so too, that he might see sound and fair dealing) desiring the Records of the *Nicene* Council, from all the principal parts of the world, from the Patriarchs of *Constantinople* and *Alexandria* they received Authentick Copies, attested with their several *known* Authorities, which agreed exactly with the Copy at *Carthage*, but disagreed with that of *Rome*; the Extract produced out of it, by the Name of a *Commonitorium*, being every word apparently forged.

Upon this the Bishop of *Rome* was condemned, his Arrogance and Usurpation suppressed by *Canons*, and his Pride chastised by *Letters*; the Letters and Canons being yet extant. This was done about the year 420.

Zozimus dying, *Boniface* and *Celestine* successively take up the Quarrel, without any Dissent appearing in the Roman Clergy: nay rather all the Interest of that *Chair* was imployed to uphold the Forgery; whereby it is evident, that it was not a *Personal* Act, but the *guilt and business of the Church of Rome*; as appear-

D   eth

eth further by all their *Successors* persisting in the Quarrel, by the multitude of her *Members* defending it and the Forgery both; and by all the Popish *Collectors* conspiring together, to maintain the Spurious and Adulterate Canons.

Epist. Concil Carthag. 6. ad Celestin.

Among other things which the Fathers wrote out of this Sixth Council of *Carthage* to Pope *Celestine*, they oppose the true Canons of the *Nicene* Council, against the *false* ones, noting that, which is alone sufficient to overthrow the Forgery, that these two Popish Canons were really *contrary* to the Canons and Decrees of the *Nicene* Council: For desiring him *no more so easily to admit Appeals, nor to receive into Communion those that were Excommunicated in other Churches*; they tell him, he might easily find *this matter defined in the* Nicene *Council: for if it seemed fit to be observed in the inferiour Clergy, and Lay-men, much more in Bishops.* They tell him, that *he should chastise and punish such impudent* Flights, *as became him:* As also, that *the Canons of the* Nicene *Council had most openly committed both the inferiour Clergy, and Bishops themselves to their own Metropolitans: wisely and justly providing, that all businesses whatsoever should be determi-*

ned

ned *in the places where they arose*; Nisi forte est Aliquis, &c. *unless perhaps there be some one who will say, that God is able to give Justice of Judgment to* one, be he who he will, *but denies it to innumerable Priests assembled in a Council.* Which was in those days held so absurd and monstrous a thing to conceive, that (however the case is altered since) they thought no man impudent enough to affirm it. In these words they cut the Popes Arrogance sufficiently, for that he being but *One*, was so highly conceited of himself, at least so behaved himself, as if he had an extraordinary Spirit of Infallibility, and were fitter to determine the Causes of the Church, than a whole Council of Bishops assembled together. Finally, they charge him with bringing *the empty puff of secular pride into the Church of Christ:* And so proceed to their Canons against him.

Notwithstanding this, the *Roman Bishops* continued obstinate, contending so long, till there was a great Rupture made in the Church upon this occasion. And if some *Records* be true; namely, those *Letters* that past between *Eulalius* and another *Boniface*, the Bishops of *Rome* grew so impudent, as to Excommunicate

the

the *Eastern Churches*, becaufe they would not be obedient to an Authority founded on fo bafe a *Forgery*. If they be not true, then there are more Forgeries in the *Roman Church* than we charge her with : For the Letters were feigned (as *Baronius* confeffeth) by fome afterwards, that were zealous of the Churches welfare ; to wit, for the better co'ouring of that *Schifm* which was made by the pride and ambition of *Rome*.

Thefe *Epiftles* were fet forth by the Papifts, and were owned at firft for good *Records* ; but upon the confideration of fo many *Saints* and *Martyrs* that fprung up in the Churches of *Africa*, during that 100 years, wherein it is pretended by thofe *Epiftles*, that they were cut off from the *Church of Rome*, it was afterwards thought better to reject them as Counterfeits, becaufe the *Roman Martyrologies* are filled with the names of thofe *African Saints* : And it is a ftated Rule, that no *Saint* or *Martyr* can be out of the *Church*. Left the *Eaftern* Churches therefore fhould out-weigh the *Roman*, by reafon of the Splendour, Multitude and Authority of thefe Eminent Saints, thefe Letters are now condemned by fome among themfelves ; *vid.* Bellarm. *de Rom.*
Pont.

Pont. lib. 2. *cap.* 25. Baron. *in Not. Mar-*
tyrol. ad 16. *Octobr. and* Bin. *in Concil.*
Carthag. 6.

This unfortunate Contest happening
so near to the Fourth Century, was the
first *Head-spring*, or Root of the *Schism*,
that is now between us: And the matter
being so, on whose side the *fault* lay, I
leave to the Reader.

How the *Roman Church* proceeded in
this business, we may learn from *Daillè,*
an able Writer of the *French* Nation:
He tells us, *that the Legates of* Pope Leo,
in the year 45 , *in the midst of the Coun-*
cil of Chalcedon, *where were assembled*
600 *Bishops, the very Flower and choice of*
the whole Clergy, had the confidence to al-
ledge the sixth Canon of the Council of
Nice, *in these very words*, That the
Church of *Rome* hath always had the
Primacy: *Words which are no more found*
in any Greek Copies of the Councils, than
are those other pretended Canons of Pope
Zozimus: *Neither do they yet appear in*
any Greek or Latine Copies, nor so much as
in the Edition if Dionysius Exiguus, *who*
lived about 50 *years after this Council:*
Whereupon he breaketh out into this
Exclamation, *When I consider that the*
Legates of so holy a Pope, *would at that*

Daillè
concern-
ing the
right use
of the Fa-
thers, lib. 1.
cap. 4.

D 3　　　　time

time have fastned such a *Wen upon the* body of so *Venerable a Canon*, I am almost ready to think, that we scarcely have any thing of Antiquity left us, that is entire and uncorrupt, except it be in matters of indifferency, or which could not have been corrupted, but with much noise, &c.

He further tells us, (in the place before-mentioned) *That whereas the Greek* Code, Num. 206. *sets before us in the* XXVIII *Canon of the General Council of* Chalcedon, *a Decree of those Fathers* ; *by which conformably to the first Council of* Constantinople, *they ordained, that seeing the City of* Constantinople *was the Seat of the Senate, and of the Empire, and enjoyed the same Priviledges with the City of* Rome *, that therefore it should in like manner be advanced to the same Height and Greatness in Ecclesiastical Affairs* , *being the second Church in Order after* Rome; *and that the Bishop should have the Ordaining of Metropolitans in the three Diocesses of* Pontus, Asia, *and* Thrace. *Which Canon is found both in* Balsamon *and* Zonoras ; *and also hath the Testimony of the greatest part of the Ecclesiastical Historians* , *both Greek and Latine, that it is a Legitimate Canon of the Council of* Chalcedon, *in the Acts of which Council, at this day also* extant,

extant, it is set down at large: Yet *not-withstanding, in the collection of* Diony=sius Exiguus *it appears not at all, no more than as if there had never been any such thing thought of at* Chalcedon. He hath other marks of *Dionysius Exiguus,* which sufficiently brand him for a *Slave to the Chair,* but omitted here, as out of our Circuit. However, I think it meet to lay down the Canon as I find it lying in the *Code* of the Universal Church.

'ccvi. Altogether following the De- *Concil.*
'crees of the H. Fathers, and the Canon *Chalced*
'of those 150 Bishops, most beloved of *Can.28.*
'God, which was lately read, which met
'under the Great *Theodosius* the Pious
'Emperour, in his Royal City of Con-
'stantinople [called] *New Rome,* we also
'define and decree the same, concerning
'the Priviledges of that most H. Church
'of *Constantinople* [that is] *New Rome:*
'For the Fathers justly gave priviledges
'to the See of Elder *Rome, Quod urbs*
'illa imperaret*, because that City was
'the Seat of the Empire : And the 150
'Bishops, most beloved of God, being.
'moved with the same consideration,
'gave equal Priviledges to the most holy
'See of *New Rome* ; rightly judging,that
'the City which is honoured with the

D 4 Empire,

'Empire, and the Senate, and enjoys e-
'qual priviledges with the Royal *Elder*
'*Rome*, ought in Ecclesiastical Affairs al-
'so, no otherwise then it, to be extolled
'and magnified, being the second after
'it, &c.

Upon this advantage, the *Patriarch*
of *Constantinople* advanced himself above
the other Patriarchs; and his *See* being
made equal to the See of *Rome*, by the
Authority of the *Church*, upon the Interest he had in the Empire then setled in
Greece, he arrogated the Title of *Uni-
versal Bishop :* Which *Gregory*, then Bi-
shop of *Rome*, so highly stomacked, that
he thundered out Letters against him,
calling the Title a proud and prophane,
Greg.lib.4. nay, a *blasphemous Title*; denying that
Epist. 30. *either himself, or any of his Predecessors
Lib. 4. *had ever used it*; and plainly affirming,
Epist. 32. that *whosoever used that Title, was the fore-
Lib. 6.
Epist. 30. *runner of Antichrist.* And to this pur-
Greg. lib.4. pose, in the 34. *Epistle of his fourth Book*,
Epist.34 he asketh, *What else can be signified by this
pride, but that the times of Antichrist are
drawing near ? For he imitates him* (says
he) *who despising the Fellowship of the
Angels in their common joy, endeavoured
to break up to the Top of Singularity.* This
he spake against *John* of *Constantinople*,
because

because he brake the Order of the Patriarchs, and despised the Equality of his Fellow-Bishops. Now whether it does not hit his own Predecessors, *Zozimus*, and *Boniface*, and *Celestine*, and *Leo*, I leave to the judgment of the Reader: They were not contented with an Equality in Power, but aspired, and that some of them by the most odious way, that of Lying and Forgery, as well as Pride and Ambition, to the top of Singularity.

Whether this *Zeal* of *Gregory* was *according to knowledge*, that is, whether it proceeded from *integrity*, or *self interest*, I shall not determine. All that I observe is this which followeth, when the Tyde turned, and the Emperour next sided with the Bishop of *Rome*, the very next Successor of *Gregory* but one, took up the *Title*, a little before condemned for *blasphemous*, which is claimed by the *Roman Bishops* to this day.

The Emperour sided with the Roman Bishop, because the Roman Bishop sided with him: For when *Phocas* had murdered his Master, the good old Emperour *Mauricius*, and usurped the Throne in his stead, the Title of *Universal Bishop* was given to the Patriarch of *Rome* by this

this Bloody Tyrant, to fecure his own; which had fo great a Flaw in it, and needed the affiftance of fome powerful Agent.

Helvic.
Chronol.

Hereupon a Council was called at *Rome* by *Boniface* 3. wherein the priviledge of the Emperour *Phocas* was promulged, and the Bifhop of *Rome* made a POPE, upon the encouragement of the *Tyrant*, by the confent of the Council: but his own, *viz.* a *Roman Council.*

Thus *Boniface* and *Phocas* were great Friends: The Imperial and Triple Crown were barter'd between them: Connivance and Commerce foiling ther both with the guilt of Murder, Simony Treafon; and if S. *Gregory* may be belie ved, with *Sacriledge* and *Blafphemy*: Fo being involved in a mutual Confpiracy they became guilty of each others crimes· to partake with Adulterers, and comply with Offenders, being imputed as fin, i the H. Scriptures.

Platina, an Eminent Writer of th Lives of the Popes, and a Papift himfel informeth us fufficiently of this bufinefs

Platin. in
vir. Bo-
nif. 3.

in thefe words, *Boniface* III. (faith he) Roman *by Birth, obtained of the Emperou* Phocas, *but with great contention, tha the Seat of bleffed* Peter *the Apoftle whic*

is the Head of all the Churches) *should be
so called, and so accounted of all: which
place the Church of* Conſtantinople *endeavoured to vindicate to it ſelf, evil Princes
ſometimes favouring it, and affirming the
firſt* See *to be due to the place where the
Head of the Empire was.*

In the Life of *Zozimus the firſt Epiſco-
pal Forger* in the Church of *Rome, Platina* mentioneth the foreſaid buſineſs at
Carthage; but ſo briefly, that it is clear
he did not like it. And to cloſe up all, in
the Life of this *Boniface* he endeavours
to ſtrengthen the Title of the *Roman* Biſhop againſt the Patriarch of *Conſtantinople*, by the *Donation* of *Conſtantine*, another Forgery, of which hereafter.

The two counterfeit Canons contained in the *Commonitorium*, which the Roman Biſhop ſent to the ſixth Council of
Carthage, are theſe, as *Fauſtinus* the Italian Biſhop delivered them in Greek, to
be read by *Daniel* the Pronotary in the
Council.

Ἤρεσεν δὲ, &c. *We are pleaſed, that if a
Biſhop be accuſed, and the Biſhops of his
Country being aſſembled together, have
judged him, and depoſed him from his
Degree, and he thinks fit to appeal, and*
ſhall

shall fly to the most blessed Bishop of the Roman Church, and shall desire to be heard, and he shall think it just that the Tryal be renewed; then he [the Roman Bishop] shall vouchsafe to write to the Bishops of the adjoining and bordering Province, that they should diligently examine all, and define according to the Truth. But if any one thinks fit that his Cause be heard again, and by his own Supplication moves the Bishop of Rome, *that he should send a [Legate or] Priest from his side; it shall be in his power to do as he listeth, and as he thinketh fit. And if he shall decree that some ought to be sent, that being present themselves might judge with the Bishops, having his Authority by whom they were sent, it shall be according to his judgment: but if he think the Bishops sufficient to end the business, he shall do what in his most wise counsel he judgeth meet.*

Here the *Roman Bishop*, nay the meanest *Priest* he shall please to send as his *Legate*, is exalted above all Councils, Bishops, and Patriarchs in the world; he may do, and undo, act, add, rescind, diminish, alter, whatsoever he pleaseth in any Council, when the Causes of the most Eminent Rank in the Church do depend in the same. All Bishops are by this

Canon

Canon made more to fear the Roman Bishop than their own Patriarch, and are
ingaged, if need be, to side with him
against their Patriarch: the Gate is open
for all the Wealth in the World to flow
into his Ecclesiastical Court, which is as
much above the Court of any other Patriarch, by this Right of Appeals, as the
Archbishops Court above any inferiour
Bishops, while we may Appeal to that
from these at our pleasure. Thus Bishops
and Patriarchs are made to buckle under
the Popes Girdle, and the Decrees of
Councils are put under his foot: And all
this is no more but half a Step to the
Popes Chair.

The other part of the Step in this *Commonitorium*, was the following Canon
concerning Priests:

Οσιος επισκοπ⊙, &c. *I ought not to pass
that over in silence, that does yet move
me: If any Bishop happen to be angry (as
he ought not) and be suddenly or sharply
moved against his Priest or Deacon, and
would cast him out of his Church, Provision must be made, that he be not condemned being Innocent, or lose the Communion. Let him that is cast out have power to
Appeal to the Borderers, that his Cause
might be heard, and handled more carefully;*

ly ; for a Hearing ought not to be denied him when he asks it : And the Bishop, which hath either justly or unjustly ejected him, shall patiently suffer, that the business be lookt into, and his Sentence either confirmed, or rectified, &c.

What is the meaning of this, *&c.* in *Binius, Labbè, Cossartius,* and the *Collectio Regia,* I cannot tell ; but doubtless the Canon intends the same in the close with the former, that the last Appeal is reserved to the Roman Chair ; which made the Fathers in the sixth Council of *Carthage* so angry as we find them, to see things so false and presumptuous, fastned upon the first most Glorious Oecumenical Council, which decreed the clean contrary, in the 4 and 5 Canons. The substance and force of which, as we gave you before, so shall we now the words of the Canons themselves.

Can. 4. Επίσκοπον προσήκει, &c. *It is fit that a Bishop chiefly be ordained by all the Bishops that are in the Province : but if this be found difficult, either because of any urgent necessity, or for the length of the journey, then the Ordination ought to be made by Three certainly meeting together, the absent* [Bishops] *agreeing, and consenting by their Writs : but let the confirmation of* of the *Acts* be given, throughout every *Province*, to the *Metropolitan.*

Can. 5. Περὶ τῶν ἀκοινωνήτων, &c. Concerning those that are *Excommunicated,* whether in the Order of the *Clergy,* or the *Laity,* by the *Bishops* in every several *Province,* let the *Sentence* prevail according to the *Canon,* that they who are cast out by some, be not received by others: but let it be required, that no man be excluded the *Congregation,* by the pusillanimity or contention, or by any such vice, of the *Bishop.* That this therefore might more decently be inquired into, we think it fit, that *Councils* should every year, throughout every *Province,* twice be celebrated: That such *Questions* may be discussed by the common *Authority* of all the *Bishops* assembled together: And so they, that have evidently offended against their *Bishop,* shall be accounted *Excommunicated,* according to to reason, by all; till it pleaseth the community of *Bishops* to pronounce a milder *Sentence* upon such. But let the *Councils* be held the one before the *Quadragesima* before *Easter,* that all *Dissention* being taken away, we might offer a most pure *Gift* unto *God;* and the second about the middle of *Autumn.*

The last *Appeal,* you see, is ordered by the

the Canon to Councils; and, as they pleafe, the Controverfie is to be ended, without flying from one to another Bifhop. Thefe are the true and Authentick Canons of the *Nicene Council*, overthrown by the Forgery.

CAP. III.

A multitude of Forgeries fecretly mingled among the Records of the Church, and put forth under the Name of Ifidore, *Biſhop of* Hifpalis: *Which Book is owned, defended, and followed by the* Papiſts.

THe *Roman Chair* being thus lifted up to the utmoſt Height it could well defire, care muſt be taken to fecure its Exaltation. After many fecret Councils therefore, and powerful Methods ufed for its Eſtabliſhment; for the increafe of its Power and Glory, (furthered by the Luxury and Idlenefs of the Weſtern Churches) of which *Salvian* largely complains in his Book *De Providentiâ* (written to juſtifie the Difpenfation of GOD in all the Calamities they ſuffered by the *Goths*, who ſacked *Rome* in the days of the forenamed *Zozimus*) there

Platin. in vit. Zo- z.p. s.

there came out a *collection of Councils and Decretal Epistles*, in the Name of *Isidore*, Bishop of *Hispalis*, about the year 790. In which Book there are neatly interwoven a great company of forged Evidences, or feigned Records, tending all to the advancement of the Popes Chair, in a very various, copious, and Elaborate manner.

That the Bishop of *Rome* had a secret hand in the contrivance and publication of them, is *probable*, if not *clear*, from divers Reasons.

1. Before they were published, *Hadrian* 1. maketh use of the *Tale* of *Constantines Leprosie*, Vision, and Baptism by Pope *Sylvester*; things till then never heard of in the world, but afterwards contained in the *Donation of Constantine*; a Forgery, which in all probability lay by this *Hadrian*, but of his own preparing, when he wrote his Letter to *Constantine* and *Irene*; which Letter was read, and is recorded in the 2. *Nicene* Council, on the behalf of Images: being *Concil. Nicen. 2. Act.* sent abroad like a *Scout*, as it were, to try what success it would find in the world, before he would adventure the whole *Body* of his Players to publick view: For if that were swallowed down without

E   being

being detected, the rest might hope for the same good Fortune: if not, the first might pass for a *mistake*, and its Companions be *safely* suppressed, without any mischief following.

2. The Emperour and the Council having *digested* the first Legend, exposed by the Pope so craftily to publick view, the other *Forgeries* were a little after boldly published in this Book of *Isidore*, together with the Legend and Donation of *Constantine :* which when *Hincmarus*, Archbishop of *Rhemes*, (upon its first publication) set himself to write against, he was taken up so roundly for the same by the Authority of *Rome*, that he was fain gladly to acquit the Attempt for e-ver: And their *tenderness* over it, is, I think, a sufficient Indication of their *Relation* to it; every Creature being natu-rally affectionate to its own *Brood*, and prone to study its preservation.

Baron. An. c. 5. nu. 6.

The Church of *Rome* was so tender of *Isidores* Edition, that, as some say, *Hinc-marus* was forced to recant his Opinion; and to declare, that he believed and re-ceived the Book with Veneration.

Baron. ibid

3. It is recorded by *Justellus*, that the forementioned *Hadrian* was careful to give *Charles the Great* a Copy of the Councils

Councils and Decretal Epiſtles, drawn up (as he affirmed) by *Dionyſius Exiguus.* *Daillè* accuſes the Book of many faults; but whether *Hadrian* or *Dionyſius* were guilty of them, is little material; only 'twas done as a *Pledge* of Reconciliation, after ſeveral Bickerings between the Giver and Receiver. *Charles the Great* having ſeveral times invaded *Rome*, and now departing thence with *Friendſhip:* which makes me a little the more prone to ſuſpect *Dionyſius* too, for one of thoſe *Danaum Dona*, which are given like *Neſ-ſus* his Shirt, when wounded by *Hercules*, to his Enemies Wife, for the deſtruction of her Husband.

Be it how it will, it ſhews that *Hadrian* I. was a buſie man, that he underſtood the influence and power of Records, what force they would have upon the minds of *Lay-men*, and that his eyes and hands were ſometimes buſied in ſuch *Affairs.*

But that which above all other Arguments diſcovers the Popes to have a hand, if not in the *Publication*, yet in the *Reception* of the Forgeries, is this; that the *Roman* Canoniſts, *Ivo,Gratian, &c.* have digeſted them into the Popes *Laws*; and they are ſo far countenanced by the

Popes

Popes themselves, that almost from the time of their publication, throughout all Ages since, they have been received for *Authentick* in the Papal Jurisdiction, and are used as such in all the *Ecclesiastical Courts* under the Popes Dominion, as the chief of their *Rules* for the deciding of *Causes*: So that they are not only *fostered*, but *exalted* by the Authority of *Rome*. The Glory which they acquired in the Throne of Judgment, advancing them for a long time above the reach of Suspition. The Veneration which is due to the Chair of Holiness was their best security.

By the influence of the Popes Authority they were received into the *Codes* of *Princes*, being (as we shall shew out of *Baronius*, in the next Chapter) introduced into the *Capitular* Books of the Kings of the *Franks* by *Benedictus Levita*; and at his instant request, confirmed and approved by the Papal Chair.

The Forgeries in *Isidore* being scattered abroad, it is difficult to conceive to what a vast Height the *Roman* See by degrees attended: The Splendour of so many *ancient Martyrs* names, together with so many *Canons* and *Decrees* in her behalf, so far wrought, that her Bishop

came

came at laſt to Claim all Power over all perſons, *Spiritual* and *Temporal*, to have the ſole power of *forgiving ſins*, to be alone *Infallible*, to be Gods *Vicar* upon Earth, the only *Oracle* in the world, nay, the ſole Supreme and Abſolute *Monarch*, diſpoſing of Empires and Kingdoms, according to the Tenour of the Doctrines contained in thoſe Forgeries; wherein he is made the ſole Independent Lord, without Controul, able to do what ever he liſted.

Some few Ages after this firſt Publication of *Iſidore*, there were other Records put forth, though lately ſeen, yet bearing the countenance of *Primitive Antiquitie*; which ſo ordered the matter, that (according to them) the *Evangeliſts* brought their *Goſpels* to S. *Peter* to confirm them; and ſeveral books of S. *Clement*, S. *Peter's* Succeſſor, were put into the Canon of the *Holy Bible*, the whole number of *Canonical books* being ſetled and defined by his ſole Authority: In token (doubtleſs) of the Power Inherent in all S. *Peter's* Succeſſors at *Rome*, to diſpoſe of the Apoſtles, and their Writings, as they pleaſe. S. *Clement's* own Canon, for that purpoſe, being numbered among thoſe of the *Apoſtles*.

Poſt. 24.

Ibid.

E 3   That

That the *Pope* was uncapable of being judged by any ; that no *Clergy-man* was to be Subject to *Kings*, but all to depend immediately upon the *Bishop of Rome* ; that he was the *Rock* and *Head* of the *Church*, was the constant Doctrine of all those Forgeries, when put together, with many other Popish Points, of less concernment, sprinkled up and down in them at every turning.

Cui bono? Among the *Civilians* 'tis a notable mark of Detection in a blind Cause, whose Good, whose Exaltation, whose Benefit is the drift and scope of things ; and 'tis very considerable for the sure finding out of the first Authors. That they are Forgeries, is manifest : Now, whose they are, is the Question in hand ; and if Agents naturally intend themselves in their own Operations, it is easily solved.

How excessively the World was addicted to *Fables* about the time of *Isidore*'s Appearance, we may see by the Contents of the 2. *Nicene Council*, Dreams, Visions and Miracles being very rife in their best demonstrations ; and among other Legends, a counterfeit *Basil*, a counterfeit *Athanasius*, a counterfeit *Emperour*, maintaining and promoting the

Adoration

Adoration of Images: As may perhaps in another Volume be more fully discovered, when we descend from these *first*, to succeeding Ages.

The *Counterfeits* in *Isidore* being mingled with the *Records* of the Church, like Tares among Wheat, or false Coyns among heaps of Gold, lay undistinguished from true *Antiquities*, and (after *Hincmarus* his ill success) were little examined by the space of 500 or 600 years. Some small opposition there was, made in particular by the Bishops in *France*, and perhaps by some Doctors and Bishops [more] sincere than ordinary, or by some Learned Lawyer that rarely appeared: but the general *Interest* of the Times, the Deluge of corrupted manners, the Ignorance of the Laity, the Luxury of the Priests, the Greatness of the Chair, and the Love of Superstition so far prevailed, that for a long time the *Court* of *Rome* luxuriantly flourished in the Light of her own Glory, and to this *Prodigious Sun-shine* owed much of its Splendour.

For the Pope having wrought himself by his first Arts into that high Reputation, the *Lustre* whereof dazled the world, it concerned him much to keep the Earth

in

Baron. An.

in a Profound Quiet, and to cherish *Ignorance*, (a Vertue highly praised in the Church of *Rome*) that as the *Tares* were *sown*, they might be permitted to *grow*, and be fruitful, *while men slept :* In which, the want of Printing much assisted him, Monks and Fryars being the only *Scribes*, or the chief ones, and all at his Devotion.

Written Copies were the only Books, which at most could be but *few*; enough indeed to preserve knowledge *by way of Record*; but being Chained up in Monasteries and Libraries, they came seldom abroad, unless by the report of such *well-affected* persons as had their Tutelage and keeping.

The Popes *Indulgence*, and the *Sloth* ensuing, made way for the *Artifice* of *Priests* in after-ages; which were not *Bookish* ones, as this is, neither were *Laymen* addicted much to *Reading*.

But upon the *Reformation*, occasioned by nothing more than the *notorious* impiety and *excess* of Popes, (unless the impudence and security of his Followers may contend for a share in it) when Libraries fell into the Protestants hands, Inquisition was made, *Archives* were entered, Books opened, *Records* searched

and

and diligently compared: Whereupon much fraud and shufling was found, and expofed to the world.

For as the Copies were enough, had they been *fincere* ; fo, though they were not fincere , by the Providence of God, they contained *Indications*, wherby clear Judgments might eafily difcern between Records and Forgeries; as I found my felf, to my great amazement, without any *Warning* ! when I firft fet my felf to read the Councils, and fimply made ufe of none but Popifh Compilers : For there is not more difference, for the moft part, between a piece of Gold and an Oyfter-fhell , than between a true Record and a Forgery.

Upon this Infpection the Popes Power began to be queftioned , and his Throne to fhake, as if it had been founded on a Quagmire : He therefore furnifheth him-felf with *Armies of Priefts*, as S. *Gregory* phrafeth it , new Orders of *Jefuites* and *Fryars* , (never before heard of) being erected for the defence of his Tottering Chair : men devoted againft the Truth, as thofe Confpirators were , that fwore *they would neither eat nor drink till they had flain* Paul ; for the Maintenance of whom, he is at great expence unto this day.

day. Above all other arts, that of providing *Seminaries* being the most costly, and the most mysterious: wherein they are secretly trained up, like *Sappho's* Birds; of whom it is reported, that being ambitious to be thought a GOD, he privately cherished a multitude, and taught them by degrees to say, Μέγας Θεὸς ὁ Σάφω: Sappho *is a great God*: which being let loose on a sudden with their Lesson, all the other Birds in the Forrest were quickly instructed in the same *Ditty*: Whereupon (he withdrawing himself) the people thought him gone to Heaven, and a Temple was erected *to the God Sappho*. Whether the Story be true, I shall not determine; I am sure it may pass for an *Embleme* of the Popes Atchievement, who by this means has *made* the World to ring of a Doctrine which *makes* him a God; or if not that, at least Lord of all *Councils*, greater than Emperours, Head of the Church, &c. His *Emissaries* issuing forth from these *mysterious* Seminaries, and filling the Earth like Locusts, or like little fraudulent and simple Birds, chirping out the Ditty: and while all the Wood learning it one of another, the Earth is full of the *Miracle*.

All

All the late *Compilers* of the *Decrees* and *Councils* seem hence to flow; *James Merlin*, *Peter Crabbe*, *Laurentius Surius*, *Nicolinus*, *Carranza*, *Severinus Binius*, *Labbè* and *Coſſartius*, the *Collectio Regia*, *&c.* being his ſworn Adjutants for upholding the Chair. The laſt is a Book of ſuch State and Magnificence, that it conſiſts of 37 Volumes, and is in price about 50 pounds: More or leſs, they all carry on the Forgeries with one conſent, which were at firſt publiſhed in the name of *Iſidore* of *Hiſpalis*; though ſome had rather, upon mature deliberation, it ſhould be *Iſidore Mercator*, or *Iſidore Peccator*, a *Merchant*, or a *Sinner*, rather than a *Saint*, and a *Biſhop*.

This Narrative of the Forgeries being thus nakedly, and by way of Hiſtory plainly given, it remains now, that the *Forgeries* themſelves be proved to be ſuch: In the detection of which, much light will *reflect* upon the foregoing paſſages: All which, if you pleaſe, you may take only for a fair *Introduction*.

Howbeit, I muſt cloſe with two or three Obſervations. Firſt of all, I do not content my ſelf with any ſingle *Collector* of Councils among the *Papiſts*, leſt they ſhould ſay, This is but *one Doctors* Opinion;

Opinion ; but I take the *Stream* of them together. Secondly, Detect not the Books of *private* men, but such as are adopted by the Church of *Rome*, being dedicated to Popes, Kings, Emperours, and coming out *cum summo Privilegio*. Thirdly, that the first of these *Compilers*, (excepting those that were imployed in the first publication and Promotion of *Isidore*) did begin with that Service not much above 130 years ago ; all of them rising up since the times of *Martin Luther*, though their Names make a great noise and bluster in the world : For upon the Reformation of the Church, so happily wrought, and carried on by the Protestants, these *Armies* of *Collectors* were marshalled together, to help a little, and to uphold the Popes Chair by Forgeries : Which intimates a *Dearth* of *Antiquities*, since they are forced to *fly* to such *shameful* expedients.

Luther appeared in the year 1517. The first that appeared after him was *James Merlin*, in the year 1535. The next was *Peter Crabbe*, in the year 1538. After him *Carranza*, in the year 1564. Then *Surius*, in the year 1567. *Turrian* follows, not as a Collector, but as a *Champion* to defend them, in the year 1573. Whom *Nicolinus*

colinus succeeded as a *Compiler* of the Councils, in the year 1585. After him *Binius, Labbè* and *Coſſartius*, and the *Collectio Regia* follow in their Order. So that it is an eaſie matter to diſcern what ſet theſe *Voluminous Writers* on work, to wit, the great and ſmart occaſion they received by the *Reformation*.

Finally obſerve, that *Iſidore* and *Merlin*, the firſt of the Compilers, whoſe Works are extant, lay down the Forgeries, ſimply and plainly, for good Records; but *Binius*, and his Followers, by reaſon of the Arguments which they cannot anſwer, begin to confeſs ſome of them to be Forgeries : So do the moſt Grave and Learned Cardinals, *Bellarmine* and *Baronius*, though they ſtill carry on the *Deſign* of the firſt *Inventers*, by ſome other Methods, which they hope will ſucceed better.

Nor is it any wonder, that a *Secular Kingdom* ſhould make men more *active* than the love of *Heaven*; ſince we daily ſee, how the Kings of the world expend vaſt Treaſures of Gold and Silver, and run through all dangers of Death and Battel, for their own preſervation, and the Conqueſt of their Neighbours. The ſame care which they take in building

Forts

Forts and Cittadels, being taken by th
Bishop of *Rome*, in maintaining *Semina*
ries , *Univerfities* , *Printing-Houfes*, &c
which depend abfolutely on him, for th
fecuring of all that *Wealth* and *Empire*
which he hath by his *Wit* and *Policy* ac
quired : It ftandeth him upon ; for i
his Religion falls, his *Glory* vanifheth, an
his *Kingdom* is abolifhed.

Gen. 34. What men will do for *Secular Ends*
beyond all the belief and expectation c
the *Vulgar*, we fee in *Hamor* and *She*
chem, the firft and moft Ancient Myrrou
of that kind in the world : who for th
accomplifhment of their defires, introdu
ced a new Religion, trou'bling themfelve
and their Citizens unto *Blood*, meerly t
get poffeffion of *Dinah* , *Jacob's* Daugh
ter.

1 Kings. *Jeroboam's* Policy is about 2500 yea
old, though much more late. When th
ten Tribes revolted from the Houfe c
David, for fear left they fhould return t
their Allegiance, if they went up yearl
to *Jerufalem*, according to the Law , h
fet up two *Calves* for the people to wo
fhip , and underwent a great *expen*
(befides the *Gold* in the Calves) in erec
ing a new Order of *Priefts*, that the pe
ple might be kept at home in their *pe*

ver

verse Obedience. He very well knew those Calves were no *Deities*, yet for fecular ends he promoted their worſhip, and was followed therein by all the *Line* of the Kings of *Iſrael*, ſeveral hundred of years together.

What *Demetrius* the *Silver-Smith* did for *Diana of the Epheſians*, and what an uproar he made, purely for *Gain*, in making her *Shrines*, all the Chriſtian World underſtandeth: But the *High-Prieſts*, Scribes and Elders of the *Jews*, in acting againſt all the *Miracles* of Chriſt, and againſt their *Conſcience*; eſpecially in giving Money to the Souldiers to hold their peace, when they brought the news of his Reſurrection, their *reſiſting of the Holy Ghoſt* at his Miraculous *Deſcent*; theſe are a ſufficient inſtance of the *incredible* obdurateneſs of mans heart, and his obſtinate perverſeneſs, allures his hopes, as the immediate Crown of his Labours.

The *Diana* of the *Romans* is much more *proſcuous* than the *Diana* of the *Epheſians*: The *fatteſt places of the Provinces*, and the *greateſt Empire in the World*, are the Game they Play. This *Dinah* animateth all their Strength to impoſe on the people: And for the eaſing
of

of their own Charge, it is a ufual thing with Popes, to permit their Priefts and Fryers, for their better fupport, to deceive the people; which Dr. *Stillingfleet*, in his Book of *Popifh Counterfeit Miracles*, does excellently open: in which, and in all other Arts and Tricks, they have a fpecial connivance, provided they keep the poor fimple Sheep within the bounds of their Jurifdiction, and contribute to the continuance of their Secular Kingdom.

This is the *truth* of the Story; and thefe are the circumftances of the whole procedure, which remains now to be proved.

CAP. IV.

James Merlin's *Editions of the Councils, who lately publifhed* Ifidore Hifpalenfis *for a good Record, which is now detected, and proved to be a Forgery.*

JAmes *Merlin's* pains was to publifh *Ifidore*, with fome Collections and Additions of his own. He pofitively affirmeth him to be that Famous *Ifidore* of *Hifpalis*, a Saint, a Bifhop, and a Father of

of the Church : though as *Blondel*
and Dr. *Reynolds* accurately obferve,
S. Ifidore of *Hifpalis* was dead 40, 50, 60
years, before fome things came to pafs
that are mentioned in that Book of the
Councils.

Blondel in a Book of his, called *Pfeudo-Ifidorus*, or *Turrianus Vapulans*, *Cap* 2.
obferves, how the loweft that write of
Ifidores death, fix it on the year 647. as
Vafæus in his Chronicle : Others on the
year 643. as *Rodericus Toletanus Hift. lib.*
2. *cap.* 18. Or on the year 635. as *the proper Office of the Saints of* Spain : or on the
year 636. when *Sinthalus* entered his
Kingdom, as *Redemptus Diaconus*, an eye-
witnefs, *De Obitu* Ifidori.

Brauleo Bifhop of *Cæfar-Auguftana*,
Lucas Tudenfis, *Baronius* the great Anna-
lift, *Mariana*, *Grialus*, and others, agree
with the laft ; which is eleven years foon-
er than *Vafæus.* So that the general prevailing Opinion is, that *Ifidore* of *Hifpalis*
died in the year 636. However, that we
may deal moft fairly with them, we will
allow them all they can defire, and calcu-
late our affair by the laft Account, which
is moft for their advantage.

Admit *Vafæus* in the right, that *Ifidore*
lived till the year 647. yet the Book

F   which

which is Fathered upon him, can be non
of his; for it mentions things whic
came to pass long after.

It is observed by *Blondel*, that *Honora
tus*, who succeeded *Isidore* in the See o
Hispalis, is found in the sixth Council o
Toledo; whereas this pretended *Isidor*
makes mention of the eleventh Counci
in the same place. He talks of the sixtl
Oecumenical Council, in the year 681. n
less than 46 years after his own death, b
the lowest account. He writes of *Boni
face* of *Mentz*, slain as *Baronius* observes
in the year 755. which was threescore an
sixteen years after *Isidores* death : Yet
Possevin, upon the word *Isidorus Hisp.* and
Hart in his Conference with *Reynolds*
contend the Author of this Book to be
the true *Isidore*, *Bishop of Hispalis*, as *Merlin* who first published *Isidore* in print, and
others did before them.

Among his Witnesses produced again[s]
this Counterfeit, the first which *Blonde,*
useth, is the *Code of the Roman Church*:
in which onely the Epistles of 13 Roman Bishops are contained, beginning
with *Siricius* : Whereas there are in *Isidore* above 6c. whereof five or six and
thirty lived before *Siricius*, and were al.
unknown until the time of *Isidore*.

His

His next Testimony is that of the Bishops of *France*, about the year 865. who concluded, that *Isidore's* Wares *then newly beginning to be sold, could not have the force of* Canons, *because they were not contained in the* Authentick Code, *or Book of Canons formerly known.*

He next citeth the Council of *Aquisgranum*, *An.* 816. the Bishops of *Paris*, *An.* 829. *Henricus Caltheisensis*, *Erasmus*, *Greg.Cassander*,*Anton. Contius*,the famous Lawyer, *Bellarmine* and *Baronius*, the Learned Cardinals.

The Testimony of *Baronius* being more largely cited than the residue, I thought it meet to search the Author, and there I found these following passages.

Writing upon the Contest between Pope *Nicholas* and the French Bishops concerning Appeals,he beginneth to shew how they complained, *that the Causes of Bishops, which ought to be tryed in Councils by their Fellow Bishops, were removed to the Apostolick Chair: And they questioned in their Letters, whether those Epistles of the more Ancient Bishops, which were not inserted into the Body of the Canons, but were written in the Collection of* Isidore Mercator, *were of equal Authority with the residue ?*

Baron. An. Christ. 865. nk. 4.

F 2   For

For the making of which Controver-
fie the more plain, and to fhew what they
mean by the *Body of the Canons*, he tells
Ibid n.u. 5. us, *It is certain, that the more Ancient
Collection of the Decretal Epiftles of the
Roman Bifhops, and the Canons of divers
Councils, acquired fuch a name, that the
Volum was called,* The Book, or Code*, or*
BODY of CANONS, *increafed by the
addition of other Councils, which were afterwards celebrated.* But the more ancient
and full collection of the Epiftles of Roman
Bifhops, and Canons of Councils, was that
of Crefconius, of which I have fpoken before, faith he: *Which being increafed by
the addition of many Canons and Epiftles,
went under the name of the Book, or* BO-
DY of CANONS. *and whereas there
were many other* Collections of Canons
*compiled, that which is the richeft of all,
made by* Ifidore *firnamed* Mercator, *containing the Epiftles of the Ancient Roman
Bifhops, beginning from* Clement, *was*
Longè recentior, *far younger than they
all; as* Hincmarus, *Archbifhop of* Rhemes,
*does teftifie: Forafmuch as it was not
brought out of* Spain *into* France, *before
the times of* Charles the Great, *by* Riculphus *Archbifhop of* Mentz: *For fo he te-
ftifies in a Letter of his to* Hincmarus Laudunenfis,

dunensis , *beginning*, Sicut de Libro, &c.
*But he who first collected Canons out of the
foresaid Epistles*, *published at first by* Isidore, *and inserted them into the books of
the Kings of the* Franks, *was* Benedictus
Levita , *as he testifieth of himself in his
Preface before the fifth book of those Canons ; who writ in the times of the Sons
of* Ludovicus Pius *the Emperour,* Ludovicus Lotharius, *and* Charles, *as we shewed,
where he saith* , *I have inserted these Canons*, &c. *to wit* , *those* WARES *of* Isidore Mercator, *which were brought* , *as
thou hast heard of* Hincmarus, *into* France
out of Spain *by* Riculphus. Nè quis ca-
lumniari possit , ab Ecclesiâ Romanâ ali-
quid hujusmodi commentum esse: *Lest
any one should slander us* , *and say* , *the
Church of* Rome *invented such a business
as this.*

I think here is enough : He looks upon it as a *Commentum*, *a meer Fiction*, and
is afraid lest any one should have the advantage of Fathering such a dreadful Bastard on the Church of *Rome.* He calls
them *Isidore the Merchants Wares* ; he
does not refel the Bishops of *France* ; he
dares not affirm they were in the Ancient
Code of Epistles and Councils ; he acknowledgeth them *far younger* than the
BODY

BODY of CANONS, and subscribes to *Hincmarus* Archbishop of *Rhemes*, citing him who writ against *Isidore*, as a good and Authentick Author. He confesseth that they were never known in *France* till the times of *Charles the Great*, that is 700 years after they first began to be written; and that they were introduced into the books of the Kings of the *Franks* by *Benedictus Levita*, in the times of *Ludovicus Lotharius*, which was about the year 850. So that the Church was governed well enough without them, and about 800 years after our Saviours Birth they were first hatcht as meer *Innovations*. This is too large a *Chink* for an Enemy to open; but he proceedeth further.

Baron. *An.*
865. *nu.* 6.

That the same Riculphus, *Bishop of* Mentz, *did live in the times of* Charles the Great, *many Monuments of that Age do make it certain; especially the Testament of the same* Charles the Great, *to which this* Riculphus *is found to have subscribed among divers others. We find that he was President also in a Council at* Mentz, *held in the year of our Redemption* 813. &c. *Since therefore the French Regions, which are nearest to* Spain, *knew not the* Collection of Isidore *before the times of* Riculphus,

Riculphus, *much less* Italy, *it is a conje-cture, that this* Isidore *did live and write not long before*; *and so it was first publish-ed by* Riculphus, *who brought it thither*; *then by* Benedictus, *who put it into the Ca-pitular books*; *and lastly, by* Hincmarus Junior, *Bishop of* Laon, *the last Collecter unto this our Age: which* Hincmarus *of* Rhemes, *a man of a keener smell, repre-hendeth in many things, defaming that collection of* Isidore *which the other used, for which cause he was accused.* For Fro-doardus, *in his History of* Rhemes, *Cap.* 16. *near the end, saith of him, that being accused because he had condemned the De-cretal Epistles of the* Roman Bishops, *he professed and protested otherwise, that he admitted, held, and approved them with the greatest honour. Upon this occasion, to wit, it appears, he was branded with a mark, because he had signified himself not to have approved that Collection of* Isidore *in all things.*

Baronius you see, who is one of the greatest Friends to the See of *Rome*, en-deavours to remove the matter of *Isidore* as far as he can from the *Roman Chair*, being sore afraid, lest the guilt of so ma-ny *Forgeries* should too apparently be charged upon her: For which cause he

will

will not have the book so much as *known* in *Italy*, nay not in *France*, which is nearer unto *Spain*, for 8cc years time, but that it came out of *Spain* first, being brought by *Riculphus*. Perhaps *Riculphus* was never there. He doth not tell us that he went into *Spain*, for ought I can find, nor upon what occasion, nor in what City, nor of whom he received *Isidore*: which putteth me in mind of *Cacus* his device, who being a strong Thief, and robbing *Hercules* of his Oxen, drew them all backward by the Tail into his Den, that the print of their heels being found backwards, they might not be tracked, but seem to be gone another way.

But he fails in his design: for as it is strange, that *Italy* should not know the Decretal Epistles of its *own* Popes for 8cc years, till *Riculphus* brought them out of *Spain*; so is it more strange, that being such *Forgeries* as he would have them, *Hincmarus* Archbishop of *Rhemes* should be accused for condemning them, and rated up, and branded in such a manner, and compelled to recant by so powerful an Enemy; for it seems he had no way to save himself, but by *renouncing* his Opinion. The jealousie of the *Roman Church*, and its tenderness over *Isidore*,

dore, appeareth most exceeding great in the *hard dealing* which *Hincmarus* met with, who though he did recant, was still *noted with infamy*; as if to speak against *Isidore*, were a Crime not to be washed off by the *Tears* of Repentance in the Church of *Rome*. Perhaps the poor Bishop was an Hypocrite in that forced Confession, and for this was branded, because he confessed a *lye*, as men upon the Rack are wont to do, for his own deliverance: for that he knew still that *Isidore* was a Counterfeit, and must therefore be reputed a rotten Member of the Church of *Rome*. This *Baronius* observes, while he ascribeth *Hincmarus* his reprehending *Isidore*'s Collection, to his *keener scent*; whereby he was able, more readily than others, to *smell* a *Rat*, and discover the *Cheat*.

Baronius proceedeth further in condemning the *collection of Isidore*, thus; But Nicholas *the Pope seemed to abstain from it on purpose: for though he was often ingaged in these Controversies, concerning Appeals to the Apostolick Chair, and there were in it many, and those most powerful, Testimonies of most holy Popes, and they Martyrs too, whose Authority might be of highest force in the Church; yet he wholly*

An 85 nu. 7.

wholly abstained from them (which that he knew to be doubtful at least, is not to be doubted) using only those, concerning which there was never any doubt in the Church of God; because the Church did not want those adventitious, and late invented Evidences, because it might receive them abundantly from other places : but Benedictus Levita *himself also, though (as you have heard from* Hincmarus, *and as he himself testifies in the Preface before his books) he took many things out of that same Collection of* Isidore; *yet being conscious in himself, that the Authority of those Epistles was not so sure, but that it nodded exceedingly, he never cited any Author of them, as he did in the other Epistles of the Roman Bishops,* Innocent, Leo, Gelasius, Symmachus, *and* Gregory; *naming the Authors of those, whose Faith was clear and certain. But further yet, with great caution, because he knew the Evidences taken from them not to be so firm, he took care, as he testifies in the end, to have them confirmed by the Apostolick Authority.*

Is not here a merry passage? *Benedictus Levita* knew the Decretal Epistles to be *false*, and therefore he got them to be *made true* by the Popes Authority; at least to be *confirmed* as *true*, whereas they

were *doubtful* before. It is the manner
of ~~Princes~~ Statesmen sometimes, to get o-
thers to propose the matters, which they
themselves design to be done; that the
business springing from the request of
others, might appear more *graceful* in
the eye of the people. We may justly
enquire, whether *Benedictus Levita* were
not *ordered* what to Petition, by private
instructions from his Holiness, before he
made his motion to the Chair: for it had
otherwise been an *extravagant impudence* to have assaulted the Chair with
such a request as that is, of craving a Confirmation of new-found Records, so feeble and suspected. Whatever the *Intrigue*
was, the *event* is clear, *Benedictus Levita*
got them *confirmed*, and so they were a-
dopted for his Holiness Children, though
Pope *Nicholas* was shy a little out of
shame and modesty, and blushed to acknowledge his poor Kindred.

It is further observable, that these
counterfeit *Epistles* were first brought in
into the Records of the *Franks*, without
naming their Authors: and that a little
after their *quiet* publication, some Favou-
rite of the Chair grew more bold, and
added their *names* unto them; this of *Clement*, that of *Anacletus*, &c. And that the
work

work was thus perfected by degrees, *Ba-ronius* shews us in the following passage.

Ibid nu. 7. *But he who first published the Decrees extracted out of those Epistles, with the Title of the* Roman Bishops, *in whose names they are recorded, was that* Hincmarus *we mentioned, the Bishop of* Laon, *as appears by an Epistle or book written against him by* Hincmarus *of* Rhemes; *who receiving that work of the Bishop of* Laon, *read it not without indignation, and in very many things reproved it. But others have followed the Bishop of* Laon, *as* Burchardus, *who writ in the following Age, and others after him, who prefixed the names of the very* Roman Bishops *before all the* Chapters, *which* Gratian *also did the last of all.*

But that those Epistles are rendered suspitious, by many things which we have said in the second Tome of our Annals, while we mentioned each in particular, is sufficiently demonstrated: Where we shewed withal, that the holy Roman Church *did not need them, so as (if they should be detected of falsity) to be bereaved of its Rights and Priviledges, since (though she wanteth them) she is abundantly strengthened and confirmed by the Legitimate and Genuine Decretal Epistles of other Popes.*

Popes. But that the Chapters *taken out of them by* Benedictus Levita, *were at first approved, as agreeable to the* Canons *(as himself testifies) by the Authority of the* Roman Bishops, *(which was done also by the latter Collectors) it happened rather by long use, than for any strength or firmness in themselves.*

Thus *Baronius* in his *Annals, An.* 865. *nu.* 5, 6, 7, 8. all together.

In Notis Martyrol. ad 4. *April.* he saith, Vasæus *is convicted to have erred, who thought this* Isidore Pacensis *that* Isidore *who collected the Epistles of the* Roman Bishops, *and the* Councils, *&c.* Hincmarus Laudunensis *also, and* Trithemius, *and others err, who ascribe that collection to* Isidore *of* Hispalis: *That Opinion is refelled; first, because* Brauleus *and* Ildephonsus, *who lived in those times, drawing up a Catalogue of his Writings, make not the least mention of that work. But further, all doubt is taken away concerning this matter, while the Author of that work, speaking there concerning the manner of holding a* Council, *recites the words of the first* Canon *of the eleventh* Council *of* Toledo, *and mentions* Agatho *the Pope in his Preface, since* Isidore *of* Hispalis *departed this life, long before the*
times

times of that Council , *and Pope* Agatho.

Had we time , we might make many curious reflexions upon thefe paffages of *Baronius* : He afterwards talks of another *Ifidore* , called fometimes *Mercator*, and fometimes *Peccator* ; but of what Parents , what Calling , what City , or what Country he was, he mentioneth nothing. So that this *Child*, among all thofe *Ifidores* and *Fathers* that are found out for it , muft reft at laft in one that is *unknown*.

All that can be gathered from this whole difcourfe of *Baronius* , is this , That a new Book of Councils, richly fraught with Evidences for the *Roman Church* and *Religion*, came abroad under the name of *Ifidore* , containing Decrees and Decretal Epiftles that were never before heard of in the world : that this Book was *falfly* Fathered upon *Ifidore* of *Hifpalis* ; and that all thofe ancient Epiftles of the Roman Bifhops, from S. *Peter* down to *Siricius* , are juftly fufpected . Nay, he confeffes them to be *infirm*, *adventitious*, and *lately invented* , or *newly found* , and to *nod exceedingly* : He oppofeth them to thofe Records which are *Legitimate* and *Genuine*, though they are of late magnified , and followed by all

the

the Collectors of the Decrees and Councils, being, though waved by some, cited and *approved* by other Popes, as well as Doctors, Jesuites, Cardinals, &c.

This is the last and best Story that can be made on the behalf of that *Book*, the Counterfeits in which, as we observed before, were, because they extol and magnifie the Popes Chair, received for good and Authentick *Laws* in the Church of *Rome:* For *Baronius* died not long since, about the year 1607. in this last Century; and when he had seen the truth of those Arguments that are urged against the Forgeries, endeavours so to handle this matter in his History, as to clear the Church of *Rome* from the imputation.

Bellarmine, that saw not into this Mystery so clearly, takes another course; which when we have intimated one or two Marginal Notes in *Baronius*, we shall declare. *Baronius* deals more fairly with us than *Binius*; for the one in his Marginal Notes contradicteth his Text, sometimes to delude the Reader: but *Baronius* fairly notes in the Margin, Isidori *collectio vulgata in Galliis.* Isidori *collectio ab Antiquis non adeo probata.* Isidori *collectio ut minùs sincera notata,*

notata, &c. Soft words for a Treatife rejected, but ftrong Indications of a Defperate Caufe. *The Ancients approved not the collection of* Ifidore. *It was not fo fincere as it ought,* &c.

Bellarm. *de Rom. Pont lib.* 1. *cap.* 14.

Cardinal *Bellarmine*, to prove the Popes Supremacy, draweth one Argument from the Popes themfelves; whofe Teftimonies he cafteth into three Claffes. *The firft,* faith he, *contains the Epiftles of Popes that fate from* S. Peter *to the year* 300. *in which* Calvin *and the* Magdenburgenfes *confefs the Primacy to be plainly afferted; and that thofe Bifhops were holy men, and true Bifhops; but they fay the Epiftles are forged and new, and falfly Fathered on thofe Bifhops.* In this Clafs he affirmeth, *Thefe Holy Fathers do clearly affert the Primacy;* Clemens *in his firft Epiftle,* Anacletus *in his third,* Evariftus *Epift.* 1. Pius *Epift.* 1, *and* 2. Anicetus *Epift.* 1. Victor *Epift.* 1. Zephirinus *Epift.* 1. Calixtus *Epift.* 1. Lucius *Epift.* 1. Marcellus *in Epift.* 1. Eufebius *Epift.* 3. Melchiades *Epift.* 2. Marcus *Epift.* 1.

After this he faith, *Quamvis aliquos Errores, &c. Though I cannot deny, but that fome Errours are crept into them, and dare not affirm that they are indubitable, yet I doubt not at all, but that they are very Ancient.*

Ancient. As if an old Deed being called into queſtion, and the matter of Fact made certain, that it was a real Forgery; he that holds his poſſeſſion by it, ſhould ſay, It has been *interlined* indeed, and *corrupted* in many places, but 'tis very *old.* Let us ſee however what his reaſon is for the Antiquity of it: He is rough with his Opponents, and telleth us, *The* Magdeburgenſes *do lye, when they ſay* Cent. 2. Cap. 7. *near the end, that no Author worthy of credit ever cited theſe Epiſtles before* Charles the Great: *For* Iſidore, *who is* 200 *years older than* Charles the Great, *in the Proem of his collection of the Holy Canons,* ſaith, *that by the advice of* 80 *Biſhops, he collected* Canons *out of the Epiſtles of* Clement, Anacletus, *&c.*

Iſidore did indeed begin to flouriſh near to the year 610. So that *Bellarmine* takes him right for the ſame *Iſidore* Biſhop of *Hiſpalis.* But had he well examined the matter, he would have forborn to give the Lye to men more in the right than himſelf, confiding in the *rotten* Antiquity of this Counterfeit *Iſidore.* For *Iſidores Preface* is a Counterfeit too, made on purpoſe to countenance the Forgeries: not 200 years older than *Charles*

G *the*

the Great, things after the Death of *Isidore,* its pretended Author, being mentioned in the same.

Confer. Cap 8. Di- *p. 3.*

Dr *Reynolds* in his Conference with *Hart,* having smartly checked him for his *fourscore Bishops* out of one *Isidore,* asked him, *About what year of Christ* Isidore *did die? How doth* Genebrard *write?* (because *Genebrard* was *Hart's* most admired Author.) He answereth, *About the year* 637. as he proveth out of *Vasæus.* Asking him, *When the General Council of* Constantinople, *under* Agatho, *was kept?* He answereth, *In the year* 681. *or* 682. *or thereabout* Then Isidore *was dead above* 40 years, faith Reynolds, *before that General Council.* He was, faith Hart, *but what of that? Of that it doth follow, that the Preface written in* Isidores *name, and set before the Councils, to purchase credit to those Epistles, is a counterfeit, and not* Isidore's: *For in that Preface there is mention made of the General Council of* Constantinople, *held against Bishop* Macarius *and* Stephanus, *in the time of Pope* Agatho, *and the Emperour* Constantine: *which being it was held above* 40 *years after* Isidore *was dead, by* Genebrard's *own confession, by his own confession* Isidore *could not tell the fourscore Bishops of it. And*

so

so the 80 *Bishops which* Turrian *hath found out in one* Isidore, *are dissolved all into one Counterfeit*, *abusing both the* name *of* Isidore, *and fourscore Bishops.* Hart was unable to answer him, and fled from the Point.

Harding, in his Book against Bishop *Jewel*, citeth these Forgeries frequently and briskly: Upon the failure of which, though *Baronius* pretends an abundant number of other *Evidences*; yet in the loss of 30 or 40 *Primitive* Bishops and Martyrs, that were so long time, for the first 300 years after Christ together, thought to speak for the Supremacy of the Church of *Rome*, one of the fairest Feathers in the Popes Crown is plucked away; and the younger *Evidences*, in which *Baronius* trusts, being none but the Malepert and Arrogant Testimonies of *Junior Popes*, in their own Causes, will make but a slight impression in the minds of men, that have found themselves deluded with more ancient pretences, of the grave and unspotted Authorities of Holy Men, that Sacrificed themselves for the Glory of God, and the good of the World, and sealed their Testimony with their latest blood; which the latter Bishops of *Rome* have been more Secular

G 2 and

and Pompous, than to be doing like their Predeceſſors.

CAP. V.

Divers Forgeries contained in Iſidore's *Collection, mentioned in particular.*

Iſidore, as he now ſtandeth ſet forth by *Merlin*, has 50 *Canons of the Apoſtles* for pure and good Records; many Decretal Epiſtles, made, as he pretends, by the firſt Martyrs and Biſhops of *Rome*; very long, and full of Popery.

He has two Epiſtles of S. *Clement* written to S. *James* Biſhop of *Jeruſalem*, that was dead before S. *Clement* came to the Chair: one to the Brethren dwelling with S. *James*, and two others in his name.

He has four Epiſtles in the name of *Anacletus*, who lived in the time of *Trajan*, and ſate in the Roman Chair, *An.* 104. In the laſt of which the Counterfeit *Anacletus* feigneth, 'That all the 'Primacies and Archbiſhopricks in the 'World were divided and ſetled by 'S. *Peter* and S. *Clement*; that the Church 'of *Rome* is the Head and Hinge of all 'the

' the Churches; and that all the Patriar-
' chal Sees were made such by vertue of
' S. *Peter*: *Antioch*, because he sate there,
' before he came to *Rome*   *Alexandria*,
' because S. *Mark* came to sit there from
' S. *Peter*: but *Rome* especially the first
' See, because it is sanctified by the death
' of S. *Peter*, and S. *Paul*. As if our Saviours Death were nothing able to sanctifie
Jerusalem, as S. *Peter*'s death was to sanctifie *Rome*: though besides the Death of
Christ, *Jerusalem* hath this advantage,
that it is the *first Church*, and the *Mother
of us all*.

That you may a little discern the deal-
ings of the Papists, note here, that *Anacletus* his first and second Epistles are
cited by *Bellarmine* for good Records,
in the very same book where he confesseth them to be Counterfeits: For though
in one *little* passage they be confessed for
the present satisfaction of a stiff *Oppo-
nent*; yet where men are minded to be
corrupt, they may serve the turn in an
hundred other places, by a *Pious Fraud*;
and the Confession being over-skipped,
they may still seem Authentick, especially
if the place happen to be unseen where
the Confession was made, as it often cometh to pass in voluminous writings.

*Bellarm.
de Rom
Pont. lib. 1
cap. 23. a*

G 3   *Isidore*

Isidore has besides these, 2 counterfeit Epistles of *Evaristus*, 3 of *Alexander*, 2 of *Sixtus*, 1 of *Telesphorus*, 2 of *Higinus*, 2 of *Pius*, 1 of *Anitius*, 2 of *Soter*, 1 of *Eleutherius*, 2 of *Victor*, 2 of *Zephirinus*, 2 of *Calixtus*, 1 of *Urbanus*, 2 of *Pontianus*, 1 of *Anterus*, 3 of *Fabian*, 2 of *Cornelius*, 1 of *Lucius*, 2 of *Stephen*, 2 of *Sixtus*, 2 of *Dionysius*, 3 of *Felix*, 2 of *Eutychianus*, 1 of *Gaius*, 2 of *Marcellinus*, 2 of *Marcellus*, 3 of *Eusebius*, 1 of *Melchiades*. All laid down without the least note of any *Fraud*: though the latter Compilers of the Councils, having their eyes opened by the Century-Writers of *Magdenburg*, and the care of other Protestants, begin to acknowledge several of them to be Forgeries.

These *Epistles* have one common blast upon them; they were first seen in a *counterfeit book*, and never known to the World, till many hundred years after their *pretended* Authors were set in their Graves. They cannot *all* be confuted at once; the Reader therefore must have patience, till we meet with them in their places. In the mean time see what Bishop *Jewel* saith concerning them, a man never answered by any, especially as to these points, wherein he chargeth them

with

with Forgery. 'Gratian sheweth, that
'the Decretal Epistles have been doubt-
'ed of among the Learned. Dr. Smith
'declared openly at *Paul's Cross*, that
'they cannot possibly be theirs whose
'names they bear: And to utter some
'reasons shortly for proof thereof, these
'Decretal Epistles manifestly deprave
'and abuse the Scriptures, as it may soon
'appear to the Godly Reader upon sight.
'They maintain nothing so much, as the
'State and Kingdom of the Pope; and
'yet there was no such State erected in
'many hundred years after the Apostles
'time. They publish a multitude of vain
'and Superstitious Ceremonies, and o-
'ther like Fantasies, far unlike the Apo-
'stles Doctrine. They proclaim such
'things as Mr. *Harding* knoweth to be
'open and known Lies. *Anacletus*, that
'was next after *Peter*, willeth and strait-
'ly commandeth, that all Bishops, once
'in the year, do visit the Entry of S. *Pe-*
'*ter*'s Church in *Rome*, which they call
'*Limina Petri*; yet was there then no
'Church as yet built there in the name of
'*Peter*. Pope *Antherus* maketh mention
'of *Eusebius Alexandrinus*, and *Felix*,
'which lived a long time after him. *Fa-*
'*bianus* writeth of the coming of *Nova-*
'*tus*

Dist. 12. De Epistolis.

Dist. 2. Tertia San-ctuum.

C 4

'tus into *Italy* ; yet 'tis clear by S. *Cy-*
'*prian*, and *Eusebius* , that *Novatus* came
'firſt into *Italy* in the time of *Cornelius*,
'who was (next) after *Fabianus*. One
'*Petrus Crab*, the Compiler of the Coun-
'cils, complaineth much, that the exam-
'ples from whence he took them , were
'wonderfu ly corrupted, and not one of
'them agreeing with another. *Gratian*
'himſelf. upon good advice, is driven to
'ſay, that al ſuch Epiſtles ought to have
'p ace, rather in debating matter of Ju-
'ſtice in the Conſiſtory , than in deter-
'mi ing and weighing the truth of the
'Scriptures. Beſides this, neither S. *Hie-*
'*rom*, nor *Gennadius*, nor *Damaſus* , nor
'any other O!d Father , ever alledged
'theſe Epiſtles, or made any account of
'them ; nor the Biſhops of *Rome* them=
'ſelves at the firſt, no not when ſuch Evi-
'dences might have ſtood them in beſt
'ſtead, in their ambitious contention for
'Superiority over the Biſhops of *Africa* :
'The Contents of them are ſuch , as a
'very Child of any judgment may ſoon
'be able to deſcry them. Here he na-
meth St. *Clement*'s writing to St. *James*
when he was dead, *Marcellus* charging
the Emperour *Maxentius*, an Infidel and
a Tyrant, with the Authority of *Clement* ;
with

with several things of this kind. In his *Reply to* Harding's *Answer, Artic.* 1. *and* 4. But I proceed with *Isidore*, or rather *Merlin*, that first printed him.

He has, besides all these Epistles, certain counterfeit Decrees of *Sylvester*, Bishop of *Rome*, in the time of *Constantine* the Great, and the *Epilogus brevis Romani Concilii post Nicænum celebrati*; which *Hincmarus*, Archbishop of *Rhemes*, is reported particularly to have excepted against, as absurd, because it ordaineth, 1. *That no Lay-man ought to accuse a Clergy-man.* 2. *That no Inferiour Priest may accuse his Superiour.* 3. *That a Prelate may not be condemned without 72 Witnesses, a Cardinal Priest not without 43, a Cardinal Deacon of the City of* Rome *not without 27, a Sub-Deacon, an Acolythite, a Reader, a Door-keeper, not without 7 Witnesses.* It is further provided, that every one of these Witnesses must be *without any spot of infamy*: no Lay-man at all, nor any inferiour Clergy man. So that upon the matter a safe Indemnity is prepared for all kind of Priests, especially the great ones, to swim in any Excess as himself listeth, provided he be not guilty of the Protestants faults; that is to say, that he doth not touch the Popes Crown, or the Monks Belly.   This

This *Decree* is most solemnly put a-
mong the Councils by *Isidore*, and *Merlin*, by *Peter Crabbe*, *Surius*, *Binius*, *Labbe*,
and *Cossartius*, and the *Collectio Regia*;
and as solemnly put among the Popes
Laws, by *Ivo* an ancient Bishop, a great
Civilian, and one of the Eldest Digesters
of the Canon Law, before *Gratian*

This brief *Epilogue* set *before* the Council, giveth you to wit, that there were
Cardinals in *Rome* in the time of *Constantine*, the first Christian Emperour. But
if you please to examine Antiquities, you
will hardly find Cardinals so ancient.

Isidore in his Preface directed to one,
whom he calls his *Fellow-servant and Father of the Faith*, mentioneth 70 Canons
of the *Nicene* Council, somewhat too affectedly: 'You 80 Bishops, *saith he*, who
' have compelled me to begin and perfect
' this work, ought to know, and so
' ought all other Priests of the Lord, that
' we have found more than those 20 Ca-
' nons of the *Nicene* Council, that are
' with us: And we read in the Decrees of
' *Julius* the Pope, that there ought to be
' 70 Chapters of that Synod. Yet when
he cometh to the Council it self, he for-
gets himself so far, as to lay down but
20; the 50 forged Canons receiving a
far

fair Countenance only, by that Preface
or Epistle, set for *shew* before the work.

He has an Epistle of *Athanasius*, and
the Bishops of *Egypt*, to Pope *Mark*;
wherein they tell him, that there were
70 Canons of the *Nicene* Council, and
desire him to send them into *Egypt* from
Rome, since all their own were burnt at
Alexandria by the *Arrians*. *Mark* was
dead 9 years before the Burning happened; howbe't, he sent them a Gracious
Answer, with the 70 Canons. The first
of these was seriously cited to m by a
Learned Son of that Church, to prove
the Bishop of *Rome* was called Pope (to
wit, by *Athanasius*, and all the Bishops of
Egypt) within the first 400 years: But
some of their latest Authors begin to
blush at it, as *Binius* and *Baronius* do in
particular.

Next to these he has three Epistles of
Julius the Pope, as very Counterfeits as
the former, yet generally cited by the
Pseudo-Catholicks, as good Records.

After these, *an Epistle of Athanasius,
and the Bishops of Egypt to Liberius*; the
oppression of the Church by the *Arrians*
being the pretended Theme, but its real
design is to magnifie the Popes Chair.

Liberius his Answer. Ejusdem farinæ.

A

A lofty Brag like the residue.

An Epistle of the Bishops of Egypt *t Pope* Felix, *concerning the cruel Persecutions of the Arrians:* An humble Address, and very Supplicatory. Though *Felix* was an *Arrian* himself, and an Usurper of the Chair, thrust in by an *Arrian* Emperour, while *Liberius* the true owner of it was banished for the Faith; yet the stile of the Epistle runneth thus, *Domino beatissimo.* &c. *To our most blessed and most honourable Lord, the Holy Father* Fælix, *Pope of the Apostolical City,* Athanasius, *and all the Bishops of* Egypt, Thebais *and* Lybia, *by the Grace of* God *assembled in the Holy Council of* Alexandria. A stile too too lofty for those purer times of humble simplicity: The usual Compellations of those days (as may be seen by S. *Cyprian*'s Letters to the Bishops of *Rome*, and some other good Records) being far more *short* and *familiar*; such as *Julio Urbis Romæ Episcopo, or, Stephano fratri, or, Cornelio Collegæ & Coepiscopo*; that is, to Julius *Bishop of the City of* Rome, or *to* Stephen *my Brother,* or *to* Cornelius *my Associate and Fellow-bishop:* Nor can we find any other, in undoubted instruments, for the first 300 or 400 years: But for an *Usurper* to be called

Most

Most blessed and honourable Lord, an *Heretick*, *Holy Father and Pope of the Apostolical City*; and that by a man who had rather die than be guilty of such a Flattery, was little suitable to the Spirit of *Athanasius*, that Great and Couragious Champion of the Church, being (as God would have it) one, that of all others was the most mortal hater of the *Arrians*.

Isidore and *Merlin* dote so exceedingly, as to make this Usurper a *Pope*, and to record his Decrees as *lawful Canons*.

After a little time *Liberius* was restored, but on very base and dishonourable terms, as *Bellarmine* himself testifieth out of S. *Hierom*, and *Athanasius*. He fainted in his Persecution, and was restored by an Arrian Emperour, *upon his Subscription to the Heretical Pravity*. After this he writeth more Decretals; and the Title of his Epistle is in *Isidore* thus, *Epistola* Liberii *Papæ, ut nullus pro Persecutionibus dum durare potestatem suam relinquat Ecclesiam*. It is Nonsense, and false Latine: but *Binius* about a thousand and three hundred years after *Liberius* his death, mendeth it thus; *Epistola* XII. Liberii *Papæ, ad omnes generaliter Episcopos, ut nullus pro persecutionibus dum durare potest suam relinquat Ecclesiam: That*

Bell. de Rom. Pont. lib.4.cap.9 Baron. An. Christ.357. Liberii 6. nu.32,33.

Bin. in vit. Liberii.

no man should forsake his Church, for persecution sake, while he was able to bear it. By the Title it should be a compassionate Letter : For if any one be wearied with persecution, as *Liberius* was , by a tacit intimation, it seemeth to permit him to renounce the Faith, as *Liberius* did : for *Bellarmine* and *Platina* consent to this, that he subscribed to the Arrian Creed ; only the one saith, he did it in the external act, *through fear* ; and the other *Sentiens*, that he thought, or *consented with them in all.* Platin. *in vit.* Liberii.

Bellarm. ut supra

Damasus his Epistle to Paulinus *Bishop of* Antioch *follows.* I fear an Imposture : *Isidore* and *Merlin* were not aware there was no such man : Their Followers are fain to mend it thus ; Paulinus *Bishop of Thessalonida.* As *Binius* , *Labbe* , &c. *In vita Damasi.*

Next the Epistle of *Damasus* to *Hierom,* and *Hierom*'s Answer , both confessed to be a Forgery, there is *an Epistle of* Stephen *the Archbishop, and of three Councils in* Africa, *to* Damasus *the* Pope, *concerning the priviledge of the* Roman Chair. Doubtless the Bishops in *Africa* were very zealous for the *priviledge of the* Roman Chair , ever since the Oppression, and Cheat of *Zozimus.* The Title is somewhat

Bin. N. in epist. 3. Damasi. & in Epist. Hieron. ad Damas.

what suspitious : *Beatissimo Domino , & Apostolico Culmini sublato, &c.* Stephanus *Archiepiscopus Concilii* Mauritanii , *&c.* In English thus ; *To our most blessed Lord, and the Apostolical Top highly lifted up, the Holy Father of Fathers , and the Supreme Bishop over all Prelates ,* Stephen *Archbishop of the Council of* Mauritania, *and all the Bishops of the three Councils in the Province of* Africa. Many men have stiled themselves Archbishops of *Provinces,* but no man (as I remember) *Archbishop of a Council.* There may be Archbishops in a Council, but not an Archbishop of the Council. *Three Councils at once in the same Province* were never heard of : One and the same *Letter sent from three Councils* is a strange thing : So is a Letter sent in the name of one Archbishop , as *President of three Councils* at a time.

After this we have 6 Epistles of *Siricius,* 2 of *Anastasius,* 19 of *Innocent,* 2 of *Zozimus,* 3 of *Boniface,* with several Answers : Among which there is inserted a *Constitution of* Honorius *the Emperour* sent to *Boniface, That if there were two Bishops of* Rome *made any more , they should be both driven out of the City :* Which shews how subject the Roman Chair is to Schismes , and the Power that
did

did of old belong to the Emperour.

There are other Epistles of *Celestine*, *Sixtus*, *Leo*, *Hilarius Simplicius Felix*, *Gelasius*, *anastasius*, *Symmachus*, *Hormisda*, &c. the most of which do much exceed our compass of the first 400 years, and are too late for our Cognizance: For since the Forgery of *Zozimus*, much credit is not to be given to the Roman Bishops: Not as if one mans fault had blasted them all; but he leads up the Van of Forgers, and they have all persisted in his Guilt, no one of them making acknowledgment or restitution, and almost all of them guilty of the like, either by doing, or suffering.

Among the rest there is an Instrument, which the Collector calleth, *Sacra* Justini *Imperatoris ad* Hormisdam *Papam*: The Sacred Writing of the Emperour *Justinus* to *Hormisda* Pope. But the word POPE is not in the superscription: The Letter it self is, *To the most Holy and blessed Archbishop and Patriarch of the Venerable City of* Rome, Hormisda. Archbishop and Patriarch we allow him; but not that *Typhus* wherewith the Fathers in the sixth Council of *Carthage* charge *Zozimus*, that *blasphemous Title* which *John* assumed at *Constantinople*, and S. Gregor;

gory so declaimed against at *Rome*.

This Letter of *Justin* the Emperour was written more than 500 years after our Saviours Birth, yet I never saw true Record, in all that time, give a Title so high to the Bishop of *Rome*. But *Justin* was a man of low Descent, a Swineherd at first, a Carpenter afterwards, then a Souldier of Fortune, and at last an Emperour : He was the more solicitous therefore to complement so Mighty a Bishop with accurate expression.

Note well. *Isidore* has suppressed all the Canons of the sixth Council of *Carthage*, as too bitter and sharp for the Popes Constitution. And so has *Merlin*, though very foolishly : for in the beginning of the Book he hath a Preliminary Tract, called, *An Annotation of Synods, the Acts whereof are contained in this book.* In which he giveth us this account : in the *Aquitan* Council, 18 Fathers made 24 Canons : in that of *Neocæsarea*, 16 Fathers made 14 Canons : in that of *Gangra*, 16 Fathers made 21 Canons : in that of *Sardica*, 60 Fathers made 21 Canons : in that of *Antioch*, 30 Fathers made 25 Canons : in that of *Laodicea*, 22 Fathers made 59 Canons : in the Council of *Carthage*, 217 Fathers made 33 Canons. I

H   had

had a long time coveted a fight of thefe Canons, and finding them numbred in fuch *an Annotation of Synods, the Acts whereof are contained in this book*, I was much comforted with hope of feeing them: But when I turned to the place, I found them not! Surely to flip out 33 Canons at a time, made by more Fathers than were in all the other Councils put together, is a lufty *Deleatur:* There was never *Deed* of more importance imbezelled in the World.

. The *Nicene Council* had 318 Fathers, that made 20 Canons: for what fecret caufe therefore he skippeth over the account which he ought efpecially to give of this, is worth the enquiry. He mentions it by the *by*, and fhuffles it off without an account, (perhaps) becaufe he was loath to fay, or unfay the ftory of 70 Canons in the *Nicene* Council. However he dealeth fairly with us in this, that having noted *Aurelius* to have been Prefident in the fixth Council of *Carthage*, he confeffeth, *that S.* Auguftine, *Bifhop of* Hippo, *is recorded to have been in that Council, in the Reign of* Honorius. *Ibid.*

Binius, and all the Popifh Compilers I could ever meet with before, clipped off that Council in the midft, without fo

much

much as fignifying the *number* of its Canons. I was glad I had a fight of their
number *here*, though I mift of themfelves:
and was confident, that however cruelly
the Pope dealt with *Aurelius* Archbifhop
of *Carthage*, S. *Aug.* Bifhop of *Hippo*, and
other holy Fathers, in cutting out their
Tongues, I fhould at laft meet with them:
And the Learned *Juftellus* with much
honefty and honour has made us fatif-
faction.

We acknowledge fome *true* Records
among thefe *Spurious* Abominations: but
a little *poyfon* fpoileth the greateft Mefs
of the moft wholefom Meat ; much more
doth a Bundle of Forgeries that over-
poyfeth the true Records in *fize* and
number.

The method which he ufeth in the
mixture of the Records and Forgeries is
remarkable : For beginning with the
Counterfeit Epiftles of *Clement, Anacletus, &c.* he firft feafoneth the Readers
fpirit with Artificial *Charms*, and *prepof-
feffeth* him with the high Authority of
the Roman Patriarchs ; and after he has
given him thofe ftrong Spells and *Phil-
tres*, compofed of *Roman Drugs*, permits
him boldly to fee fome true Antiquities,
his eyes being dazled in the very *Entry*,

H 2   with

with Apparitions of Popes, and such other *Spectres*.

Left the *Tincture* should decay, he reserves some of the Forgeries till afterwards; that the *true Records* might be compassed in with an *Enchanted Circle*, and the last *Relish* of Antiquity go off as strong as the first, and be as successful as the *prepossession*. Thus he cometh down with Forgeries to *Melchiades*; and then he breaketh off the *Decretal Epistles*, to make room for the *Councils*, beginning with the *Nicene*, under pretence of its Excellency, and putting the Councils before it in time, after it in order, that he might get a fit occasion to introduce them here; so running down in a disorderly manner, from *Ancyra* to *Neocæsarea*, *Gangra*, *Sardica*, *Antioch*, *Laodicea*, *Constantinople*, *Ephesus*, *Chalcedon*, among the *Greeks*, and then up again to the *Latine Councils*, many of which preceded divers of the other; as the first, second, third, fourth, fifth, sixth Council of *Carthage*, all which were before the Council of *Constantinople*, *Ephesus*, and *Chalcedon*: From the seventh Council of *Carthage*, he runneth down to the thirteenth Council of *Toledo*, which happened long after *Melchiades*, *Silvester*, Pope *Mark Liberius*,

us, Felix, &c. were dead. Then he cometh (in the second part of his Work) up
again to *Sylvester*, and so downwards
with more Decretals, that he might Huf-
band his Forgeries well, and not glut us
with them altogether. And remarkable
it is also, that he doth not give us the
least syllable of notice of any Fraud a-
mong them : Nay, even *Constantine's Donation* set in the Front before the *Nicene*,
and in the midst between the first Order
of Counterfeits and the Councils, paf-
seth with him silently and gravely for a
true and sacred Instrument, which is of
all other the most impudent Imposture.

Let *Baronius* say what he will, it was
impossible to *debauch* all Antiquity and
Learning with so much *Labour* and *Art*,
without some deep *Counsel* and *Design*.
What use *Merlin* puts all these things to,
and how much he was Approved in the
Church of *Rome*, you shall see in the next
Chapter, and how highly also he extolleth
this Book of Forgeries.

How plainly he fathereth it upon S. *Ifidore* Bishop of *Hispalis*, is manifest by the
Coronis of the first Part, wherewith it
endeth.

*Give thanks to industrious and learned
men, studious Reader, that now thou hast*
at

at hand the *Acts of the* Councils, *as well as of the* Popes; *which* Isidore *the Bishop of* Hispalis *collected into one Volume,* &c. What shall we believe? The *first* Edition of the Book it self, or *Baronius* his Testimony? Old *Merlin* fathers it upon *Isidore* before Baronius was born, and all the World was made to believe the Bishop of *Hispalis* was the Author of it; though now for shame, and for a shift, they fly to another *Author.* Now if *Isidore* were dead before the Booke was made, it must needs be a Cheat; which, as * *Merlin* saith, *honest* Francis Regnault, *the cunning Printer*, *ended at* Paris, *in the year of our Lord* 1535, which unusual form of *Concluding*, instead of allaying, increaseth the suspicion.

Ibid.
* *Clausula insueta suspicionem pariuns.*

CAP. VI.

What use Merlin *makes of* Isidore, *and the* Forgeries *therein. How much he was approved in the* Church of Rome. *How some would have* Isidore *the Bishop to be a Merchant, others, a Sinner.*

HOw false and fraudulent soever the Collection of *Isidore* be, yet its Title is very Splendid, and its Authority Sacred in the Church of *Rome.*

JAMES

~~Roman Forgeries.~~

JAMES MERLIN'S
COLLECTION
OF THE
Four General Councils;

The NICENE, *the* CONSTANTINO-POLITAN, *the* EPHESINE, *and the* CHALCEDONIAN:

Which S. Gregory *the* Great *does Worship and Reverence as the Four Gospels.*

TOM. I.

Of 47 *Provincial Councils also; and the Decrees of* 69 POPES.

From the APOSTLES *and their* CANONS, *to* ZACHARIAS.

ISIDORE *being the Author.*

ALSO

The GOLDEN BULL *of* CHARLES IV. *Emperour; concerning the Election of the* KING *of the* ROMANS.

PARIS:

At Francis Regnault. 1535.

All we shall observe upon this Title, is this; If *Gregory the Great* did Worship

H 4   *and*

and Reverence the *Four General Councils*
as the *Four Gospels*, they were the more
to blame that added 50 Canons to one
of them; and they much more, that
ftain them all with the Neighbourhood,
and Mixture of fuch hateful Forgeries.

But who could fufpect that fo much
Fraud could be Ufhered in with fo fair
a Frontifpiece? or fo much Sordid Bafe-
nefs varnifhed over with fo much Magnificence! I have heard of a Thief that
robbed in his Coach, and a Bifhops *Ponti-*
ficalibus; of the *German Princefs*, and of
Mahomet's Dove: But I never heard of
any thing like this, that a *Patriarch*
fhould trade with Apoftles, Fathers, Emperours, Golden Bulls, K'ngs, and Councils; under the fair pretext of all thefe,
to Cheat the World of its Religion and
Glory.

His *Grandeur* is rendered the more re-
markable, and his *Artifice* redoubted, by
the Greatnefs of his *Retinue*: *Riculphus*
Archbifhop of *Mentz*, *Hincmarus Lau-*
dunenfis, *Benedictus Levita*, the Famous
Ifidore, and his fourfcore Bifhops, *Ivo*
Cartonenfis, *Gratian*, *Merlin*, *Peter Crab*,
Laurentius Surius, *Carranza*, *Nicolinus*,
Binius, *Labbè*, *Coffartius*, *the* COLLEC-
TIO REGIA, *Stanislaus Hosius*, Cardi-
nal

nal *Bellarmine, Franciscus Turrianus*, &c.
Men that bring along with them Emperours and Kings for Authority, as will
appear in the Sequel : Men who think it
lawful to Cheat in an *Holy Cause*, and to
lye for the Churches Glory : These aug-
ment the Splendour of his Train. Their
Doctrine of *Pious Frauds* is not unknown : And if we may do evil that
good may come, certainly no good, like
the Exaltation of the *Roman Church*,
can possibly be found, wherewith to justifie a little evil.

The *Jesuites Morals* are well understood : Upon their Principles to do evil,
is no evil, if good may ensue. Perjury it
self may be dispenced with by the Authority of their Superiour. An illimited
Blind Obedience is the *sum* of their Pro-
fession. To equivocate and lye for the
Church, that is, for the advancement of
their Order, and the Popes benefit, is so
far from sin, that to murder Heretical
Kings is not more Meritorious.

It is a sufficient Warrant, upon such
grounds, to *James Merlin* our present
Author, that he was commanded to do
what he did, by great and eminent Bishops in the Church of *Rome :* as he
sheweth in his Epistle Dedicatory, *To*
the

the *most Reverend Fathers in Chrift*, *and his moft excellent Lords*, Stephen *and* Francis, *&c.* the one of which was Bifhop of *Paris*, and the other an Eminent Prelate, who ordered all his work by their care, and made it publick by their own Authority.

Conceiving nothing (faith he) *more profitable for the Commonwealth*, *I have not diffembled to bring the Decrees of the Sacred Councils and Orthodox Bifhops*, *which partly the bleffed* Ifidore *fometime fince digefted into one*, *partly you*, *moft Reverend Fathers*, *having confirmed them with your Leaden Seal*, *gave me to be publifhed in one Volume* : *For every particular appeareth fo copioufly and Catholickly handled here*, *which is neceffary for the convicting of the Errours of mortal men*, *or for the reftoring of the* now almoft ruined World, *that every man may readily find wherewith to kill Hereticks and Herefies*.

The *Proteftants* being grown fo dangerous, that they had almoft ruined the *Popifh World*, by reforming the Church; nothing but this *Medufa's Head* of Snakes and Forgeries was able to affray them. The nakednefs of the *Pontificians* being difcovered, they had no Retreat from the Light of the Gofpel, but to this Refuge

fuge of Lies : *Where every one may readily find*, faith Merlin, *wherewith to kill Hereticks and Herefies, to deprefs the roud, to weary the voluptuous, to bring down the ambitious, to take the little Foxes that fpoil the Vineyard of the Church.* By the proud and ambitious, he meaneth Kings and Patriarchs, that will not fubmit to the Authority and Supremacy of the *Roman Church*; and by the *little Foxes*, fuch men as the Martyrs in the *Reformed* Churches; the driving away of which was the defign of the publica-ion. That he meaneth *Kings* and *Patri-rchs* in the former, you will fee in the Conclufion.

And if any one fhall hereafter endea-our to fray, and drive away thefe Mon-iers from the Commonwealth, what can be iore excellent, faith he, *than the ftones of David, which this Jordan fhall moft copi-ufly afford? If any one would fatisfie the lefires of the Hungry, what is more fweet ind abundant than the Treafures which his Ship bringeth from the remoteft Regi-ns? but if he defires the path and fplen-our of Truth, by which the clouds of Er-our (with their Authors) may beft be di-elled, and driven far away; what is ore apparent than the Sentences of the*
Fathers,

Fathers, which they, by the Inspiration of the Holy Ghost, have brought together into this Heap? For here, as out of a Meadow full of all kind of Flowers, all things may be gathered with ease, that conduce to the profit of the Church, or the suppressing of Vices, or the extinguishing of Lusts. Here the most precious Pearl, if you dig a little, will strait be found, &c. Here the Tyranny of Kings and Emperours, as it were with a Bit and Bridle, is restrained. Here the Luxury of Popes and Bishops is repressed: If Princes differ here peace sincere is had: If Prelates contend about the Primacy, here THE ANGEL OF THE GREAT COUNCIL *discovers who is to be preferred above the residue,* &c.

Are not the *Roman Wares* set off with advantage here? How exceedingly are these *Medicines* for the Maladies of the Church boasted by these Holy *Mountebanks?* The stones of *David* that kill *Goliah,* the River that refresheth the City of God, the Food of Souls, the Ship, the very *Argonaut* of the Church, that comes home laden with *Treasures* from unknown Regions, are but mean expressions; the Inspirations of the Holy Ghost, the Pearl of Price, *Angelus ille Magni Concilii,* the Angel of the Cove-

nant

nant are hid here ; and all (if we believe this dreadful Blasphemer) declare for the Pope against all the World. Here is a Bit and Bridle for Kings and Emperours, a Rule for Patriarchs, and what not?

The *Councils*, and true Records, we Reverence with all Honour due to Antiquity : And for that very cause , we so much the more abhor that admixture of Dross and Clay , wherewith their Beauty is corrupted. Had we received the Councils sincerely from her, we should have blest the Tradition of the Church of *Rome* for her assistance therein : But now she loveth her self more than her Children, and the Pope (which is the Church Virtual) is so hard a Father , that he soweth Tares instead of Wheat, and giveth Stones instead of Bread , and for Eggs feedeth us with Scorpions : We abhor her practices, and think it needful warily to examine , and consider her Traditions

What provisions are made in *Merlin's Isidore* for repressing the Luxuries of Popes and Bishops, you may please to see in *Constantines Donation* , and the *Epilogus Brevis*. In the one of which so many Witnesses are required before a Bishop be condemned ; and in the other,

care

care is taken for the *Pomp* of the *Clergy*, even to the *Magnificence* of their *Shooes*, and the *Caparifons* of their *Horfes*.

As *Merlin*, (who was a Doctor of Divinity of Great Account) fo likewife all the following *Collectors* among the Papifts, derive their Streams from this *Ifidore*, as their Fountain. And for this caufe I was the more defirous to fee the *Book*, which is very fcarce to be found; and the more fcarce, I fuppofe, becaufe if the Fountain be unknown, a greater Majefty will accrue to the Streams. The Bookfellers-Shops afforded me none: but at laft I met with two of them; the one with the Learned Dr. *Barlow*, *Margaret Profeffor*, and *Provoft* of *Queens Colledge* in *Oxford*, the other in the *Bodleian* Library: The one was Printed at *Collein*, *An.* 1530. The other at *Paris* beforementioned. Either had all, and both affirm *Ifidore Hifpalenfis* to be the Author.

Though fome afterwards are careful to diftinguifh *Ifidore Hifpalenfis* from *Ifidore Mercator*. The one failing, the other is obtruded as the Author of the Work: the latter *Collectors* unanimoufly leaving out *Hifpalenfis*, and calling him only by the Name of *Mercator*. But how the Name of *Ifidore Mercator* fhould

come

come before the Book , the Wifeft Man in the World , I fuppofe , can fcarcely *Divine*.

It is faid, that Eulogius *Bifhop of Cor- duba had a Brother, whofe Name was Ifi- dore, whofe condition of Life Banifhment, whofe Nation* Spain, *whofe Trade was Mer- chandize*: And *that this Spanifh Mer- chant flying out of his Country , upon the account of Religion , chofe rather to in- truft this moft precious Treafure, which he had faved from the Luft of Barbarians, to the care of the Germans, than to expofe it to the Rage of thofe Wafters and Deftroyers wherewith* Spain *was at that time infefted, as the Monks of* Mentz ; *at leaft , who, upon his having fojourned there , took oc- cafion to put his Name before the Book that was then in their hands , would have the World really to believe*. This is *Blondel's* conjecture , which he raifeth from the real exiftence of fuch an *Ifidore*. But he excufeth himfelf for *conjecturing barely* in fuch an affair , becaufe the Work is *a Work of Darknefs* , and they that did it, hated the Light , becaufe their Deeds were evil : *And the Patcher up of thofe Epiftles coming forth in the Vizor of ano- ther Name*, in fuch *a bufinefs* a conjecture may fuffice. Let them that impofed the Name,

Blondel, cap.6.

Name, give us a Reafon why they did it: it is not incumbent on us to render an account of what other men are pleafed without reafon at any time to do.

It is not impoffible, but a Knave, called *Ifidore*, might be fent abroad with the Book, being pickt out on purpofe, that the Famous *Ifidore*, Bifhop of *Hifpalis*, might be believed to be the Author. He might come to *Mentz*, and fojourn there under the notion of a *Spaniard*, and give *Riculphus*, or the Monks, a fight of the Book, as a rare ineftimable Treafure: For *Sinon* was let loofe, with as little Artifice as this, to the Deftruction of *Troy*. Thus, whence it came really, could hardly be difcovered; and the Thing too would be the more admired, becaufe it came from the *fartheft Regions*, as *Merlin* fpeaks, being faved fo Miraculoufly from the hands of *Barbarians*. But where did this Traveller find it? this Merchant, of whom did he receive it? For *morally* fpeaking, it is impoffible, that a Merchant fhould be the Author of it; efpecially at that time, when the Records lay fcattered perhaps in an hundred Libraries, and were all to be fought in obfcure *Manufcripts*. An Afs may be expected to meddle with an Harp, as foon as a Merchant

chant with the Myſterious Records of
the Church. How come *Lay-men* to be
ſo Judicious? Had any Merchant ſo great
a Skill as this imports? It is improbable
fourſcore Biſhops ſhould know it; much
more that they ſhould urge him to do
that, which their own Learning and Fun-
ction fitted them to do far better : Yet
Iſidore in his Preface writeth thus, *You
Eighty Biſhops, who urged me to begin and
perfect this Work, ought to know, as ought
all other Prieſts of the Lord alſo, that we
have found more than thoſe 20 Chapters of
the Nicene Council,* &c. It is a ſhame to
the Church of *Rome*, that a Lay-man
ſhould be the Fountain of all her Records; and that in very deed, the greater
part of them ſhould be in no Manuſcript
nor Library in the World, being never
ſeen, nor heard of, till *Iſidore* brought
them out of *Spain* : That no man can
tell what *Iſidore* made the Book, which
is now the Preſident, and the ſole Store-
houſe of all their Collections, is a little
infamous; eſpecially ſince they believed
of old unanimouſly, that the Biſhop *Iſidore* of *Hiſpalis* was its ancient Author.

Baronius when he had irrefragably di-
ſproved *him*, puts nothing certain in his
ſtead : but having a Wolf by the ears,

I   and

and being willing to say something, raises a dust, and goes out in the Cloud.

Baron. in
Not Mar-
tyr Lat.
April.

In the ancient Manuscripts, saith he, *we find this Isidore, the Collector of the Councils, surnamed Mercator; as in those which we have in our Library: but in the Inscription of the Books lately Printed, he is stiled not Mercator, but Peccator, according to the manner of some of the ancient Fathers, who for humility sake were wont to superscribe, and subscribe themselves so. I conceive it crept in by a mistake, that Mercator was written for Peccator: but since the Author of that Collection reciting the General Councils in his Preface endeth with the sixth, it is evident that it lived after the sixth Council, and before the seventh.*

What Hypocrisie is here? He had before that manifestly detected the Collection for a Cheat, and yet he now gravely troubles his Brains, to know what *Isidore* this might be. It is a blind *Isidore*, that has left no mark of his Life behind him, but only that which lies in this counterfeit Preface; an *Isidore* that can no where else be found, by the great Annalist, *Baronius*. He has no other help to know the time about which he lived, but the Preface: Whether *Peccator*, or *Mercator*,

Mercator, is but a superficial Controversie; whether any *Isidore* made the Book, is a deeper enquiry : The old Manuscripts of *Baronius*, are Books of yesterday, all written since the counterfeit *Isidore* was published. The variety shews, that the Papists can rest no where : And the liberty they take to alter what they see in *Manuscripts*, as they please, is an ill sign of a large Conscience, which studies not what is *faithfully* to be published, but *conveniently*. For because the Name of *Mercator* did smell too strong of the *Wares*, lest the World should wonder how the Inscription of a *Merchant* should come out before the Councils, they thought it fit to strain the courtesie of a Letter, and (because *Peccator* is an humble Name) to turn the Merchant into a Sinner. That it was a *Sinner*, I dare be sworn, and a sly *Merchant* too; lucky Names both of them : but the last is capable of a finer pretence, no Cheat being so vigorous and unavoidable, as that of a penitent weeping Sinner. The Pride of *Rome* comes cloathed in Humility, after the example of her Supreme Head, who stileth himself *the Servant of Servants*, while he aspires (by these very Records) to be the *King of Kings.*

L 2

Isidore

Iſidore and *Merlin* being two of the firſt Collectors of the Councils among the Papiſts, I have taken the more liberty to be ſomewhat copious in them, that I may conveniently be more brief in peruſing the reſidue.

CAP. VII.

Of Francis Turrian *the Jeſuite: With what Art and Boldneſs he defendeth the Forgeries.*

NOtwithſtanding all the weakneſs and uncertainty of *Iſidore, Francis Turrian,* the Famous Jeſuite, appears in its defence, about 40 years after the firſt publication of it by *Merlin.* The *Centuriators of Magdenburg* having met with it, to his great diſpleaſure, he is ſo Valiant, as not only to maintain all the Forgeries therein contained, but the whole Body of Forgeries vented abroad by all the *Collectors* and *Compilers* following, till himſelf appeared.

His Book is expreſly formed againſt the Writers of the *Centuries,* and is a ſufficient Evidence, that as ſoon as *Iſidore* came abroad by Dr. *Merlin's Labour,* and the

the Bishop of *Paris Command,* it was sifted by the Protestants.

It is dedicated *to the most Illustrious and most Reverend D.D.* Stanislaus Hosius, *Cardinal of the Holy Roman Church, and Bishop of* Collein. Printed by the Heirs of *John Quintel,* and approved by *Authority, An. Dom.* 1573.

He defends all the Canons of the Apostles which are recounted by other *Collectors.* That you may know the *Mettal* of the Man, I will produce but two Instances. *Vid.* Turrian.

The last of those Canons, which he maintaineth to be the Apostles, is this which followeth.

Qui Libri sunt Canonici, &c. *Let these Books be Venerable and Holy to you all: Of the* Old Testament, *five Books of* Moses, Genesis, Exodus, Leviticus, Numbers, Deuteronomy; *one of* Joshua *the Son of* Nun, *one of* Judges, *one of* Ruth, *four of* Kings, *two of* Chronicles, Hester *one, three of the* Macchabees, *one of* Job, *one Book of* Psalmes, *three of* Solomon, Proverbs, Ecclesiastes, *and the* Song of Songs; *one of the* 12 *Prophets, one of* Isaiah, *one of* Jeremiah, *one of* Ezekiel, *one of* Daniel : *And without, let your young men learn the Wisdom of the Learned* Syrach. *Can.* 84.

I 3 *But*

But of ours, that is, of the New Testament, *there are four Gospels,* Matthew, Mark, Luke, *and* John : *fourteen Epistles of* Paul, *two Epistles of* Peter, *three of* John, *one of* James, *one of* Jude, *two Epistles of* Clement, *and the Ordinations of* Me Clement, *set forth in Eight Books to you Bishops, which are not to be published to all, because of the Mysteries contained in them : and the Acts of our Apostles.*

This is the eighty fourth Canon, and in some Accounts the eighty fifth ; where you see the *Epistles* of *Clement,* and *Eight Books of his Ordinations,* put into the Body of the Bible : As for the difference of the Accounts, he sheweth you the way how to reconcile them.

If this be one of the Apostles Canons, then *Clement* was an Apostle, or had Apostolical Power : But if it be a Forgery, then not only the Apostles Canons, but the very Text of the Holy Scriptures is interlined and forged by the same.

He maintains all the *Decretal Epistles,* and among the rest S. *Clement's:* Whose genuine *Epistle to the Corinthians* they leave out, as making nothing to their purpose : but five *Spurious* ones they record ; the two first of them being written to S. *James,* and the last *to the Brethren*

thren dwelling with him at Jerusalem.

It is good sport to see how like the *shot* of a great Gun, the Discovery of the Protestants comes in among them: Their keenness in detecting *the time of* S *James his Death*, shatter the Knots; and whereas before they were all united, they now fly several ways, every man shifting for himself, as he is best able.

Baronius dislikes such Arts of upholding the Church, not as impious and unlawful, but as inconvenient and pernicious. *Bellarmine* affirms the Epistles to be Old, but dares not attest them: *Isidore, Merlin, Peter Crabbe, Nicolinus, Carranza,* and *Surius*, own them freely without any scruple: For saying nothing of the Quarrel, they lay them down simply as good Records. *Binius, Labbè,* and the *Collectio Regia,* confess some of them to be false; and in particular, that S *James* was dead seven years before S. *Clement* could write his first Epistle to him. And to salve the sore, they say, that it was not written to *James,* but to *Simeon,* who was also *Bishop of Jerusalem,* and *Brother to our Lord;* and that the Name of *James* crept into the Title *Mendosè,* by Errour and Mistake, for that of *Simeon.* But honest *Turrian* maintains plainly, that

I 4   S. *Peter*

S. *Peter* and S. *Clement* knew very well that S. *James* was dead before they wrote unto him ; yet nevertheleſs they did very wiſely, both S. *Peter* in ordering the Epiſtle , and S. *Clement* in writing it. And his Reaſons, as he bringeth the matter about, are pretty ſpecious.

For my part , I proteſt , that ſuch a High Piece of Impudence was to me incredible : But that you may ſee the rare Abilities of a *Jeſuite* to argue well for the *abſurdeſt Cauſe*, turn to his Book, and read his Comment on S. *Clement's firſt Epiſtle*, and there you ſhall ſee *Wit* and *Folly* equal in their height : Wit in *managing* , but Folly in *attempting* ſo mad a buſineſs.

For the ſake of thoſe who are not able to read, or get the Book, I will give you a Glympſe of his Demonſtrations. Firſt he obſerveth, how *Reaſon it ſelf compelleth us, eſpecially being confirmed by ſo many and ſo great Teſtimonies of the Ancients, to confeſs the Epiſtle to be S.* Clement's, *whoſe it is reported to be.* He ſophiſtically pretendeth here , that there were great Authorities of the Ancient Fathers extant to prove it : *Whence,* ſaith he *it began to be had in every mans hand, to be read by the Catholicks , to be put a-mong*

mong the Decretal Epiftles, and produced and cited in Ecclefiaftical Caufes and Judgments. The latter part of which Claufe is true: For (as we before obferved) *Gratian*, *Ivo*, and the reft of the Popes Minifters, have brought the *Decretals* into the Body of the *Canon-Law*, which maketh the matter more *fatal* and abominable; for being really cited in their *Ecclefiaftical Courts*, and ufed both in matters of Controverfie, and in cafes of Confcience, they are forced either to defend them, or to pluck up their Cuftoms by the very Roots; and fo further expofe the Church of *Rome* to the fhame of Levity or Fraud; yet for this very caufe, it is far more impious and wicked to retain them: So that not knowing which way is beft, fome of them retain them, and fome of them renounce them. But you muft wink at all this, and believe what *Turrian* fays, for the Authority of the Roman Church (which hath feated the Forgeries in the Chair of Judgment) is a greater Argument, to them that believe her Infallible, than any one Doctor can bring againft them: *Neither was bleffed* Peter *ignorant, when he commanded to write to the Dead, nor* Clement, faith he, *when he wrote by the Command-*

ment;

ment; but that the Readers would presently fee, the Epistle to be written to him, whom all men knew to be dead before S. Peter: they being about thereupon, to enquire diligently into the cause thereof, and seeking to find it: *Nay, this was the design of the blessed Peter, and therein he imitated the Holy Scripture.* Whether to counterfeit, or blaspheme the Scriptures, be the worse, I cannot tell: but of this I am sure, that they who think such courses lawful, (as this faftned on S. Peter, and the Holy Scripture here) will ftick at nothing which they take for their advantage. For that it was lawful to counterfeit S. *James* his Name, he proveth afterwards very largely ; and now he is giving the reafons of it: One intention was to ftir up all people to Enquiry ; their admiration at fo ftrange a thing, being very prone to make them diligent to learn the caufe of it : Another was, that all Bifhops might fee the more clearly, that they were taught in the perfon of *James* : For *James* being dead, and uncapable of receiving the inftruction, it is evident, that he was not intended thereby ; and therefore it muft be for others in his capacity. A third reafon was the preventing of envy : for had
S. *Peter*

S. *Peter* vouchfafed (being our Saviours *Vicar*, and *Head* of the *Church*) to write to any Bifhop alive, the Honour done unto that Bifhop had been fo great, that all the reft had been tempted to maligne him fhrewdly for that advantage : *His intention was*, faith he, *to transfigure these things in the perfon of* James, *after the manner of the Holy Scripture ; and that as well for other Bifhops as efpecially thofe that fhould fucceed him in the Church of* Jerufalem, (*whence the preaching of the Gofpel began, according to the Prophefie of* Ifaiah) *that they might thus think with themselves ; If the Prince of the Apostles commanded* Clement *to write thefe things to* James *the Brother of our Lord, whom* Peter, James *and* John *did first of all ordain, who now ceafed to be a fhepherd, and was rewarded with his Crown ; he certainly did not command him to write for his fake, but for us, to whom* Solomon *faith, Look diligently to the face of thy Cattel, and confider thy Herds*, &c. *Let this*, faith he, *be one caufe of the Transfiguration, or counterfeiting a perfon in this Epiftle.* Having noted how S. *Paul* transferred a certain bufinefs on himfelf and *Apollos* by a Figure, he concludeth thus : *Why therefore may we not think, that*

S. Peter

S. Peter *for the same reason commanded* Clement *to transfer his Epistle concerning his Death and Doctrine, pertaining in common to every Bishop, by a Figure to* S. James *already dead?* left *if he should have commanded him to have written to* Simon *the Bishop of* Jerusalem, *who succeeded* S. James, *or to any other, as to* Mark *the Bishop of* Alexandria, *or* Ananias *of* Antioch, *or any other, he should then perhaps seem to love him, or honour him, more than the residue?*

Much more he faith to this purpose but all made vain, with one small observation: Whereas he pretends that *Clement* knew S. *James* to be dead, there is a fifth Epistle written by the same *Clement, To his most dearly beloved Brethren dwelling at* Jerusalem, *together with his dearest Brother* James, *his Fellow-Disciple.* So that S. *James* after all, was still thought to be alive, by those that *transferred* this Epistle on S. *Clement* by a *Figure.*

S. *Peter's* influence over the Bishop of *Jerusalem,* and *our Lords Brother,* was thought a considerable Circumstance for the Establishment of the following Popes: And till the Protestants discovered the *Fraud,* let *Turrian* say what he will, there was scarce a person in the World,

World, that thought not the Letter *timed* well enough for the purpose.

And whereas he pretendeth *so many and so great Testimonies of the Ancients, confessing the Epistle to be S.* Clement's; he is not able, nor does he so much as attempt to name one, from S. *Clement* downward, till this *Spurious Isidore*, that affirmed any such matter. Howbeit, he quotes *Origen, Theodoret, Gregory Nazianzen,* &c. to prove the lawfulness of a Transfiguration, and makes great Ostentation of the Fathers, in shewing that S. *Peter* and S. *Clement* did wisely in the business.

CAP. VIII.

Of Peter Crabbe's *Tomes of the Councils: Wherein he agrees with, and wherein he differs from* Isidore *and* Merlin.

BEsides the Forgeries that are in *Merlin* and the Bastard *Isidore*, *Peter Crabbe*, whose Tomes of the Councils were published eight years after the *first Edition of Merlin*, published more, of as great importance as the former; not omitting those of *Isidore* and *Merlin*, but recording

recording and venting them altogether.

He pretends to give an account of all those Councils that have been from S. *Peter* the Apostle, down to the Times of Pope *John* II.

He wrote before *Turrian*, as *Carranza* and *Surius* did, whom it is *Turrian's* business to defend.

The End being proposed before the Means, with what design these Editions of the *Councils* are so carefully multiplied, we may conjecture by a *Treatise* that is set in the Front of them, *concerning the Roman Primacy*. Almost all the Compilers, after *Peter Crabbe*, having prefixed the same with one consent before their Work, as the Aim of their ensuing Labours.

It is extant in *Crab*, *Surius*, *Nicolinus*, *Binius*, *Labbe* and *Coffartius*, and the *Collectio Regia*. *Carranza* hath it not nor *Paul* V.

Paul V. *in his own Work*, *published at* Rome, *Anno Dom.* 1608. touches the Forgeries but very sparingly. It does not become the Majesty of a Pope in his own Name to utter them: It is moreover a thing of hazardous consequence for *him* to appear in Person in such a disgraceful business: It befits his Holiness to act rather

ther

ther by Emiſlaries and Inferiour Agents, as all great Statesmen and Polititians do, being unſeen themſelves in matters that reflect too much upon their ſafety : that Method (you know) is more ſtately, as well as more Honourable and ſecure. Yet he approveth others at a diſtance, as his dear Son *Severinus Binius* in particular, who dedicated all his Tomes to Pope *Paul* V. in the year 1608. and has a particular Letter of Thanks from Pope *Paul* himſelf, as a Badge of his Favour before the Work. As for *Carranza*, he is but an Abſtract, or brief *Compendium*.

This *Treatiſe of the Primacy*, thus put before the Councils, containeth a Collection of Teſtimonies out of Counterfeit Epiſtles of the Primitive Biſhops and Martyrs of *Rome*, proving under the Authorities of moſt Glorious Names, *that the Holy Apoſtolical Church obtained the Primacy, not from the Apoſtles, but from our Lord himſelf: that it is the Head and Hinge of all the Churches ; that all Appeals are to be made thereunto ; the greater cauſes, and the contentions of Biſhops, being to be determined only by the Apoſtolical See: that ſhe is the Mother of all Churches ; and as the Son of God came to do the Will of his Father, ſo ought all Bi-*
ſhops

shops and *Priests to do the Will of their Mother: that all the Members ought to follow the Head, which is the Church of* Rome *: that the first See ought to be judged by no man, neither by the Emperour, nor by Kings, nor by the People : that it was granted to the Church of* Rome *, by a singular priviledge, to open and shut the Kingdom of Heaven to whom she would : that none may Appeal from her to any other : that the Apostolical See may without any Synod unbind those whom a Synod or Council hath unjustly condemned.* Of which Sentence she is to be the Judge, whether it be just ; for she may judge all, but none her : *that the Church of* Rome *is the Foundation and Form of all the Churches* ; so that no Church hath its Essence without that of *Rome : that from her all the Churches received their beginning.* Doctrines as true, as the Authorities by which they are confirmed ; and to say no more, as true as the last : For the Christian Churches received their beginnin from *Jerusalem,* before the Church of *Rome* had any Being.

Consider it well, and you shall fin this the removing of a *meer stone* of high est importance, an Encroachment upon the Territories of other Patriarchs, a

Usurpatio

Usurpation of all Spiritual and Secular Power, to the subversion of Emperours, Kings and Councils.

For if all are to obey her, as Jesus Christ did his Eternal Father; if it be granted to the Roman Church, by a singular Priviledge, to open and shut the Kingdom of Heaven to whom she will; if no King, Emperour or Council, hath power to judge the Pope, while he hath power to judge all; Kings, Emperours and Councils are made Subject to him, and nothing can escape the Sublimity of his Cognizance.

Besides this *Treatise of the Primacy, Peter Crab* has 34 new *Canons of the Apostles* more than *Isidore* and *Merlin :* So that Antiquities are daily increasing in the Church of *Rome* , and Records are like Figs, *new* ones come up instead of the *old* ones.

The last of these Canons is that of *Clement,* about the *Canon* of the Bible: a Forgery of more *Scriptures* , added to the former, in the names of the Apostles; defended by honest *Turrian* zealously, and magnified by *Nicolinus* as the *Coronis* of the Apostles Canons. *vid. C.r.ll*

He has the *Roman Pontifical* , a Treatise of the Lives of Popes, fitted exact-

K ly

ly to the *Decretal Epiſtles*, and accordingly, moſt richly ſtored wtih all kind of Forgeries and Lyes. It is a *new* Book Fathered upon Pope *Damaſus*; which *Iſidore* and *Merlin* (I think) were ignorant of, for it is not in them; and I admire where he had it. It is the Text on which he commenteth, as a Great Record; he uſeth it as a great proof in doubtful matters, and according to it the Method of his *Tomes* is ordered. You will ſee more of it hereafter.

He has the counterfeit *Council of Sinueſſa*, a new Piece, which I find not in *Merlin*: But I verily believe, he ſcraped it up ſome where elſe, and 'tis not his own, 'tis ſo full of nonſenſe: A Council ſitting in the year 303. and defining from that Text, *Ex ore tuo juſtificaberis, & ex ore tuo condemnaberis*, that no Council can condemn a Pope, nor any other Power, but his own mouth: For becauſe our Saviour has ſaid, *Out of thine own mouth thou ſhalt be juſtified, and out of thine own mouth thou ſhalt be condemned*; therefore no body can condemn the Pope but himſelf alone: for which purpoſe they repeat the Text over and over again, very feebly and childiſhly, even unto nauſeating: And the example of *Marcellinus* is
made

made an inftance in the cafe; who being
called to an Account for offering Incenfe
to an *Idol*, could not be condemned by
this Council, and was therefore (becaufe he was Pope) humbly implored to
condemn himfelf.

It is a Council of great value, becaufe
of the Prefident we have in it, how Scriptures may be applied to the Bifhop of
Rome; and how places that belong to all
the World, muft peculiarly be afcribed to
him alone: Howbeit *Crab* makes a fowre
face on't, and is fain to promife this Premonition to the Reader.

*By reafon of the intollerable difference
and corruption of the Copies, whereof the
one was old and faulty, though written in
the beft Parchment and Character; the o-
ther more old, but equally depraved (as the
Beholders might difcern with their eyes)
fo far, that what they mean fometimes cannot be underftood, we have fet both the
Copies, without changing a fyllable of them,
in two Columns; fetting the Letter A over
the firft, and C over the other: but the
middle Column over which B is placed,
for its capacity, or rather conjecture, endeavours as much as it is able, to reconcile
the other two fo very divers, and bring
them to fome fe*—

He does not tell you plainly, that he made the middle Copy; but 'tis eafie to conceive it, fince he found but *two*, and they were fo full of nonfenfe, that he added one, which is the third, to reconcile them. Yet *Crabbe's* Invention is now recorded by the *Collectio Regia*, and the two old ones, for their horrid *Barbarifmes*, are thrown out of the Councils, and (for very fhame) are caft away: for proceeding in his Apology, *Crab* a little after faith, *Nemo ergo caput fubfannando moveat*, &c. *Let no man therefore wag his Head in derifion, who having either gotten more correct Exemplars, or being of a more Noble and clear apprehenfion, is able to mend thefe: but rather let him patiently bear with what is done, and reduce it himfelf into better form.*

This is a fufficient Light, wherein to fee the diffimilitude between Forgeries and true Records: For whereas the *undoubted* were made in great Councils of Holy Men, and are all of them clear and pure, and well-advifed, full of Uniformity, Senfe, Gravity, Majefty, Smoothnefs, Order, Perfpicuity, Brevity, Eloquence and Verity; it is the common Fate of thefe Inftruments which we accufe as *Forgeries*, being made in a *Dark Age*,

Age, by men not so Learned as the Church of *Rome* could desire, (and sometimes in a Corner by some silly Monk) to swarm with Absurdities, Errours, Tautologies, Barbarismes; to be rude and tedious, empty and incoherent, weak and impertinent: yet some of them we confess to be more pure in Language, and better in sense than others.

This Council of *Sinuessa* is more ridiculous than it is possible well to imagine, before you read and consider it.

He has the Counterfeit *Edict of the Emperour Constantine* for a good Record. It is more warily made than the other, and better Latine, but of *Swinging Importance*: 'Tis but a Deed of Gift, wherein the first most Christian Emperour is made to give all the Glory of the Western Empire, with its Territories and Regalities, to the Bishop of *Rome*. We shall meet with it in others: for the Collectors of the *Decretal* Epistles, all of them, harp upon this String most strangely.

As Pope *Paul* V. so *Peter Crab* has but 20 Canons of the *Nicene Council*; wherein he agrees with *Isidore* and *Merlin*, and differs much from some that follow him: Nay, he agrees and disagrees with *Isidore*

K 3   at

at once, in this very thing: He agrees with *Isidore* in his Book it self, (on the *Nicene* Council) but disagrees with him in his *Preface*.

But then he maketh amends for the Omission; for he hath the Synodical Epistle of the *Nicene* Council, a *new* Record, which I find not in *Isidore*, or in any before him: It is an humble Address of the *Nicene* Council to Pope *Sylvester*, beseeching his Holiness to *ratifie* their Decrees: To shew that no Council is of any value, unless it be approved by the Bishop of *Rome*: And he has a Gracious Answer too by the same Pen, or I am sorely deceived; for they are both alike so full of Barbarismes and false Latines, that another Dunce can hardly be found like the first to imitate them. In good earnest, they are the most feculent Forgeries that ever I saw. To speak much in little, is, they are worse than the *Sinuessa* Council.

They are without Greek Copies, which (where all the rest is in Greek) is an evil sign: But as they are, you shall have them, when we come to *Binius*, that the more Learned may judge of their Excellency.

He has a *Pseudo-Catholick* Council at
Rome

Rome under Pope *Sylvester*, with the same *Premonition to the Reader*, word for word, which he set before the *Sinuessa* Council, *Propter Exemplariorum intolerabilem nimiamque & Differentiam, & Depravationem*, &c.

He has the other Forgeries of *Isidore Mercator*; and among the rest, the *Epilogus brevis* concerning the number of Witnesses.

He defaces and suppresses the sixth Council of *Carthage*, as well as his Predecessor.

What with blotting out, and putting in, he so disguizes the Face of Antiquity, that unless it be to very clear eyes, the Primitive Church appeareth not the same.

Yet are his Voluminous Tomes dedicated *to the Invincible Emperour* Charles V. being Printed in the year 1538. by Peter Quintell. *Cum Gratiâ & Privilegio tam Cæsario quam Regio Colloniæ.* That is, *At* Collein *by the consent and Authority both of the King and Emperour.* So far even Monarchs are deluded sometimes with a shew of Piety, and the Light of Depraved and Corrupted Learning.

CAP. IX.

Of Carranza : *his Epitome of the Decrees and Councils. He owneth the Forgeries.*

CArranza, being but a short *Compendium*, was Printed at *Paris*, *An.* 1564. to wit, very fitly, for the more general spreading of the corrupted Councils : All the other *Collections* being great Volumes, but this a little Informer, or Companion for the Pocket.

It was dedicated *to the Illustrious* Diego Hurtado Mendoza, *Orator in the State of* Venice, *and his Imperial Majesties Vicegerent in the Holy Council of* Trent.

He lays down all the *Apostles Canons* for good Laws, even the last it self being not excepted ; and selects Decrees out of the *Decretal Epistles* for good and Catholick *Canons.*

The Decretal Epistles themselves would be too long for so short a Compendium ; and therefore he has not the Decrees themselves, but Excerptions.

He has the *Pontifical* of the Popes Lives, but more modesty than to ascribe it to *Damasus :* It is a part of his Text however.

He

He has but 20 Canons of the *Nicene* Council, and skippeth over the Council of *Sinuessa.*

He omits the *Epilogus Brevis*, but owns the Council to which it is annexed.

He followeth *Isidore*, and exceeds him a little.

CAP. X.

Of Surius *his four Tomes, and how the Forgeries are by him defended. He hath the Rescripts of* Atticus *and* Cyril*, by which Pope* Zozimus *was condemned of Forgery in the sixth Council of* Carthage.

LAurentius Surius was a Monk of the Order of the *Carthusians*: He wrote four Tomes: He pretends to have all the Antiquities of the Church at large, and to *mend* and *restore* the defects of the Ancient Manuscripts. What their *mending* and *restoring* is, you begin to discern. He dedicates the whole Work to *Philip* King of *Spain*, *Sicily*, and *Neapolis*, &c. and directeth it in another Epistle *to the most August and Invincible Emperour* Charles V. It was *Printed at* Collein

lein *by* Geruvinus Galenius, *and the Heirs of* John Quintell, *in the year of our Lord* 1567.

He has the counterfeit Preface of *Isidore Mercator*, before detected ; *The Treatise of the Primacy of the Roman Church*, all the 84 *Canons of the Apostle* , and the *Apostolical Constitutions* of Pope *Clement* (newly added to the Tomes of the Councils) for good Records ; though *Isidore Mercator* , some of the *Apostles Canons*, and *Clement*'s *Constitutions*, are rejected by some of the best of his most able Followers, (as you shall see hereafter :) not I suppose upon mature deliberation , but inevitable necessity.

The *Liber Pontificalis* of Pope *Damasus*, that notorious Cheat, is the groundwork upon which he commenteth. It so exactly containeth the Lives and Acts of the Bishops of *Rome* , that when I first approached it, I apprehended every *Life* to have been recorded by some person *contemporary* with the Pope, of which he was writing : for it nominates the time of their Session to a Year, a Moneth, a Week, and a Day , from S. *Peter* downward : Which being done for no Episcopal Chair beside, it made the *Roman See* seem of more Eminent Concernment than the

the refidue from the very firft beginning;
fuch a peculiar and extraordinary care
being no mean Indication of its High
Exaltation above all other Chairs, that
were not for a long time together fo accurately regarded. But a little after, I
found *a fhrewd fign*; for befide the errours and contradictions noted before,
in the midft of all this exactnefs, he mif-
feth fometimes· 3, 4, 5, ·, 9 years together. This fhall be proved hereafter,
with more than we yet fay, when we
come to *Binius*.

He has all the *Decretal Epiftles*, and the
Donation of Conftantine for good Records. *The Epiftle of* Melchiades *concerning the Munificence of* Conftantine; the
Spurious *Roman Council under Pope* Sylvefter, with the *Epilogus Brevis*; *the Letters between* Athanafius *and Pope* Mark,
concerning the number of the *Nicene* Canons: Thofe Letters tell us the Canons
of the *Nicene* Council are 70. and yet he
records but 20 of them.

The moft of thefe Great Appearances
are rejected afterwards, by *Baronius*, *Binius*, *Labbè*, and the *Collectio Regia*.

By good fortune he has the *Refcripts of*
Atticus, and S. *Cyril*, the Patriarchs, con-
cerning the *true Records* of the *Nicene*
Council,

Council, sent to the sixth Council of *Carthage*, upon the occasion of *Zozimus* before related.

The Letter of that Council to *Celestine* the Bishop of *Rome* concerning that Controversie.

And a Scrap of the Council it self: but he omits the Decrees.

Did I follow them throughout all Ages, my work would be endless. We should find much foul Play in following Councils and Records of the Church: but for several weighty Reasons I have at present confined my self within the compass of the first 400 years next after the Death of our Lord, whose Name is not to be mentioned without praise and glory.

Note well: I go on thus, to observe particularly what Forgeries every Collector of the Councils owneth, and what Emperours, Kings, and Popes, their Books are dedicated to; and what priviledge, in all the principal parts of the Popes Jurisdiction, they come forth withal; and especially what a multitude of men have been encouraged to carry on this Design, that you might see the Conspiracy of the Members with the Head, and the general Guilt of that Church in so

Enormous

Enormous an Affair. To which we might add the innumerable *Armies* of Learned men that have cited them in that Church, and the **Company** of **Captains** that have defended them : But it had been better for them that they had never medled with the Proteſtant Objections, for they have made the matter worſe than they found it , and bewraid themſelves in all their Anſwers ; nay, they have made the *Frauds* more eminent and notorious , by diſturbing the Reader , while they give him Warning by their *Notes*, though the intent be to defend them. This I ſpeak eſpecially upon the laſt , from *Binius* downward.

CAP. XI.

Of Nicolinus *his Tomes , and their Contents for the firſt* 420 *years. His Teſtimony concerning the ſixth Council of* Carthage.

Nicolinus is printed in five Volumes, *Sixti V. Pont. Max. feliciſſimis Auſpiciis,* as himſelf phraſeth it : I think he means, *By the favourable Permiſſion and Authority of Pope* Sixtus V. He dedicates

his

his Tomes *to the* same *most Holy Lord* Sextus, *&c.* which were printed at *Venice*, *An.* 1585.

Among other things in which I should say he is peculiar, had not *Merlin* in his *Isidore* done the same, he sets a counterfeit *Epistle of* Aurelius, *Archbishop of* Carthage, *to* Damasus *the Pope*, and the Popes *Answer*, in the Front of his Work. The Epistle requesteth a Copy of all the *Decretals* that were made by the Bishops of *Rome*, from S. *Peter* downwards. The Answer intimates a Copy, commanding him to preach and publish the same.

In both these *Collectors* the Epistles are displaced above 300 years out of their due order, meerly that they might face the Forgeries with the great Authorities of *Aurelius* and *Damasus*, who were both dead 300 or 400 years before the Counterfeits were made: Howbeit, the Pageant does well to adorn the Scene; it entertains the Spectators as a fit *Præludium*, to make the way more fair for these disguized *Masquers*.

In the last of these Epistles, the Counterfeit Decrees are Fathered on the *Holy Ghost*, and whosoever speaketh against them, is charged with *Blasphemy*.

Yet for all this, though the Epistles were

were defired by *Aurelius*, and fent by *Damafus*, and commanded to be preached and publifhed throughout the world, they were never heard of by the fpace of 700 or 800 years after their firft Authors, nor for 300 or 400 years after this *Damafus* and *Aurelius*; though pretended to be the Canons of the Holy Fathers, fo Sacred, and fo Divinely infpired by the Holy Ghoft.

This is that *Damafus* upon whom the Famous Pontifical is Fathered : He fate in the Chair *An.* 370. The Forgeries were unknown till about the year 800.

This *Aurelius* is he who tafted the Decrees of *Zozimus*, and had experience of their fincerity, when he refifted the Encroachments of the Roman Chair.

But to return to *Nicolinus*; he has *Ifidore*'s Preface, *The Treatife concerning the Primacy of the Roman Church*, containing fo many Teftimonies out of forged Bifhops, Martyrs, and Fathers: *All the Apoftles Canons*, of which he maketh S. *Clement*'s the Top and *Coronis*, concluding that Impious Counterfeit with this affected phrafe, *Coronidis ipforum Canonum Apoftolorum finis* : *The end of the Coronis of the Apoftles Canons*.

Francis Turrian is in fo much efteem

with

with him, that he hath Eight Books of *Clement's* Conftitutions, with *Turrian's Proem*, and *Explanatory Defences* upon them.

The *Liber Pontificalis*, drawn from the beginning like a *Vein* of Lies, through the tedious length of 800 years, infect-ing all thefe Ages with Forgery: It is his Text in like manner.

He has all the *Decretal Epiftles* without Exception; *the Council of* Sinuella, *or condemnation of Pope* Marcellinus, with the fame *Premonition* you faw in *Peter Crab* to the *Reader*; *The Donation of the Emperour* Conftantine, which by this time one would think to be a found and admirable Record, having fo many Hands fubfcribing it, and fo many Pens inferting it among the *Councils*, without the leaft note of any *dubioufnefs* or *blemifh* in it.

He has *threefcore and eighteen Canons* of the *Nicene* Council, and profetteth himfelf to be the firft which added them thereunto: And he had them of *a cer-tain man* that brought fourfcore of them in *Arabick* to *Alexandria*, as his *Printer* does witnefs for him to the Reader. But furely had there been fo many, Pope *Paul* V. and all the Collectors before him, had not omitted them.

Nicol. Epift.
Dedicat.
ad Sixt V.

Some

Some 40 years hence we may expect fourscore more: for as for those *naked and vulgar Canons*, (as he calleth the Old and Authentick Records) they will not serve the turn; nor yet the old *Seventy* mentioned by *Isidore*, *Athanasius*, and Pope *Mark* : by which you may see they are always growing, and may come to a *Million*, if the continuance of the World permit it, and their need require it.

What say you? In good earnest, methinks, the year 1585. is very late, for the finding of *eight and fifty Canons of the Nicene Council* : That Council was assembled in the year 327. and made its Canons above *one thousand and two hundred years* before *Nicolinus* time : They were written in *Greek*, and these lay dormant in *Arabick*, so many Ages, no man can tell where. But the *blessed* Jesuites, or *one of the same Society*, luckily found them the other day.

Nicol. Typogr. Lecte. ri.

Nicol. Typogr. Lecte. ri.

Here and there he has a true Record, and among the rest a piece of the sixth Council of *Carthage*, though mangled too : where concerning the two Counterfeit Canons of Pope *Zozimus*, he saith, *The African Fathers not finding any such* Canons *as these, in the* Codes *which they had of the* Nicene Council,

L   *both*

both in Greek *and* Latine, *promised that they would keep them only so long, as the time would be, that they might get the true* Copies *out of* Greece: *Which when they had been sent for, and were brought from* Cyril *of* Alexandria, *and* Atticus *of* Constantinople, *they were found imperfect, as not containing but only those* 20 Canons, *which were extant also among the* Latines; *in which nothing is contained concerning Appeals to the* Roman Bishop: Nay, *those* African Fathers *from the fifth and sixth of those* Canons *gathering the contrary, did earnestly beseech* Celestine *the* Pope, *that succeeded* Boniface, *who was the* Successor *of* Zozimus, *that he should not admit Appeals: which (they said) as it was most prudently and justly provided for by the* Nicene Council, *so they found it in no Synod of the Fathers, that any should be sent from the side of his Holiness. What* Boniface *and* Celestine *answered, it is not certain:* Acta enim illa valdè concisa sunt, & mutila, *For those* Records *are cut very short, and maimed; and therefore the matter is the more obscure.*

No Lega-
tus à La-
tere.

Who maimed those Records is worth the Enquiry: Some-Body that was concerned in them, and whose influence must
be

be exceeding great for the attempting of such a thing, hath *cut them fhort*, that Records fo offenfive and pernicious to him, might be made *obfcure*. But as Thieves, by dropping fome of the Goods by the way, are oftentimes detected, or Murderers by forgetting the Knife behind them; fo doth the Great and Juft GOD infatuate the Pope of *Rome*, againft whom this Council was afiembled, and fmite his Agents with blindnefs here; and at other times their heart faileth them, becaufe of *Guilt:* fo that not daring to make *thorow work* with the Councils, they faulter, and are detected.

Here is a rare cafe, all the Copies of the *Nicene Council*, throughout the World, were *imperfect* 1200 years ago, both among the *Greeks*, and among the *Latines*, only thofe at *Rome* were valid and Authentick. For the Councils of *Carthage* were reckoned among the *Latines*, as you may fee by *Ifidore*, and *Merlin*, placing them in that number, and that juftly; for the *African* Fathers that pertained to *Carthage*, wrote in *Latine*, as S. *Auguftine, Fulgentius, Tertullian, &c.* They were Naturalized fo far, that *Latine* was almoft their Mother-Tongue, as *Juftellus* obferves out of S. *Au-*

L 2   *guftine:*

gustine : and yet these that were Allied to the See of *Rome* so near, were at one with the *Greeks* in the Records contro= verted : None were good at *Carthage,* *Constantinople,* or *Alexandria,* &c. but only those which the Pope produced in his own Cause : Nor were any like his upon the Face of the whole Earth be- sides.

At first I admired to see those Canons of *Carthage* so abruptly cut off by *Bini- us,* where I happened first to miss them : but when I afterwards found them, by the help of *Justellus,* I saw the reason : The *Roman Bishop* was curbed; though that of *Anacharsis* concerning Laws pro- ved true; *Laws are like Spiders Webs, they detain Flies, but Hornets break through them.*

Nicolinus having intimated the lame- ness and obscurity of the Narration, go- eth on thus : *It is probable that* Celestine *wrote back sharply, and would have the Appeals of Priests, from their own, to the bordering Bishops, and of Bishops them- selves to the* Roman Chair *established and valid.* The Pope would have it so, not- withstanding all contradiction : *Foras- much as they were founded on Right and custom, and upon the* Nicene Canons, *which*

Nicol. ibid.

which were kept entire (it is credible) in the Roman See, as they were extant in the time of Mark.

It is credible: Was ever such Impudence known before! They were not able to urge one Argument why it should be *credible*, and yet this *credibility* muſt overthrow all the Evidence in the whole World.

But they were kept entire *in the Roman See, as they were extant in the time of* Mark. This ſpoileth all! for by referring you to *Mark*, he appeals to the Epiſtles of *Athanaſius* to *Mark*, and of Pope *Mark* to *Athanaſius, concerning the number of the Nicene Canons.* Which Epiſtles of *Mark* and *Athanaſius*, by invincible reaſons urged by *Binius*, as well as the Authorities of *Baronius, Labbè*, and the *Collectio Regia*, are evidently proved to be very Forgeries.

He gives you more of theſe audacious *Gueſſes*; He ſays *it is credible, that they were contained alſo among the Canons of* Sardica *which* Celeſtine *ſent, it is probable, unto them: But that the Afric. ns reſted not ſatisfied, either becauſe they ſuſpected thoſe Canons to be corrupted, or for ſome other cauſe; it is ſhewn in the Epiſtle of* Boniface *the* II. *to* Eulalius *of* Alex-

L 3 andria,

andria, *concerning the Reconciliation of* Carthage, *which happened about* 100 *years after.*

The more you ftir this bufinefs, the more it ftinks. The *Epiftles* made in the name of *Eulalius* and *Boniface*, concerning the *Excommunication of the Churches of* Africa *for* 100 *years*, paft down fo fair to *Nicolinus*, that he took them for good Records; and doubtlefs he thought it well enough, that the African Fathers were Excommunicated for oppofing the Popes Opinion: So that the Quarrel rofe very high, or, what we before obferved was very true, thefe Epiftles of *Boniface* and *Eulalius* were invented to colour the Popes Caufe, and difgrace the Fathers. Take it which way you pleafe, it fmells ill: *Baronius* and *Bellarmine* had rather they fhould be Counterfeits.

His *probability* about *Celeftine's* fending the Canons of *Sardica* to *Carthage* fares little better: *Celeftine* knew very well the Canons of *Sardica* would not do in that Council: *Nicolinus* cannot produce one fyllable in proof, to make it *probable*, that he fent them thither; and his fly-ing to *Sardica* is in an evil hour; for it is oppofed by 217 Bifhops, fo great, that they have frighted *Rome* out of her Excommunication,

communication, who altogether teſtifie,
no leſs than twelve hundred years ago,
*that no Synod of the Fathers made any
ſuch Canons.* And if *Sardica* were no
Synod, what will its Canons ſignifie?
The Popes then living and concerned,
never attempted ſo vain a ſhift, but po-
ſitively affirmed and maintained ſtill,
that they were the *Nicene* Canons: only
the Council of *Sardica* is pretended of
late, and ſome *new* men, now the buſineſs
is over, perſwade us they did all miſtake
while the *matter* was in agitation, both
at *Rome* and *Carthage*; and that themſelves have more clear and piercing judgments (to ſee into a buſineſs ſo far off
better) than all the Fathers.

Admit thoſe Canons were made at
Sardica, it was a groſs Errour to Father
them upon the *Nicene* Council: for the
Authority of *Sardica* is not to be compared with that of *Nice*. *Sardica* was
unknown to all the Council at *Carthage*.
S. *Auguſtine* thought it an Arrian Council;
as *Binius* in his Notes upon it obſerveth:
and *Bellarmine* puts it among *the partly
Reprobated*. And that which induceth *Bell. de
Concil. &*
me to believe thoſe Canons now extant *Eccleſ.lib* 1
cap ⁙
in the name of *Sardica* to be forged, is,
that they were firſt produced in *Zozimus*

L 4   his

his Counterfeit, and Fathered upon *Nice*. And there being a *Council* once, it is now pretended that there were two there; that these Baſtards diſowned at *Nice*, might have a Sanctuary ſomewhere, and find ſome Fathers. My conjecture is made conſiderable, becauſe the Canons now Fathered upon *Sardica* are *contrary* to thoſe of *Nice:* And it is not probable, that two *Catholick Councils* ſo near, ſhould ſo ſuddenly Decree things contrary to each other: nor that the *ſame Fathers* that were at *Nice*, when they came to *Sardica*, ſhould change their minds with the place of their Seſſion. That there were no Canons of *Sardica* known till the time of *Dionyſius Exiguus*, is very probable, becauſe they were not in the *Code of the Univerſal Church*, nor in the *African Code*, till *Dionyſius · Exiguus* put them in; as *Jacobus Leſchaſſerius* moſt excellently proveth.

Whether *Dionyſius* or *Hadrian* put them in, is to me uncertain: But *Hadrian* I. firſt gave the Copy of *Dionyſius* to the Emperour *Charles*, whence the *old Manuſcripts* were tranſcribed, which are now extant in ſeveral Libraries; and in which the Dedication of Pope *Hadrian* is contained in Verſe, *To his moſt Excellent*

lent *Son King* Charles, *&c.* The firſt Letters of the Verſes being put together, make this Acroſtick , EXCELL. FILIO. CARULO. REGI. HADRIANUS. PAPA. The Verſes are found in the Copies yet extant of *Dionyſius Exiguus.*

This ſhews that ſome *New* Thing was put into the Book, and that *Hadrian* had a finger in it , which reach'd perhaps farther than the beginning. If the Book was as new as the Acroſtick, *Dionyſius* was far enough from being its Author. What Faith we are to have in the Papiſts, when they tell us who were the Ancient Compilers of the Councils, you may ſee by *Baronius,* who giving us an Account of their Order, reckons *Iſidore* (a known Counterfeit) for *one* ; *Dionyſius Exiguus* for the *firſt* , *Ferdinandus Diaconus* for the *ſecond* , *Martinus Bracarenſis* for the *third* , *Creſconius* for the *fourth* ; and after all theſe, *Iſidore* for the *fift.* As certain as *Iſidore* was a Collector of the Councils, ſo certain is it that *Dionyſius* was one, but further certainty yet I can ſee none.

In Not. Martyrol. ad. 4. April.

Charles the Great , perhaps having never ſeen the like before, was pleaſed with the Acroſtick; and the putting of his Name in Capital Letters before the *Coun-*

cils

cils was delightful to him. *Syrens* fing fweetly, while they deceive bloodily. *Hadrian* 1. knew well, what was a Gift fit for a *Scholar*, and a *Pope* of *Rome*.

If I fhould produce but one paffage which I found in it, the matter would be more effectual: For after he has done with the Councils, he lays down the Decretal Epiftles of **13** Roman Bifhops, beginning with *Syricius*, who lived in the year 385. In his Epiftle to *Himerius*, there is this paffage: *Such is our Office*, faith he, *that it is not lawful for us to be filent, for us to diffemble, upon whom a Zeal greater than that of all others, of the Chriftian Religion, is incumbent: We bear the burdens of all that are oppreffed; nay rather the bleffed Apoftle* Peter *beareth them in us: who as we truft, protecteth and defendeth us his Heirs in all the things of his Adminiftration.*

Of GOD he faith nothing here, but his confidence is all in *Peter.* There is not a word like it in all Antiquity: and thofe words *protecteth and defendeth us,* feem to relate to thofe Jars that had been before between *Hadrian,* and *Charles* the King, or Emperour.

Thefe obfervations carry me to believe what I met with in *Daille,* fince *Dionyfius*

is

is gone from under my hands: and having searched into the Book since, I am further confirmed.

About 74 *years after the Council of* Daillé pag. 45. &c. Chalcedon, Dionysius Exiguus, *whom we before-mentioned, made his collection at* Rome, *which is since Printed at* Paris, cum Privilegio Regis, *out of very Ancient Manuscripts. Whosoever shall but look diligently into his collection, shall find divers alterations in it; one whereof I shall instance in, only to shew how Ancient this Artifice hath been among Christians. The last Canon of the Council of* Laodicea, *which is the* 163 *of the* Greek Code *of the Church Universal, forbidding to read in Churches any other Books than those which are Canonical, gives us withal a long Catalogue of them.* Dionysius Exiguus, *although he hath indeed inserted in his collection,* Num. 162. *the beginning of the said Canon, which forbiddeth to read any other Books in the Churches, besides the sacred Volumes of the* Old *and* New Testament; *yet hath he wholly omitted the Catalogue, or List of the said Books; fearing, as I conceive, lest the Tail of this Catalogue might scandalize the Church of* Rome, &c. A little after he saith, *the* Greek Code *represents unto us* VII Ca-

nons

nons of the first Council of Constantino
ple. which are in like manner found bot
in Balſamon, and in Zonoras, and alſo i
the Greek and Latine Edition of the Ge
neral Councils, Printed at Rome. Th
three laſt of theſe do not appear at all in th
Latine Code of Dionyſius, though the
are very conſiderable ones, as to the buſi
neſs they relate to, which is the order o
proceeding, in paſſing judgment upon Bi
ſhops accuſed, and in receiving ſuch per
ſons, who forſaking their communion wit
Hereticks, deſire to be admitted into th
Church. It is very hard to ſay, what ſhould
move the Collector to Gueld this Counci
thus: But this I am very well aſſured of
that in the ſixth Canon, which is one o
thoſe he hath omitted, and which treatet
of judging of Biſhops accuſed, there is no
the leaſt mention made of Appealing to
Rome; nor of any Reſerved Caſes, where
in it is not permitted to any, ſave only t
the Pope, to judge a Biſhop: The power o
hearing and determining all ſuch matter
being here wholly and abſolutely referred t
the Provincial Synods, and to their Dio
ceſans.

Another inſtance which he hath is this.
After the Canons of Conſtantinople, there
follow in the Greek Code VIII Canons o
                                        the

the General Council of Ephesus, *set down also both by* Balsamon *and* Zonoras, *and Printed with the Acts of the said Council of* Ephesus, *in the first Tome of the Roman Edition : but* Dionysius Exiguus *hath discarded them all,* &c. *Daille in his Treatise of the Right of the Fathers.* Cap.4. pag.45,46,47.

This being true, the Authority of *Dionysius* is very small, relating to the matter of the Council of *Sardica.* If any man hath any thing to say against it, let him, when he answereth this Charge of ours, produce what he is able in Defence of *Dionysius,* as to the points whereof he stands accused by *Daille* ; but we proceed to *Nicolinus.*

CAP. XII.

Nicolinus *his Epistle to* Pope Sixtus. *His contempt of the* Fathers. *He beginneth to confess the Epistle of* Melchiades *to be dubious, if not altogether* Spurious. *He overthrows the* Legend *about* Constantines *Donation.*

That you may know the *Genius* of the Man a little better, how much he he was devoted to the fervice of the Pope, and how little he valued the Authority of Councils and Fathers, I have thought it meet to give you his *Epiſtle*; and his *Admonition to the Reader*, recorded by him in the words following.

To our Moſt Soveraign Lord, *Sixtus V.* High-Prieſt.

'It fell out conveniently for me, Moſt 'Bleſſed Father, in the Univerſal Joy of 'the Chriſtian World, for your Elevati- 'on to the Sublimity of the Apoſtleſhip, 'that in ſo great a multitude flowing 'from every place to honour you, I al- 'ſo, among the Oldeſt Servants of your 'Holineſs, had ſomething near at hand, 'which is unworthy neither of the Ma- 'ſty of your Name, or Authority; and 'yet very fit for my Occaſions to offer at 'your feet, as ſuitable to the Office of 'my Gratitude and Veneration It is a 'new Edition of the Councils: for the 'remarkable addition of two Councils 'eſpecially, the *Niſene* and the *Epheſine*, 'never publiſhed ſo entire and full, as 'now.

Things put into the Councils of Nice and Epheſus by Nicolinus.

'For to whom may the Councils of the 'Church, aided by the Inſpiration of the 'H. Ghoſt, according to the ſeaſonable- 'neſs

'nefs of various times, for the repairing
'of her Ship, more fitly be Dedicated,
'than to her Chief Mafter, to whom it
'is given from Heaven to call and con-
'firm them? efpecially him, who is fo
'well verfed in all Scholaftical Difci-
'plines, and Ecclefiaftical Hiftory !

'I have ufed all diligence, according
'to my weak ability, fparing no coft, o-
'mitting no labour; the moft Catholick
'and Learned Divines of our Age, being
'affembled alfo from every Quarter, e-
'fpecially the moft Excellent Father *Do-*
'*minicus Bollanus*, a Noble-Man of *Ve-*
'*nice*, of the Order of Preachers, never
'enough commended for his excellent
'parts; who by his Induftry, Care, and
'Learning, was a vaft help both to me,
'and to the Work.

'And that I may in one word fignifie
'my ftudy and pains beftowed thereup-
'on, left I fhould feem to draw the Saw
'backward and forward too often upon
'the fame Line, I have taken care to per-
'form whatever could be done by one
'man, and he a private perfon, that this
'Edition might come forth from me, and
'be offered to you, more Copious and
'Illuftrious than any other Publications
'hitherto fent abroad: In which I truft,
'that

‘that as a juft and knowing Judge, you
‘will difcern fome Accomplifhment:
‘Wherefore I fuppofe I may affirm, that
‘nothing is perverfly, or too concifely
‘expreft; but all things moft rightly and
‘clearly, as far as was poffible, according
‘to their Primitive Candour.

‘This my Gift therefore, from which
‘men may receive fo great profit and be-
‘nefit, fince both thofe things that be=
‘fore were wanting, and thofe that have
‘hitherto been difperfed, may be had to-
‘gether in it; and this Work of mine,
‘not of lefs coft in Printing (the great
‘expences of which may eafily be proved
‘by the magnitude of the Volume) than
‘labour: to which I was not fo much
‘prefent, as prefiding; earneftly defi-
‘ring that it fhould come forth moft free
‘from Errour and Faults, for the benefit
‘of the Studious, I doubt not but ac-
‘cording to your Humanity, you will
‘accept it with a willing mind, as fome
‘kind of Token of my will to ferve you;
‘even as I defire with all my Soul, and
‘humbly pray, that your Holinefs may
‘receive it. In the mean time, Holy Fa-
‘ther, I defire that all things may fall out
‘profperoufly to your Bleffednefs: And
‘I pray, that you may long be preferved
‘in

' in health, and more plentifully adorned
' with Heavenly Gifts, for the good of
' the whole Church. *Venice* VI. Kal.
' *Octob:* M. D. LXXXV.

Here you see one of the Popes Old
Servants laying down all the Councils
at his Holiness Feet, boasting of additions to the *Nicene* and *Ephesine* Councils,
never before published, ascribing the
Councils to the Inspiration of the Holy
Ghost; and yet adding, for the good of
the *Roman* Church, eight and fifty Canons to the most glorious of them all,
ascribing the power of calling and confirming Councils, to the Pope, sparing
no cost (though he draws the Saw too
often upon that point, which as if he
were enchanted, he cannot leave,
throughout all the Epistle) assisted, as
himself confesseth, with a confluence of
the best Popish Divines, permitted to
come forth under the Popes Nose, with
all these Abominations. By which you
may perceive, it is not the work of a
private Doctor, but the Disease of the
Church of *Rome*.

His *Typographus Lectori.*

His contempt of the Fathers appears
in his *Printer to the Reader*: for by one
of *Turrian's Transfigurations*, he covers

M   that

that *Admonition* with the Printers Name, though too Learned for any Printer, and evident enough to be his *own*: for he there unfoldeth the matter, order and use of the Work, far above a Printers reach; and especially notes its *Correĉions and Emendations* to us : which he reduceth to four Heads.

I. *To the observation of the time wherein Councils were held, and under what Pope.* Whereupon we note, the manner of ordering the Councils *under such and such a Pope*, seemeth a new thing : *Nicolinus* else arrogates too much to himself, in ascribing this to his own Invention. Certainly the custom of *computing times by the Popes Lives*, is of no long standing, but an Artifice lately taken up by his Flatterers, to dazle the eyes of their Readers; for it adds much to the Splendour of the Chair, to see Kings and Councils marshalled under the *Reign*, as it were, of this, and that, and the other Pope, down from S. *Clement*, throughout all Ages. But from the beginning it was not so.

2. *To the truth of History and Aĉions : As when various Authors are often cited, either for the confirmation of Sentences, or to shew the variety that is among Writers,*

ters, or to reprehend some falsity, *Quod interdum, parcè tamen, & timidè fecimus.* In his Dedicatory Epistle he told the Pope, *that he did nothing perversly, but all things most rightly and clearly, as far as was possible, according to their Primitive Candour :* As you see before. But here he confesseth, the business of reprieving falshoods to be a tender work, which he went about with great caution and trembling. Some he detected, but *timerously and sparingly :* he durst not meddle with them all.

3. *To the confutation of some contumacious and rebellious persons ; who lay hold on the lightest occasions, and oftentimes wrest the plainest matters, to the disgrace of the H. Roman Church. As when from a slight contention of the African Fathers, about Appeals to the Church of* Rome, *they forcibly conclude against the very truth of the Acts, and the Faith of the History, that those Fathers did not acknowledge, but refuse its Primacy over them.* In the Body of his Tomes, he citeth the Epistles of *Boniface* and *Eulalius,* as good Records, testifying the Excommunication of all the African Churches by the Pope ; yet here he calleth it a light contention : Himself wresteth the plainest matters for-

M 2 cibly

cibly againſt the very truth of the Acts, and chargeth the fault on the Proteſtants : For in this very place he pretendeth that the African Fathers did not refuſe the Primacy of *Rome*, but acknowledge its Supremacy, or its *Primacy over them*. Yet is all this but a Copy of his countenance, a common flouriſh in the Frontiſpiece of their work : For if they ſubmitted to the Popes *Primacy over them*, why ſhould they be Excommunicated? He knows well enough, when we come cloſe to the matter, that theſe *Rebellious Proteſtants*, and thoſe *Catholick Fathers*, were of the ſame judgment, and acted the ſame thing. By way of proviſion therefore he addeth, that *this was far from the mind of thoſe Fathers; but if they had conceived ſo, it would have redounded to their Infamy, and not at all have tended to the leſſening of the Supreme Authority of the Roman Church, ordained and eſtabliſhed by God.*

Two hundred and ſeventeen Biſhops in an ancient approved Council, even the *ſixth Council of Carthage*, proteſted againſt the *Popes* Supreme Authority, *to their perpetual Infamy*; as *Nicolinus* would have it : for ſhould all the Biſhops in the World joyn together, they would but

daſh

dafh themfelves againft that *Rock*, and do things *to their Infamy*, and there's an end. This is, the value which Papifts have for the Councils and Fathers, when they ftand in their way : And this Impudence comes abroad by the confent of *Nicolimus*, and the Pope, without *Elufhing*.

His fourth Head is Addition. His Emendations are referred *laftly to Addition*, either *by making thofe things perfect and entire, that before were imperfect and maimed: as when the Canons of the Canons of the* ...... *and* ... *Acts of that Coun* ... ... *of a Greek Book* .... *into Latine by* .... *a Jefuite; and fourfcore* ... ... *into Latine out of an Arabick Book brought to Alexandria by another man of the fame Society.*

I once thought a certain man had *had* the Book at *Alexandria*; but now it feems a Jefuite, brought it thither. He does not tell you *who*, nor *from whence*. Jefuites are the Popes *Janizaries*, and fit to be fo imployed : And the *Vatican* is an admirable Storehoufe doubtlefs for the Greek too, a very Pit of Witneffes for the Popes Supremacy. As if *Perkin Warbeck* fhould have brought Evidences

M 3   out

out of his own Closet to prove himself King of *England*. If no body but he must be believed, the veriest Cheat in the World must needs prevail. *Greek* and *Arabick* are strange amusements: else a Book out of the *Vatican*, in its Matters own Cause; or *another man without a* name, that *brought an Arabick Book to A-* lexandria, *with fourscore Canons of the* Nicene Council *in it*, would scarcely be regarded against the Evidence of the whole World; especially in a matter so upheld by Forgeries.

Two things there are wherein he adventures to be a little cordial; *Licèt parcè & timidè :* though *seldom*, and with fear.

1. Whereas *Isidore*, and *Merlin*, and *Peter Crab*, and *Surius*, &c. have the Epistle of *Melchiades* without any Note of its dubiousness, he confesseth it can be none of *Melchiades*, *because mention is made therein of the* Nicene Council, *and of other things that were done after* Melchiades *Death*.

2. Whereas *Einius* lays a Dreadful Reproach upon *Constantine*, the first most Excellent Christian Emperour, as if after all his Glorious Acts done for the Church and State of *Christendom*, he were

an

an Apoſtate, a Murderer, a Tyrant, a Per-
ecutor, a Parracide, ſmitten with Leproſie for notorious Crimes, for killing *Licinius* unjuſtly, and his own Son *Criſpus:*
And all, that he might uphold the *Counterfeit Donation*, *Nicolinus* begins the
firſt Book *of the Acts preceding the Nicene
Council*, (*tranſlated out of an Ancient
Greek Book in the Vatican*) thus.

> *De Geſtis poſt Sublatum impium* Licini-
> um, *& de Imperio Regis* Conſtan-
> tini, *& de Pace Eccleſiarum Dei.*

'*Conſtantine*, when he had conquered
'his Enemies, ſhewing himſelf an Empe-
'rour by the Wiſdom given him of God,
'took care to better the Affairs of the
'Chriſtians day by day, more and more.
'And this he did ſeveral ways, having a
'moſt flaming Faith, and faithful Piety
'towards the God of all: And the whole
'Church under Heaven lived in pro-
'found peace. Now let us hear what *Eu-
'ſebius*, that moſt excellent Husbandman
'of the Churches Agriculture, ſirnamed
'from the moſt Famous *Pamphilus*, ſpeak-
'eth here. In his tenth Book he ſaith,
'What *Licinius* ſaw long ago to befall
'wicked Tyrants with his eyes, he now
'ſuffered himſelf, like to them; and that
'deſervedly: for he would neither re-
'ceive

' ceive Discipline, nor be admonished at
' any time to learn wisdom by the punish-
' ment of his Neighbors, *&c.* But *Constan-*
' *tine* the Conqueror being adorned with
' all kind of Piety, together with his Son
' *Crispus*, the Emperour beloved of God,
' and in all things like his Father, redu-
' ced all the *East* into his Power, and
' brought the Empire of the *Romans* into
' one, as it had been of old, and obtain-
' ed an Universal Kingdom, from the ri-
' sing of the Sun, to the utmost borders
' of the *West*, and to both the other Re-
' gions of the *North* and *South*, in perfect
' peace: Then the fear of Tyranny where-
' with men were before oppressed, was
' utterly taken away from the life of
' men; then frequent Assemblies were
' held, and Festivals kept; then all things
' abounded with gladness and joy; then
' they that were before of a dejected
' countenance, and sorrowful, looked
' with a pleasant face, and with joyful
' eyes; then with Dances and Hymns,
' throughout all Cities and Fields, they
' proclaimed first, that God was truly
' God, and the Highest King of all:
' next, they magnified the Emperour and
' his Children, more dear unto God.
' Then there was no remembrance of the
' former

'former evils; then all Impiety was for-
'gotten; then there was a sweet enjoy-
'ment of present goods, and a joyful
'expectation of future: Then finally,
'not only the Decrees of the Emperour,
'the most Illustrious Conquerour, full of
'Humanity and Clemency, but his Laws
'also glorious in Magnificence, and
'fraught with Tokens of true Piety were
'published in all places: So the remotest
'Spot of all Tyranny being purged away,
'and wholly blotted out, *Constantine* a-
'lone, and his Children, thenceforth pos-
'sessed the Helm of the Empire, which
'by Right pertained to them; it being
'made secure by his Authority and Go-
'vernment, and freed from all envy and
'fear. Hitherto *Eusebius Pamphilus*, of
'all Ecclesiastical Writers most worthy of
'belief.

Thus their own Record in the *Vatican*
justifieth *Eusebius*: and thus *Nicolinus*
produceth it, who also defendeth *Eusebius*, though himself holdeth the *Donation of Constantine* firm; not discerning
how that History overthroweth the same.
But *Binius* who saw the inconsistence better, crys out of *Eusebius* for a Lyar, a
Flatterer, an Arrian, because he stands in
his way. Thus all of them, here and there,
serve

ferve the Fathers : For *Eufebius* lived in the time of *Conftantine* himfelf, and was Honourable in his eyes : He was Bifhop of *Cæfarea-Cappadocia*, and an individual Friend of *Pamphilus* the *Martyr*, a Father in the *Nicene Council*, and one of thofe that difputed there, in perfon, againft *Phædo* the *Arrian* : As *Binius* alfo himfelf recordeth in the Difputation, extant in his *Tomes*. But of fuch Legends as this, and the Tragical Story of *Conftantine*, we have more than good ftore in Popifh Writers *:* As you may fee at large in Dr. *Stillingfleet* his Book of *Popifh Counterfeit Miracles.*

CAP. XIII.

The Epiftle of Pope Damafus *to* Aurelius, *Archbifhop of* Carthage, *commanding him to take care, that the Decretals of the Roman Bifhops be preached and publifhed abroad: Wherein the Forgeries of the Church of* Rome *are Fathered on the Holy Ghoft.*

DAmafus, *to his moft Reverend Brother, and Fellow-Bifhop* Aurelius. *We have received the Epiftle of your Holinefs* ness with due Veneration: Wherein we understand how your Reverence and Prudence thirsteth, as is fit, for the Apostolical Decrees. Concerning which Affair, we have sent some of those which you desired, and desire to send more when you shall send unto us. Yet we have past by none of our Predecessors, from the Death of Blessed ter, Prince of the Apostles, of whose Decrees we have not sent somewhat to you under our certain Seal by Ammonius the Priest, and Falix the Deacon: Which we both desire you to keep, and command to be preached and published to others; that they may inviolably be kept with due Veneration of all, and inviolably observed, and diligently reverenced by all future Ages.

Because the voluntary Breakers of the Canons are heavily censured by the H. Fathers, and condemned by the H. Ghost, by whose Gift and Inspiration they were dictated: Because they do not unfitly seem to blaspheme the H. Ghost, who being not compelled by any necessity, but willingly (as was before said) either do any thing perversly, or presume to speak against the same Holy Canons, or consent to them that will; for such a presumption is manifestly one kind of blaspheming the H. Ghost: Because (as was even now promised) it acteth

against

against him , by whose grace and impulse the same Holy Canons were set forth. But the wickedness of the Devil is wont to deceive many , and so doth very oftentimes delude the imprudence of some by a similitude of Piety, that he perswadeth them to take hurtful things for healthful.

Therefore the Rule of H. Canons which are made by the Spirit of God, and consecrated by the Reverence of the whole World, is faithfully to be known, and diligently to be handled by us ; lest by any means the Decrees of the H. Fathers should without inevitable necessity (which God forbid) be transgressed : but that we walking most faithfully in them , may by their Merits, God assisting, deserve the glory of a reward, and the heap of our labour.

A Loop-
hole for
the Popes:

These therefore being rightly considered, and upon our deliberation brought to the knowledge of your Churches, it most highly becometh you to obey the Rules of the same H. Canons , lest the sloth of some should make them in any thing to walk contrary to them. But let your wise and wholesome Doctrine, which desires you in all things to please God, shew them these faithful Fellow-workmen in their Thrones, the coheirs and partakers of the Cælestial Kingdom. Dated XVI. Kal. *Jun.* Gratian *and* Cyricius *being* Consuls.   The

The cloſe of the Epiſtle (if not clear nonſenſe) is very obſcure. The meaning of it is, that *Aurelius* ſhould ſhew men the Decretal Epiſtles of *Clement, Anacletus,* &c. *thoſe faithful Fellow-workmen in their Thrones, the coheirs and partakers of the Cœleſtial Kingdom,* that are now in Heaven, to the intent they may obey them, and come to the ſame Eternal Glory. A goodly deſign doubtleſs. But we have a croſs Proverb, *Woe be to the ſheep, while the Fox Preacheth.* This piety in the Cloſe is but the Sheep-skin to cover the Fox, who needs not more cunning in Preaching, than concealing himſelf. We have a more ſacred ſaying, *In the Pit which he made for others, is himſelf fallen.* And it is not impertinent: for while he chargeth others with the unpardonable ſin, himſelf *blaſphemes the Holy Ghoſt.* For to make the Holy Ghoſt the *Father of Lies,* is (I think) to blaſpheme him.

Damaſus, we confeſs, never made the Epiſtle; but that makes the matter worſe. Some other in *Damaſus* his Coat, is guilty of this accurſed buſineſs; that while he Fathers the Frauds, which himſelf invented, on the H. Ghoſt, has not *ignorance* to *excuſe,* but *malice* to *condemn* him. And whether the Forgeries

are

are not so Fathered still on the Hol
Ghost, may be a proper Question. *Bi
nius*, I think, was afraid of these Epi
stles.

Nicolinus in his *Printer to the Reader*
pretendeth an exact *observation of th
time, under what Pope* things were done
but for once he varies the method, an
sets this in the Front of the Forgeries, t
countenance all.

He knows them perhaps to be wha
they are, yet clearly owns them.

There is some Errour in the date o
these Epistles; an usual Symptom of th
Disease in such Instruments. Instead o
the xvi. *Kal. Jun. Nicolinus* putteth it th
xi. Some hidden reason compels him, o
he would never be so nice: for *Cyricius
Siricius* a small mistake: But the next i
greater, for *Gratian, Equitius*. As i
Damasus the Pope could not tell wh
was *Consul* at *Rome* when he wrote hi
Letter.

I wonder at *Damasus* for one thin
much; he tells us of *the wickedness ⌐
the Devil, who deludes men with a shew ⌐
Piety*, and forces in that expression ⌐
the *Devils perswading men to take hur
ful things for healthful* so affectedly, tha
it would make one to think his Guilt pt
hi⌐

him in memory of such a saying. But his design in charging all that impugn them, with the dreadful and unpardonable sin of blaspheming the Holy Ghost, was more clearly to deter men from writing or speaking against these pretended Canons. And perhaps he declaims against *the wickedness of others, that delude the imprudence of some with a similitude of Piety*; and so loudly inveigheth against the Guilt of *perswading men to take hurtful things for healthful*, to remove the suspition from himself. Whatever 'tis, no man is more guilty of the Fraud in the World.

You may note a contradiction in the Letter: The Canons of the H. Fathers, and Bishops of *Rome*, were *consecrated by the Reverence of the whole World*; and yet upon *Aurelius* his desire, were newly *brought to the knowledge of the Churches*, and now first ordered to be *published and preached.*

They past the *deliberation* of our present *Damasus* before they came abroad, *being rightly considered, and upon due deliberation brought to the knowledge of the Churches.* Doubtless they were well weighed, and what was most agreeable to the *Roman Chair* was pickt out, and chosen for the purpose. CAP.

CAP. XIV.

Counterfeit Canons of the Apoftles defended by Binius. *A Glympfe of his Pretences, Sophiftries, and Contradictions. A Forged Council of Apoftles concerning Images, defended by* Binius *and* Turrian.

SEverinus *Binius*, a late Collector of the Councils, is grown fo famous, that his Voluminous Tomes have been Printed thrice; he is approved by an Epiftle of Pope *Paul* V. inferted among other Inftruments before his Work, and fo highly efteemed, that he is exactly followed by *Labbe* and *Coffartius* in 17 Volumes, and taken in, word for word, by the COLLECTIO REGIA; lately publifhed by the care of a King in 37 Tomes. The reafon why they follow *Binius* fo exactly, the *Collectio Regia* giveth in the words, fet next to the Title-page of the Book, for our better information. *We thought fit to follow the laft collection of the Councils put forth by* Binius, *and illuftrated with his Notes; and to Print it nicely, as that which of all others is moft richly ftored.* Wherein they have done

done *Binius* as great Honour as one can well imagine: for it shews his Notes to be the best and most convenient that can be gotten in the Church of *Rome*, and that all the Collectors since (which were very many) have not been able to devise better.

Hereupon it followeth, that in one Work we may the more concisely treat of *Binius*, *Labbe*, *Coßartius*, and the *Collectio Regia* together.

I once intended to give you a Copy of the Popes approbation, with the other Authorities by which *Binius* is approved; but as the case standeth it is superfluous.

He pretendeth in *Prefaces and Provisos*, to justifie all the Canons, Councils and Decretal Epistles, and maketh a glorious shew, setting them down afterwards with great *Titles* of Splendour and Majesty; in such sort, that a man would take them all for Authentick Records: But when he cometh to his *Notes*, he many times deserteth his design, and confesseth the Imposture. But his *Notes* are Pen'd in more obscure and inconsiderable Letters, and those his acknowledgments hidden from a Transient Eye in little room.

In his Letter to *Paul* V. he layeth all his Labours at the Popes Feet. So that we are like to have good on't, when the Malefactor (accufed) is made fole Lord and Judge of the Witneffes.

He hath feveral Prefaces to the Reader, and to Perfons of the Higheft Rank and Splendour: in which he pretends to magnifie the Decrees and Canons following, as good Records.

He prefixeth *Ifidore*'s Counterfeit *Preface* before His Collection.

Over the Canons of the Apoftles, in a Splendid manner, he fets this Title.

THE CANONS
OF THE
HOLY APOSTLES
WITH ALL VENERATION
TO BE FOLLOWED.

According to

The Ancient Edition
OF
DIONYSIUS EXIGUUS.

A man would think now there fhould no more *Canons* be laid down, than *Dionyfius*

nyſius Exiguus hath in his Ancient Edition : But as if he intended to bear the
Mark of the Beaſt in his Forehead, he
puts under this Title *eighty four Canons
of the Apoſtles*, whereas *Dionyſius* hath
but 50. Certainly 'tis not well done ſo
to Cheat his Reader with a Lye; but in
ſome blind Corner or other he will make
us ſatisfaction.

Over againſt this he puts a Note in the
Margin, thus: Francis Turrian, *of the
Society of* Jeſus, *hath publiſhed a very
clear Book in Defence of the Apoſtles Canons*. He approveth the Book, yet rejecteth two of the Canons which *Turrian*
defendeth: but that is concealed till afterwards.

It is his cuſtom, in the top of his Pages, Chapters and Margins, eminent and
conſpicuous places, to put Notes or Titles, defending thoſe Counterfeit Antiquities, which in ſome little Gloſs hidden
in the Text, he really ſlighteth: For the
Potentates of the World, with their
Lords and Councellors, not having
time enough to ſearch into the bottom,
may by ſuch means as theſe neatly be deceived; while they think no man ſo impudent, as in the ſame Leaf, to contradict
his *pretences*. So that the very greatneſs

of the Crime is their greatest security.

Another Artifice like this, is that of putting the Preface of *Dionysius Exiguus* before these Tomes of his own, the better to countenance the ensuing Frauds. Though *Dionysius* were dead 1000 years before he wrote them, and never intended, nor thought of the greater part of them.

But Lyars are intangled always in the Bryers: what is convenient in one respect, being inconvenient in another.

For in that his Preface, *Dionysius* speaking for himself, saith only this: *In the beginning we have placed those Canons which are said to be the Apostles, translated out of Greek: which because the most do not easily acknowledge, I thought meet to acquaint your Holiness with the same.*

He doubts them all you see; yet speaketh only of his own fifty, which he hath in the Code which himself digested: He does not meddle with those that make up the number of 84. no more than *Isidore* and *Merlin* do: Howbeit *Binius*, when he comes to his Notes upon the word *Canones Apostolorum*, speaketh thus, after his large Copy in three Columns of all the 84. *Those Canons made by the Authority of the Apostles, and by Tradition*

from

from them delivered to us, Clement *of*
Rome, *S. Peter's Disciple, wrote in Greek;
and* Dionysius Exiguus, *an Abbot of*
Rome, *translated them into Latine; in the
time of* Justinus *the Emperour.*   An. 520.

He does not prove that *Clement* wrote
them, unless by the last Canon, which
hath *Per me Clementem* in it: nor by that
neither; for that he ought also to be a
Forgery. *Dionysius* the same, in his
before *Bittius*, does not say that *Clement*
wrote them, but rather the contrary:
He suspects them all, and knows *Clement*
could not write them all; since himself
has but fifty, and those only by Rumour,
not Tradition

Nay *Binius* himself, you will see presently, rejected some; and yet here he
pretendeth the whole number to be
written, both by *Clement* in Greek, and
by *Dionysius* in Latine: For of all his
Catalogue, he saith, *These Canons*, &c.
Clement *of* Rome, *S. Peter's Disciple,
wrote in Greek, and* Dionysius Exiguus,
an Abbot in Rome, *translated them into*
Latine; as if it were not sufficient to
write a Lye in the Front, unless he clo-
sed up the Canons with a Lye in the
Tail.

It would be worth the Enquiry to
know

know where they had the 34. which were unknown to the Ancient *Dionyſius?* For after all this, he ſeems to reject them in the paſſage following.

Horum quinquaginta priores, &c. ſaith he, *Only the firſt fifty of theſe (the laſt of which is of dipping thrice in Baptiſm) containing nothing but ſound Apoſtolical Doctrine, and approved by Ancient Biſhops, Councils, and Fathers, are received as Authentick,* Cap. 3. Diſt. 16. *And according to that common Rule of the Holy Fathers, becauſe the Author of them is unknown, they are rightly believed to flow unto us by Apoſtolical Tradition. The reſidue by Pope* Gelaſius, Can. Sanct. Diſt. 15. *are accounted Apocryphal, both becauſe their Author is unknown, as alſo becauſe by the* 65. *and the laſt Canon, it is evident, that ſome of them are craftily put in by the Grecians, and ſome of them corrupted by Hereticks.*

This paſſage deſerves one or two remarkable Obſervations.

1. If the Tradition of the Apoſtles, though committed to *writing,* be capable of corruption; what ſecurity can we have of *Oral Tradition,* which is far more looſe, and liable to danger?

2. If the Church of *Rome* were una-

Ilc

ble to secure the *Apostles Canons* from the Leven of the *Grecians*, and other *Hereticks*; or so careless, as not to keep one Copy, or Record *sincere*: what assurance can we have of her care and ability in the residue? This shews the weakness of these inconvenient Shifts, and pitiful Answers.

But the reason why some are *received as authentick*, and others *accounted Apocryphal*, is most fit to be marked. The reason why it is highly to be presumed, that the first 50 Canons should be Apostolical, is, *Because the Author of them is unknown*: And the reason why the residue are rejected, is, *Because the Author of them is unknown*. So that the same reason (as Fire hardens Clay, and softens Wax) will prove contrary things. And by reasoning in such a Latitude, it will be easie to prove the Sun *black*, and the Sky a Molehill.

Howbeit for these reasons, *Gelasius* an Ancient Pope rejecteth some of them: But *Binius* takes the liberty to put his judgment in the other end of the Scale; and outfacing us with a Counterfeit *Clement*, and Pretended *Dionysius*, will have all but two, to be Authentick Canons: All but two; namely, *the 65. and the last Canon; by which it is evident, that some*

of

of them are craftily put in by the Grecians, and some of them corrupted by Hereticks. Some of them *put in* by the Grecians, must at least be two: and some of them *corrupted* by Hereticks, must at least be two more; yet they are all of them, except two, Authentick.

Let his reason be what it will, we observe, 1. That the Church of *Rome* is in a tottering condition, when a poor Canon of *Collein* shall take upon him to refel the Sentence of an Ancient Pope, and fourscore Bishops: for so many did *Gelasius* use in discerning the *Apocryphal* from *Genuine* Books; and this Sentence was Definitive by a Pope in his Council: So that 2. A Pope in his Council is not Infallible. 3. If *Binius* be right, *Gelasius* and fourscore Bishops did err exceedingly in condemning the Code of the Canons, which S. *Clement* wrote from the mouth of the Apostles. 4. The Church of *Rome* is divided, the New and the Old Church of *Rome* are against each other. The New is all for Additions, and the very Apostles Canons, allowed in *Gelasius* his time, which was 1260 years ago, are not sufficient, unless more be added.

But let us now consider *Binius* his reasons.

reasons. *Quia tamen ex his posterioribus fere omnes præter prædictos duos, &c.* But because all these latter almost, besides the two forementioned, are either by the Authority of the Roman Bishops, or by the Decrees of other Councils, or by the Sentences of some Fathers, confirmed and approved, as is manifest by these our Marginals and Annotations: (So that it may not lightly or rashly be doubted, whether they were taken hence by the Bishops, Councils, and Fathers, or rather translated hither, and put here out of their Writings:) Hereupon they may and ought rightly and deservedly all, except the two excepted, to be taken for Authentick.

How perplexed his discourse is, I suppose you see. His courage fails in the midst, and it becomes thereupon so rough and difficult, that it is scarce intelligible. The occasion of its Incoherence is that Parenthesis (thrust into the middle.) For *Binius* foreseeing a strong Objection to the Discourse he was going to make, claps it Sophistically into the midst of his Argument; hoping thereupon, that it would never more be retorted upon him: Which you may easily see, both by the Nature of his Argument, and by the resolution of his words. For

For his Argument is this; which if you lay aside the Answer to it, runs smoothly. *Almost all these latter Canons, besides the two forementioned, are either by the Authority of Roman Bishops, or the Decrees of other Councils, or the Sentences of some Fathers, confirmed and approved (:) hereupon they may and ought rightly and deservedly, all except the two excepted, to be taken for Authentick.* Now the Answer is the *Parenthesis* in the midst. Certain Sentences like to these Canons are in the Fathers writings, but so contained there, *that it may not lightly or rashly be doubted, whether they were taken hence by the Bishops, Councils, and Fathers, or rather translated hither, and put here out of their Writings. To doubt a thing rashly* is nonsense; but it may justly be feared, that these Canons are Sentences pickt out of other Books, and packt into a Body, bearing the name of the *Apostles Canons.* His Conscience did convict him, and he replieth not a word, though it be an important consideration in the case.

But there is a worse fault in his *Logick*; he argues from *Particulars* to *Universals*: for having said, *Ferè omnes preter prædictos duos,* he comes to conclude,

clude, *Omnes præter prædictos duos.* Almost all except two are approved; therefore all except two are Authentick.

Such Tricks as these he hath often: And sometimes affects an obscure kind of speaking, on purpose to blind the Reader; especially when he is intangled with some difficult Argument: He then Clouds himself, like the *Cuttle,* in his own *Ink,* that he might vomit up the *Hook* in the dark, and scape away.

He might have produced a General Council, if he pleased, to confirm all the 84 Canons, and that *under the Name of the Apostles too,* which had been more to the purpose: but then he must have confessed the last Canon of *Clement* to be true, and consequently that his eight Books of Constitutions, and his two Epistles, are part of the Bible; or else that the Decree of the Council, confirming these, was *Spurious*; or else of necessity, that the Pope and Council did *err.* But he had more kindness for the Pope than so, and therefore perhaps let the Council alone.

He would inure you by his words to believe that Popes are equal to Councils. *Because they are,* saith he, *either by the Authority of Roman Bishops, or other Councils,*

cils, or *some Fathers confirmed, they may and ought to be taken for Authentick*. *Some Fathers* is a dwindling expreſſion. He very well knows that 217 were rejected together in the ſixth Council of *Car-thage*. *Roman Biſhops*, and *other Councils* are words of ſome weight: But what can *other Councils* do, if the *Roman Biſhops* pleaſe to reject them? The *Roman Biſhops*, and *other Councils*, are ſo put in contradiſtinction, that the Authority of *Roman Biſhops* is ſet before that of *other Councils*: And perhaps the proportion being obſerved, the *Roman Biſhops* muſt be thought as far above *other Councils*, as *other Councils* above *ſome Fathers*.

In other places they affirm a Pope with his Council to be Infallible: Here, that *the Roman Biſhop is a Council:* Otherwiſe it is nonſenſe to ſay, *The Roman Biſhops, or other Councils.* The Roman Biſhop hath a Council in himſelf: And indeed it is requiſite, that he of all other ſhould be the greateſt Council, when ſtanding alone, he is to judge of a Council, and to determine, even whether an Oecumenical Council ſhall be approved, or diſapproved.

This is a Taſt of *Pinius*, an Elephants Clee, a Scrap of five large Volumes, full

full of the fame integrity and perverfe=
nefs.

The fwelling words which they talk
of, *approved* and *difapproved Councils*, are
all to be underftood, of Councils approved, or difapproved by the Roman Bifhop.

From his Canons we proceed to his
Council : for *Binius* hath a Council of
Apoftles too, on a Prodigious Theme!
the fetting up of Images. It is but a fhort
one, and hath but one Canon, and that
is the *eighth*. It is fet forth in this form.

ANTIOCHENA SYNODUS
APOSTOLORUM.

Canon. 8. *Ne decipiantur Salvati ob
Idola : fed pingant ex Oppofito Divinam
Humanamque manufactam Impermixtam
Effigiem Dei veri ac Salvatoris noftri Jefu
Chrifti, ipfiufque Servorum, contra Idola
& Judæor. Neque errent in Idolis, neque
fimiles fiant Judæis.*

This is all : and fure it is old, for the
Latine is very bate. If you conftrue it,
it fpeaketh thus, but hath no Greek
Copy.

A COUNCIL of the APOSTLES
at ANTIOCH.

Canon. 8. *Let not the Saved be deceived*

*ved for Idols : but let them paint on th
Opposite, the Divine and Humane unmin
gled Image of the true God, and of our Sa
viour Jesus Christ, made with hands, an
of his Servants. Neither let them err i
Idols, nor be made like the Jews.*

The first Authority he hath to prov
it, is the 2 *Nicene* Council, 800 year
almost after the Apostles. And he col
lecteth it thence by a blind conjecture
not by any evident Assertion of theirs.

Besides this he citeth one *Pamphilus*
who testifieth that he found it in *Origen'*
Study, as *Turrian* saith against the Wri
ters of *Magdenburg*. So that all this rest
eth upon *Turrian*, an impudent Corrup
ter, as the World hath any. Where w
first observe, that *Origen* had no Image
himself, neither adored any. 2. That I
mages were forbidden in the H. Scrip
ture, especially in the Old Testamen
3. The Apostles were wont to allure th
Jews, and not to offend them. *To th
Jews*, saith S. Paul, *I became as a Jer
that I might gain the Jews*. Whereas t
set up Images, was the only way to driv
them out of the Temple. 4. That all o
ther Councils, *Nice, Constantinople, 1
phesus, Chalcedon, Arles, Eleberis, Antioc
Laodicea, Sardis, Jerusalem, Alexandri*

Rom

Rome, &c. during all the time of 800 years, were silent of this Apostolical Canon.

Concerning which, I beseech you to consider further: 1. That admitting it were in the 2 *Nicene* Council, that was an Idolatrous Council, addicted to Fables, and full of Forgeries; for which it is rejected by all the knowing and sounder part of the World. 2. The Apostles were not obeyed in this Commandment, neither in their own Age, nor in divers Ages after. 3. *Binius* himself seemeth conscious of its unsoundness, for he putteth it not among the Councils of the Apostles, which are before their Canons altogether, but in another place stragling by it self, in his own Notes, and after the Apostles Canons. 4. Since the Apostles wrote in Greek, this is rendered suspitious by wanting a Greek Copy. 5. No Collector produceth one word besides himself, in the whole Circuit of the first 400 years, on the behalf of Images. 6. The Fathers unanimously write against Images in the Church of GOD. 7. You may perceive by the dulness of the Sense out of what Storehouse this Fragment came, and by the horrid incongruity of *making a Divine and Humane Image un-*
mingled

mingled with hands: The Divinity and
and Humanity being Natures infinitely
diftant, cannot be painted in the fame
Picture. But for want of a better, this
Mufty Evidence muft ferve the turn.

CAP. XV.

*Of the Pontifical Falfely Fathered upon Da-
mafus, Bifhop of* Rome, An. 397. *How
the Popifh Collectors ufe it as their Text,
yet confefs it to be a Forgery full of Lyes
and contradictions.*

THe *Liber Pontificalis* is a Legend fo
ftuffed with Lyes, that the very *Title*
of it is notorious: The very firft Infcrip-
tion of the Book mifcarries ; not fo as to
need, like the former Counterfeits, either
thofe of the *Apoftles Canons*, or their
Council, or the *Preface of Ifidore*, a long
Circuit of Deductions to prove the Forgery ; *Binius*, *Labbe*, and the *Collectio
Regia*, immediately confefs it. It beginneth thus.

THE

THE BOOK OF POPES,

From Pope Peter *down to Pope* Nicholas *of that Name the First; in which their Acts are described: The Acts of the first Popes by Pope* Damasus *: The rest by other * Ancient Men, and * worthy of credit.*

Upon this Title *Binius* noteth, *Hujus libri Pontificalis* Damasus *Auctor non est, &c.* Damasus *is not the Author of this Pontifical: but rather it is patched up of two divers Authors: as may be proved by this, that almost in every Popes Life, it contains things fighting with themselves: And so no account can be given of Things and Writings clashing with one another.* And for this he cites *Baronius, An. Christ.* 69. *nu.* 35. *An.* 348. *nu.* 16. *& 17. Anton. Possevin. Apparat. Sac. on the word* Damasus.

Now a man would expect he should lay aside the Book, and refuse to make use of such an odious Pamphlet : But for want of a better he takes it in, as his most Learned Companions do; and so they labour all under the miserable Fate of making a Forgery, the Text upon which their Notes and Volumes are the Commentary.

O P

It is meet before I pass, to make some use of what is given us: for Observation is the Life of History, Reflexions digesting the Objects that are before us, and turning them into nourishment.

What is here said, concerneth not a Page, but a whole Book, stuffed with Legends, and Lives of Popes.

It was set forth as a Book made by *Damasus*, a Learned, Grave, and Ancient Bishop of *Rome*, that his name might give colour and Authority to the same.

Because it could not be believed that *Damasus* should write of Popes that followed after he was dead, part of it is ascribed to *other ancient men, and worthy of credit*; naming no body, for the greater Reverence, and shew of Antiquity, and the more pious estimation of unknown persons.

How ancient, and how worthy of credit they are that are such Cheats, and what a Mystery of Iniquity they make of Antiquity, you may easily conjecture.

Sometimes Forgeries are thrown upon the Greeks and Hereticks: but here is one made and compiled by the more Famous *Romans*.

Erasmus knew it to be a Forgery by the bareness of the Stile; *Consarcinatus est,*

It

It was patched up. That is his word; a Metaphor implying, the Taylors were but Botchers that made it. Secondly, By the contradictions that are in it, he knew they were divers Authors, because they jangle, and cannot agree. The parts of it are so irreconcileable, that the Story will by no means hang together.

It is a Vein of Lyes, reaching from S. *Peter* to *Damasus*, and from *Damasus* to *Nicholas* 1. containing the Lives of above 100 Popes, from S. *Peter* to the year 860.

About the time of this *Nicholas* 1. the Popedom was exalted above the Clouds, and was (of necessity) to be secured by as evil means, as it was gotten: When loe the Witch of *Endor* raises up *Samuel* in the good old *Damasus*, to tell the World that *Peter* was a Prince, and all his Successors *Universal* Heads of the *Catholick Church.*

Nicholas 1. began to sit about 50 years after the death of *Hadrian* 1. the Pope that is suspected by us to be the Father of the Forgeries. So great an Impression therefore being made by the Publication of *Isidore*, a little before, it was thought good to follow the Blow by this *Pontifical:* and a more ancient Father than *Isi-*

O 2 *dore*

dore must be awakened out of his duft to juftifie *him*. For as Light anfwered Light in *Solomons Buildings*, fo do the *Lives* and *Letters* of the Popes; their Lives in the *Pontifical*, and their Letters in the *Decretal*.

The Artifice fhews contrivance, and the defign of it a deep and hidden Correfpondence.

The World has been cheated for fo long a time, by the attempt of wicked and deceitful men.

Peter Crab, *Carranza*, *Surius*, *Nicolinus*, the Elder Compilers of the Councils, ufe it boldly and freely, without warning their Readers to fufpect it, or confelling it to be a Forgery; though *Binius*, and the laft Compilers, upon neceffary Conviction, are forced to do it.

Ifidore and *Merlin* have it not at all: we may juftly wonder therefore where thefe latter Collectors got it.

The Forgery is not about mean matters, but things moft Sacred, the Rights of the Church, and the Souls of men.

Here the Papifts are detected by their own confeffion: and he that is once taken is ftill fufpected.

The Works of Darknefs are feldom difcovered, fo that more are committed than are known. All

All thefe Forgeries that are now ac-knowledged, did pafs about 200 years ago for good Records, excepting fome perhaps that were fince invented: And if the laft two Ages brought fo many to light, an Age or two more may, through Gods bleffing, accomplifh Wonders.

The Secular ftate and fecurity of the Pope, with his Adherents, which *Binius* in his Epiftle to Pope *Paul* V. calls *Honor & Augmentum Ecclefiæ*, was the end of all. And if men excogitate Titles to Crowns, and patch up Genealogies with fome Flaws, yet ferviceable enough with the help of a Long Sword; then a Chair fo Politick is able to do it more neatly, having had the ftrong Holds of the Church fo long in their hands.

Now we fhall note fome few of thofe many Errours that are in the *Pontifical*; which, though it be a duty circumftance to have fuch a Text to glofs on, is the ba-fis of their Difcourfes, and the Rule of their Method, both in the Popes and Councils. It beginneth thus.

Peter the bleffed Apoftle, and Prince of the Apoftles, the Son of John, *of the Pro-vince of* Galilee, *of the City* Bethfaida, *the Brother of* Andrew, *fate in the Chair of* Antioch *feven years*. In the end it telleth

C 3   us

us how long S. *Peter* Reigned, juſt *twent five years, two moneths, and three days Binius* tells us with the conſent of *Baro nius*, it was rather twenty four years five moneths, and eleven days.

The Pontifical ſaith, *Peter was Mar tyred with Paul on the ſame day:* Thougl *Prudentius* and S. *Auguſtine* ſay, *It wa not the ſame year. Binius* reconcileth them, *They* were ſlain the ſame *day* in deed, but not the ſame *year:* Therefor ſay we, *Peter* was not Martyred witl S. *Paul.*

The Pontifical ſays, *It was 28 years af ter the Paſſion of our Lord.* More truly th 35. ſaith Binius, *in the 12 year of* Nero *and the 69 after the Birth of Chriſt.*

S *Peter's Name* is the Patron and Bul wark of the Roman Church; and there fore inſerted like a Shield in the Front Next his Notes on S. *Peter's* Life. *Biniu inteats the Treatiſe of the Roman Churche. Primacy,* Ex antiquo Codice: *out of a Old Book,* without any name at all Which puts me in mind of the *Gibeonite eld Bottles, clouted Shooes, and mould Bread,* and the notable Cheat whicl thereby they put on the *Iſraelites.* Al is Old and Ancient in the Church o *Rome:* and this *Old Book* of the Prima

cy

cy set before the Councils according to the Rules of Art, because the *End* is to be proposed before the *Means*.

After this *old Treatise* of the *Primacy*, he cometh to S. *Linus, Pope and Martyr.* He is pleased to call him *Pope*, as well as *Pope Peter*; not as if his Contemporaries called him so, but because the Modern Title will not fit well on the present Popes, unless it be given to S. *Peter*, and the first Bishops of that *See.* And ever and anon he begins with a known Lye in the top of the Chapter, formally set by it self, the more pleasingly to take the eye, after the manner of a Title, *Ex Libro Pontificali* Damasi *Papæ*;

OUT OF THE PONTIFICAL OF POPE *DAMASUS*.

This course he continues from Life to Life throughout all the Popes, so far as the Pontifical lasteth, intermixing the *Decretal Epistles* first, and then the *Councils*, in the Lives of the several Popes: or to use his form, *under the Pope in whose* Life they happened. And all his Tomes being moulded into that form, it makes every Pope seem, to him that is not aware of the fetch, the Supreme over all Councils from the beginning. And with this Method he always goes on, *Ex libro*

bro

bro Pontificali Damasi *Papæ*, hoping perhaps that in long tract of time, he should be at last believed.

In all the Book, there is scarce a Life, wherein there are not as many Errours, as in S. *Peter's*. As in example.

An. 70. Linus *sate eleven years, three moneths, and twelve days,* saith the Pontifical: *Binius* saith, *It was eleven years, two moneths, and twenty three days.* A days difference, where the exactness is pretended to be so great, shews all to be Counterfeit.

An. 81. He saith, Cletus *sate twelve years, one moneth, and eleven days :* *Binius* rails on him for the mistake; though he agrees with him in the main, *that* Linus *and* Cletus *sate some twenty three years between* Peter *and* Clement. So that on this account, S. *James* was dead above 27 years before S. *Clement* (who wrote a Decretal Epistle to him) came to the Chair: For before he was Pope he might write an *Epistle,* but not a *Decretal Epistle.*

Cletus (saith *Binius*) *was by* S. Irenæus, Ignatius, *and* Eusebius, *called* Anacletus, *which* Baronius *thinks was a mistake among the Greeks, occasioned by the Errour of Writers and Libraries.* What shifts will a man be driven to by a desperate Cause *!*

Cause! Three of the best and most Ancient Fathers were cheated *with the Errour of Writers and Libraries*, concerning a mans *Name* that was alive, either not long before, or together with themselves. S. *Irenæus* and *Ignatius* are extremely Ancient. *Ignatius* lived before *Anacletus* was Bishop of *Rome*, much more before his Name was put into *Libraries*, and much more yet, before it could be corrupted there by the *mistake of Scribes and Writers*. But such *Errours of Writers and Libraries* are a good hint, how capable they are of them, and how much the Church of *Rome* is acquainted with them.

Binius is at last terribly provoked with the nonsense of the *Pontifical:* for whereas it saith, Cletus *was in the Church from the seventh Consulship of* Vespasian, *and fifth of* Domitian, *to the ninth of* Domitian, *and the Consulship of* Rufus; that is, from the 70 year of *Christ*, to the 85. *Binius* speaking as if he were present, takes him up finartly, *Errorem igitur Errori addis, quisquis hujus Pontificalis Authores*, &c. *Whoever thou be that art the Author of this Pontifical, thou addest Errour to Errour: For if* Cletus *began to sit in the forementioned Consulship, in the 78*

year

year of Chrift, how did he immediately fucceed Linus, *dying, as thou faidft, in the* 69 *year of Chrift,* Capito *and* Rufus *being Confuls? How wilt thou excufe a* 9 *years Interregnum in the Chair, made only by thy Authority contradicting it felf? How fayeft thou that* Cletus *fate twelve years, whofe continuance thou doeft circumfcribe by two Confulfhips, in the fpace of* 7 *years diftant from themfelves? How, which is more intollerable and abfurd, doeft thou fay, that* Clement *fate from the Confulfhip of* Trachilus *and* Italicus, *even to the third year of* Trajan; *which is from the* 70 *year of Chrift to the* 102. *and fo to have adminiftred the* See 33 *years, whom in his Life thou affirmeft to have continued only* 9 *years? Thus far* Binius.

When *Cato* faw the Southfayers faluting one another in the *Roman* Marketplace, he faid, I wonder they can forbear laughing, to think how delicately they cheat the people! *Hence therefore, faith* Binius, *O Reader, thou mayeft perceive on what Rocks he fhall dafh, whofoever fhall fuppofe the writings of this Book to be taken up upon Truft, without any Inquifition!* Yet when the fit is over, in the very next line, he is at it again, THE LIFE, EPISTLES, AND DECREES OF CLE=
MENT,

MENT, EX LIBRO PONTIFICALI DAMASI P. The Pontifical is (afresh) ascribed to *Damasus*: For Friends may quarrel, without falling out eternally. But if they are so angry, what make they together? What have Scholars to do in so scandalous a Fellows Company? Why of all Books in the World do they take this to follow? All of them from *Peter Crab* to the *Collectio Regia*? Why not the Grave, Sincere, and Learned? Why not a true Record? Why do they chuse a Counterfeit so *full of lyes and contradictions*? It is the highest Symptom of a deadly cause, that they take such a Fellow to be their Copy to write after, their Text to gloss on, their Guide to follow. For all these gross mistakes are committed within the compass of some 30 or 40 lines, in four Lives of *one hundred and six*: And in every Life almost throughout, they are exercised in the same manner. If this be the best Record they can find for the purpose, and all their Antiquities be like this, they are as mouldy and rotten as can well be desired.

CAP.

CAP. XVI.

Of the Decretal Epistles forged in the Names of the first holy Martyrs and Bishops of Rome. The first was sent (as they pretend) from S Clement, by S. Peter's order, to S. James the Bishop o Jerusalem, seven years after he was dead; and by the best Account 27. S. Clement's Recognitions a confessed Forgery.

TO stumble in the Threshold is O-minous: If the first of all the Decretals be a Forgery, it is a leading Card to the residue.

Binius his Title, and the Text of the *Pontifical,* is represented thus.

THE LIFE, EPISTLES, AND DE-CREES OF POPE *CLEMENT* I.

Out of the *Pontifical* of Pope
D A M A S U S.

*.He made two Epistles that are called Ca-*nonical. *This man, by the Precept o* S. Peter, *undertook the Government o the Church; as by* Jesus Christ *our Lord the Chair was committed to him. In the Epistle which he wrote to* S. James, *you*
shall

shall find after what manner the Church was committed from S. Peter. Linus *and* Cletus *are therefore recorded to be before him, because they were made Bishops by the Prince of the Apostles himself, and ordained to the Priest=like Office before him.*

NOTES.

(After the Method of *Binius.*)

He made two Epistles called Canonical.] These words are adapted to the 84th Canon of the Apostles, where two Epistles of *Clement,* and his eight *Books of Ordinations*, are made parts of the Canonical Scripture.

In the Epistle which he wrote to S. James] Here the Pontifical openly voucheth his Epistle to S. *James;* which *Binius* afterwards tells you was written to *Simeon.* If the *Pontifical* be right, *Binius* was overseen, in saying, the name of S. *James* crept by corruption into the Title of the Epistle, for that of *Simeon.* The Tales do not hang together.

They were made Bishops by the Prince of the Apostles, &c.] You understand here, that S. *Peter* out of his superabundant care for the Church, made three Bishops of *Rome* in his own life time: So that *Rome* had four Popes at once, S. *Peter,* S. *Clement,* S. *Linus,* and S. *Cletus.* Some think

think that *Linus* and *Cletus* were S. Cle=
ment's Adjutants in External Affairs :
Some, that they succeeded each other in
order : Some, that they presided over
the Church together. Some say, that
Clement out of modesty refused the
Chair, till he was grown older belike.
It is a world to see, what a variety and
puzzle they are at in this matter : The
confusion springeth from two causes:
The first is the obscurity of the State of
Rome in the beginning : The second is the
ignorance of the Forger that made S. Cle-
ment's Letter to S. *James* : For happening so heedlesly to Father it on S. Cle-
ment, he has made all the Story inconvenient. S. *Clement* saith not one word of
refusing the Chair in his Epistle, nor of
Linus and *Cletus* coming between him
and it; but with a very fair Hypocritical
shew, pretendeth in his Epistle to S. *James*,
that he was chosen by S. *Peter*, and succeeded him accordingly. Whereupon,
they that will have this Epistle to be a
good and true Record, are forced of necessity to say, that S. *Peter* did himself ordain *Clement*, though they very well
know that *Linus* and *Cletus*, or *Anacletus*, were both in their Order Bishops
before him : For a sure Token, either
that

that the Church of *Rome* was little con-
fidered in the dawning of the Gofpel, or
that their ignorance marred her Officious
Impoftors, nothing is more obfcure and
doubtful than the order and manner of
her firft Bifhops. The Pontifical undertakes to reconcile all; and does it luckily, were it not that it contradicts it felf.
For he faith of *Clement*, that *he under-*
took the Government of the Church *by the*
precept of Peter And yet of *Linus* and
Cletus it faith, they *are recorded to be be-*
fore him, *becaufe by the Prince of the A-*
poftles they were made Bifhops before him.

Be that a contradiction or no, it was
neither *Linus* nor *Cletus* it feems, but *Cle-*
ment who writ the Epiftle to S. *James*
about the death of *Peter*.

He made many books.] *Binius* upon
thofe words obferves, that *before his Epi-*
ftles he wrote the Conftitutions of the A-
poftles, &c. *He did not make, but write*
the Apoftles Canons in Greek, &c. It is
much he did not make them, for the *Co-*
ronis of them, as *Nicolinus* calleth it, hath
by me Clement in it; and for ought I
know a *Pope* that hath the *fulnefs of*
power Apoftolical, may make Apoftles Canons at any time. It is an odd obfervation, *He did not make, but write the Apo-*
ftles Canons.　　　　　　　　*Among*

Among his other Monuments (faith Binius) *there are ten books of the circuits of*
Peter; *which by some are called,* The Itinerary of Clement, *by others his Recognitions :* Which *since they are stuffed with*
Loathsome Fables, *and the Fathers abstained from the use of them, as* Gelasius
also in a Roman Council *rejected them for*
Apocryphal; *all wise men will advisedly
abstain from reading them. It is a Tradition, that* Clement *left the Rite of offering Sacrifice to the Church of* Rome *in
writing. It is reported also, that many
pieces are falsly published under the Name
of* Clement.

Forgeries are (you see) thick and
threefold in the Church of *Rome :* but
this of *Clement's Itinerary*, which *Binius* diffwadeth all men from reading, e-
ven ten Books, *Cum insulsis fabulis re-
ferti sunt, since they are stuft with loathsome Fables,* I desire you to take special
notice of ; because this Confession of his
will discover him to be either a false man,
or a Fool. It is a delicate Snare, and
will detect S. *Clement*, and S. *Binius* together.

As for B*inius*, who defendeth *the first
Epistle of* Clement *to* S. James for a good
Record ; if he did read the Epistle, and

note

note what he read, he was a falfe man
for defending it againft his Judgment
and Confcience. He that fo mortally hated *the Itinerary of Clement*, could not
but know the *Epiftle* to be Forged, if he
read it with any diligent obfervation:
If he trufted others, he was an unwife
man, to be fo confident in maintaining
it, upon the report of thofe that read and
tranfcribed it for him: For their inad-
vertency hath deceived him.

For S. *Clement* himfelf (if that Epiftle be his) owneth the Forgery of
S. *Clement*'s *Itinerary*, which *Binius* fo
extremely abhorreth. It muft needs be a
Forgery therefore, becaufe in this cafe,
nothing but a Forgery can defend a Forgery: no Author (if a Saint) acknow-
ledging thofe Forgeries for his, which he
never made.

After a long Oration which S. *Clement*
fendeth to S. *James*, in that Epiftle out
of S. *Peter*'s mouth, concerning the Dignity and Excellency of the Roman Chair,
he has thefe words, fpeaking of S. *Peter*.

*When he had faid thefe things in the
midft before them all, he put his hands on
me, and compelled me (wearied with fhame-
facednefs) to fit in his Chair. And when
I was fate, again he fpake thefe things un-*

P   10

S. Peter's order a-bout the Itinerary.

to me: I beseech thee, O Clement, before all that are present, that after (as the Debt of Nature is) I have ended this present life, thou wouldst briefly write to James, the Brother of our Lord, either those things that relate to the beginning of thy Faith, or those thoughts also which before thy Faith thou hast born; and after what sort thou hast been a companion to me from the beginning, even to the end of my Journey, and my Acts; and what, being a Solicitous Hearer, thou hast taken from me disputing through all the Cities; and what, in all my preaching, was the order either of my words or actions: as also what End shall find me in this City, as I said; all things being (as thou art able) briefly comprehended, let it not grieve thee to destine unto him: Neither fear, that he will be much grieved at my End, since he will not doubt but I endure it for piety. But it will be a great solace to him, if he shall learn, that no unskilful man, or unlearned, and ignorant of the Discipline of Ecclesiastical Order, and the Rule of Doctrine, hath undertaken my Chair: For he knows, if an unlearned or an unskilful man take upon him the Office of a Doctor without, the Hearers and Disciples being involved in a Cloud of Ignorance, shall be drowned in destruction. Where-

Wherefore I my Lord James, *when I had received these precepts from him , held it necessary to fulfil what he commanded, informing thee both concerning these things, and briefly comprehending , concerning those , which going through every* City, *he either uttered in the word of preaching, or wrought in the vertue of his deeds. Though concerning these things I have sent thee more, and more fully described already, at his command, under that very Title which he ordered to be prefixed; that is ,* Clementis Itinerarium , The Itinerary of Clement, *not the preaching of* Peter.

In these words he telleth us, how S. *Peter* taking his leave of the World, placed him *in his Chair,* and by that Ceremony installed him in the Episcopal Throne in the presence of them all : What a charge he gave him in that moving circumstance of time, just before his piercing and bitter Passion, to write to S. *James* : How he ordered him to make an *Itinerary* of his Circuits throughout the World , and furnished him at the same time with the *Materials* and *Title* of the Book ; The *Itinerary of* Clement, *not the preaching of* Peter. S. *Peter*'s modesty (as is to be supposed) giving the Honour of the Title, not to himself that was the *Subject* , but

P 2

to

to the *Author*: How S. *Clement*, according to this *commandment*, had sent to S. *James*, not only this Epistle, but the Book it self long before it; wherein the *Journeys and the Acts* of Peter *were more fully described*: And the great care which S. *Peter* took, lest the dead man should be grieved, by the Solace he provided in the Tydings sent unto him, concerning the perpetual certainty of *Skilfulness* and *Learning* in all his Successors, securing at once both the Church, and *his* Chair, is very remarkable. All these things, out of the very Bowels of the Epistle, disgrace the Chimera's of *Binius* and *Turrian*. For what Saint being well in his Wits, would tell the World, that S.*Peter* commanded him to make a *Forgery*, nay a putid Forgery, *stuffed with loathsom Fables*! S. *James* his Name is over and over in the *body* of the Epistle, not only in the *Title*. The Epistle was not sent to S. *James* by a *Figure*, but it plainly tells S. *James*, that he had sent him the *Itinerary* before; which consisting of *ten books*, must be some considerable time after S. *Peter's* Death in making, some time in going from *Rome* to *Jerusalem*, and some time must be spent in coming back with the Answer, that certified him of

S. James

S. *James* his receiving it. After all which, this new Letter was written to S *James*, impertinently giving him an account of the same business: And yet all this while S. *James* was dead before S. *Peter*. For as *Binius* observes, S. *Peter* was put to Death in the thirteenth year of *Nero*, and S. *James* in the seventh.

The Compiler of this Epistle, finding S. *Clement* s *Itinerary* extant in the World, several hundreds of years before himself, and being not aware of its unsoundness, took it up as a good Record, and so fitted the Epistle and Fable to the purpose in hand, being himself cheated with a Forgery, as many others are, and not expecting to be detected so clearly, as it hath since happened.

But to make the matter more absurd, they have a second Letter to S. *James*, *De Sacratis vestibus. vel vas.* Wherein he divides the *Priesthood* (as *Pius* in his Decretal afterwards does) *into three Orders, of Presbyter, Deacon,* and *Minister:* With what design I cannot tell, unless he would have us think *the Pope the only Bishop.* Wherein he also takes care about the *Lords Body;* orders the Priests with what Ceremony of *Fasting* and *Reverence* it shall be *consumed:* Gives Com-

mands

mands about the *Pall*, the *Chair*, the *Candlestick*, and the *Vail:* speaks of the *Altar*, the *Worship of the Altar*, the *Doorkeepers*, the *Vails for the Gates*, the *covering of the Altar*, &c. As if there were stately Temples, Attires, Ornaments, and Utensils, in those early days of poverty Persecution, when a Den or a Cave was both *Sanctuary* and *Temple*. Among other things, he orders that no man should *through ignorance believe a dead man ought to be wrapt in a* * *Fryers Coul*; a Novel, superstitious Errour. All which he speaks out of the mouth of S. *Peter*, whom he calls the *Father and Prince of the Apostles*. In the end of the Letter, he denounces a Curse against all them that will not keep S. *Peter*'s *Commandments*. So that *Peter*'s Name, and *Peter*'s Authority, is used for every thing appertaining to the Chair, and all the Apostles to be ordered by S. *Peter*'s Successors, as S. Jam ⸳ ⸳⸳⸳⸳ of *our Lord* was.

CAP.

CAP. XVII.

Of Higinus *and* Pius, *as they are repre=sented in the* Pontifical; *and of a notable Forgery in the name of* Hermes: *Where you have the Testimony of an Angel, concerning the Celebration of Easter, cited by no body, while the matter was in controversie.*

Higinus *sate,* saith the Pontifical, *four years, three moneths, and four days.* Binius saith, *He sate four years, except two days;* counterfeiting as much exactness as the other. *If we should follow him in his Consuls,* saith he, *we should make Higinus sit twelve years.*

But the Pontifical is guilty of a more arrogant and *ambitious* errour: *The Hierarchy of the Church,* it saith, *was made by* Higinus, *to wit, the Order wherein Presbyters were inferiour to Bishops, Deacons to Presbyters, the people to Deacons.* Binius mendeth it as well as he is able, interpreting it only of a Reformation of Collapsed Discipline. But it suiteth so exactly with the distinction before made in S. *Clement's* second Epistle, who will have the Priesthood divided into *the Order*

P +   *der*

der of *Presbyter, Deacon, and Minister,*
that the design seemeth deeper than so.
He doth not say, the Hierarchy of the
Church was *corrected,* but *made* by *Hyginus:* which strikes at the Root of E-
piscopacy; as if it were not of Divine,
but Humane Institution : and being *made*
by the Pope alone, depended only on the
Popes pleasure.

Binius is not able to name the time
wherein the Discipline of the Church
was (in this respect) corrupted so, as to
need the Reformation pretended.

Next after *Hyginus,* the Pontifical
bringeth in *Pius, an* Italian, *the Brother
of a Shepherd. He sate nineteen years,
four moneths, and three days, in the times
of* Antoninus Pius. Hermes *his own Brother wrote a book, in which a Commandment was contained, given him by an Angel of the Lord, coming to him in the Habit of a Shepherd, that* Easter *should be
observed on the Lords Day. This man ordained, that an Heretick, coming from a-
mong the* Jews, *should be baptized,* &c,

This *Hermes,* saith *Binius,* in his Notes
on the place, *is the same whom S.* Paul
mentioneth in his Epistle to the Romans.
*Salute Asyncritus, Phlegon, Hermas, Pa-
trobus, Hermes,* &c. He was at Mans E-
state

ftate when S. *Paul* faluted him, and a very old man fure for a Writer of Books in the time of *Pius*.

Binius is not willing to have him fo obfcure as a Shepherd, but faith, *He was called* Paftor, *either becaufe he was of the Family of* Junius Paftor, *who in the third year of* Aurelian *was Conful, or more probably, becaufe the Angel appeared to him in the form of a Shepherd.* In this his Guefs he is upon the brink of rejecting the Pontifical. Howbeit he quits it not of a Lye: for inftead of nineteen years which the Pontifical giveth him, *Binius* faith, *he fate but nine years.* A fmall miftake in this Learned Pontifical.

Concerning the Book which *Hermes* the Shepherd wrote, he faith, *It was almoft unknown among the Latines, but very famous among the Greeks*: Which was very ftrange, confidering he was the *Popes Brother*: A Book made by fo eminent a perfon, and fo near home, *unknown among the Latines*! But his meaning is perhaps, it was better known than trufted. For a little after he faith, *The Latines efteemed it Apocryphal, as* Tertullian, Athanafius, *and* Profper *witnefs, and as* Gelafius *decreed*; Can. Sanct. Dift. 15.

Now becaufe their unmannerlinefs doth

doth reflect a little upon the Pope himfelf, who in his Decretal Epiftle annexed, owns his Brother with an Honourable mention of the Angelical Vifion ;
Binius to difplay more Learning on the
behalf of the *Pontifical*, and *Pius* his *Decretal*, tells you ; that *the Book of the true
Hermes Paftor, praifed fo much by* Tertullian, Origen, Athanafius, Eufebius, Jerome,
&c. *is not now Extant. Which is evident*
(he faith) *becaufe in that we now have,
there is no Mention at all of Eafter. Nay
the Author of it faith, he was admonifhed
to deliver it to* Clement *the Pope, by whom
it was to be fent to forreign Cities.* They
have as good Luck at *Rome* , as if they
held Intelligence with *Purgatorie.* The
Dead and *they* have as intimate a Correfpondence, as if the Pope knew the Way
to fend his *Bulls* thither. Here is another
Forgerie detected, by its Dedication to
S. Clement who by no unufual Providence is ferved juft in his own kind, for
he difturbed *S. James*, and another dif-
turbes him, in his *Grave.* Yet *Binius* is
very much inclined to this Opinion, for
from hence he gathereth, it was *longè
ante hæc Tempora Scriptus, a Book written
long before the time of* Pius. As no doubt
it muft, if it be not the fame that was
                                        praifed

praised by *Tertullian, Origen, Athanasius*, *&c.* For all Forgeries must be old and True, or they are not worth a farthing.

But how comes *Tertullian* and *Athanasius*, *&c.* to esteem it Apocryphal, and yet to praise it so much, in the same Breath? It is *Binius* his Breath, not theirs. They poor men are made like *Stage players* to say whatsoever the Poet listern. Or else as *Binius* observes there were two Books of *Hermes* (though it be double dealing thus to have two of a Sort :) the one right, and the other *Apocryphal*.

But then *Gelasius* did very ill, there being two of a Sort, to condemn the one, and not tell us of the other. And so did *Ivo.* For this *Pastor* is one of the Catalogue we told you of in the Beginning.

But *Binius* has a fetch beyond this ; He teaches you a way, how to take *both* these persons for the same man : and what you may say in defence of your self, if you so do. *However* (saith he) *if any one be disposed to take them for the same Author, Ex Sententiâ Illustriss. Card. Baronii dicendum est,* &c. *He must necessarily say, as Baronius gives his Opinion, that they were two commentaries, written at divers times, whereof the first was more famous among the Greeks, the later more obscure a-*

mong

mong the Latines. A brave Antithefis *!*
So that upon the point the *Latines* had
none. *The more obfcure among the Latines*
was obfcure every where: *the more famous*
among the Greeks and *the more obfcure a-*
mong the Latines ! The *Antithefis*
makes a fhew of giving you fome So-
lid matter, but when you grafp it in
your hand, it turnes to Air. Unlefs perhaps you will learn thereby, that the
more obfcure among the Latines was a
Book made in an inftant, by a meer Conjecture and a pretty Mockery to gull the
Reader, as a fhadow at leaft of fome
proof that the Pontifical and the Decretals are not Lyars.

Among other Things their Allowances
are confiderable: for they are good honeft
reafonable men, and will let you think
what you will of the Book, fo you confent to the main, and believe *the Popes*
Supremacy. And next that, their Art of
Inftruction is to be weighed, Whether it be true or no, no matter : If the
Difciple can but defend himfelf by a Dif-
tinction, and efcape the Conviction of an
Abfurdity, it is enough ; *Bellarmine* is at
fuch *Dicendums* often. Though 'tis a
Secret among themfelves, they teach their
Difciples *What to fay,* not *What is* True.

But

But I thought we had been agreed before, that of these *Hermes* one at least was a Forgerie.

It seems by Pope *Pius* his Letter, that *Hermes* was a *Doctor*, and not a *Shepherd*, for in these Days, he saith, *Hermes a Doctor of the faith, and of the H. Scriptures shined among us.* Not of old, but *in these Days.* Yet it is pretended, that the Book of old was by some order from on high, to be *delivered to Clement the Pope, by whom it was to be sent to forreign Cities.* Notwithstanding all their Contrivance, there Wit failes them sometimes, that are so accustomed to Lying. They have so many Irons in the fire that some of them miscarry, whether they will or no.

Nevertheless *that Hermes received this Commandment from the Angel Tertullian witnesseth, in his third Book of verses against Marcion* saith *Binius.* I have not heard much of *Tertullian's* Poetrie. I have his Works, put forth with the Notes of *Beatus Rhenanus*, and cannot find any such *verses* among them. If he hath, all that *Binius* pretendeth out of them, is that *Hermes spake Angelical Words*; Therefore he saw the Angel.

Pius in his Decretal Epistle applieth this Scripture, *Not holding the Head from which*

which all the body by joynts and bands
having nourishment miniſtred, and knit together, increaſeth with the increaſe of God,]
to the Pope of Rome. Whereupon, he
ſaith, *We inſtruct you all by our Apoſtolical
authority, that you ought to obſerve the
ſame Commandments, becauſe we alſo obſerve the ſame. And ye ought not by any
means to divide from the Head.*

The Commandment was given to *Hermes* by an Angel. Whereupon Pope *Pius*
after the firſt complement, beginneth very unluckily with *forbidding the Religion
or worſhipping of Angels.* Whereas upon
this occaſion ſome eminent matter ought
to have been ſpoken concerning Angels.
But becauſe of the words following, he
puts them together. *Let no man beguile
you of your reward in a voluntary humility
of worſhipping Angels, &c. Not holding
the Head from which all the body by joynts
and bands, &c.* Where he taketh off the
Eternal Head, and puts a *New* one on the
Churches ſhoulders. *For in theſe dayes*
Hermes *a Doctor of the Faith and of the
Holy Scriptures ſhined among us : And
though we obſerved Eaſter on the foreſaid
day, yet becauſe ſome doubted, for the confirming of their Souls, an Angel of the
Lord appeared to the ſame* Hermes *in the*
ſhape

Coloſ. 2. 18,
19.

shape of a Shepheard, and commanded him that the Passeover should be celebrated by all on the Lords day: Whereupon we also instruct you all by our Apostolical authority, that you ought to observe the same Commandments. (Not because an Angel brought them, or GOD sent him ; but) *Because we also observe the same, and ye ought not by any means to divide from the Head.* And because the business is to promote the Apostolical Authority above all the Angels, instead of extolling and magnifying them, which had been the natural method on such a Topick : as if he would enervate the evidence of the Angel, he biddeth them *take heed,* and that *diligently, least any one seduce you, by any Astrology, or Philosophy, or vain Fallacy, according to the tradition of men : after the Rudiments of this World, and not after Christ's and true Tradition.* As if no more heed were to be given to an *Angel,* than to an Asse, unless the *Pope* first approved the Vision : Nor is Philosophy, nor the Tradition of men, nor any thing else to be valued in opposition to him, and his *true Tradition ; for in him dwelleth all the fulness of the Godhead bodily : that ye may be repleat in him, who is the Head of all Principality and Power, and who hath com-*
manded

commanded this *Apostolical See, to be
the Head of all Churches, saying to the
Prince of the Apostles*, Thou art Peter,
*and upon this Rock will I build my
Church.*

What it is to walk *after Christ and
true Tradition*, you may see Cleerly, by
this Gloss upon our Saviours Text. They
that do not *hold the Head, from which
all the Body by Joynts and Bands having
nourishment ministered, and knit together,
increaseth with the increase of God*, are in
extream peril of damnation. And our Saviour who is *the Head of all Principality
and Power*, hath commanded this Apostolical See to be the Head of all Churches;
Therefore, Whosoever holdeth not to
this Head is in extream peril of damnation. For the Pope is not the Head
of all Principality and Power *in himself*,
but only by Derivation he is made the
Head, &c. And consequently, 'tis as
necessary to cleave unto him as to *Christ*
himself. Since he *in whom all the fulness
of the Godhead dwelleth Bodily*, dwelleth
in his *Vicar*, even as *S. Peter* does in like
manner. So that all Angels and Traditions of men, Reason, Philosophy *&c.*
are but feeble Threeds for him that hath
Plenitudinem Potestatis, the *fulness of*
Power

Power, and may *open the Kingdom of Heaven to whom he will*

. It is a Cross Observation to note the little Authority of the Popes *Custome.* For though it it was the Practice of all the Roman Church to Keep Easter in such a manner before, yet *some doubted,* that is, all the *Eastern Churches* were of another Opinion: till an Angel came to teach them otherwise. Yet when he came, he must not be believed for his own sake, but the Popes: nor be obeyed for himself: so jealous was the Pope of his Apostolical Authority.

Euseb.

How weak both the Popes Authority and the Angels were, (which thus mutually needed each others assistance) appeareth by the Event, for notwithstanding the Testimony of *Pius* and the *Angel,* this Controversy was it undetermined till the *Nicene* Council.

It continued above *set* years after Pope *Pius* his days. Yet through all that considerable Tract of time, this *Testimony* of the *Angel* was cited by no Body. Only as *Ovid* makes use of the *Cock,* and his *Crowing* in the Morning, to introduce the fable of *Alector;* this wicked *Pius* maketh use of this Controversy, for the fable of the Angel. But it was a little

Q

Suspicious

Suspicious that the *Angel* should appear to no body but the *Popes Brother*, and the matter be published by no body but the Pope himself. It smelleth of the Forge out of which it came, being proved by the Pontifical of Pope *Damasus*

CAP. XVIII.

A Letter fathered on Cornelius Bishop of Rome in the year 254. concerning the Removal of the Apostles Bones: giving Evidence to the Antiquity of many Popish Doctrines, but is it self a Forgery.

THE forgery made in the Name of *Pius*, is fitted to the year 158. You shall now see one made in the Name of *Cornelius* Bishop of *Rome* in the year 254. 100. years after the former excepting four. Not as if there were no forgeries between this and that, there is scarce a year upon which they have not fastned some thing, but should we trace them all, through the weary Length of so many Ages, our Travail would be Endless. We have chosen one, or two, as Exemplars of the residue.

THE

THE FIRST EPISTLE

Of Cornelius *the Pope.*

*Concerning the Translations of the Bo-
dies of Peter and Paul, &c.*

'Cornelius, the Bishop, to his Dear and
'most Beloved Brethren, the Sons
'of the Holy Church of God, and to all
'them that Serve our Lord in the right
'Faith.

'Considering the Benevolence of your
'Charity, because we are Lovers of the
'Apostles and hold their Faith and Do-
'ctrine, I determined to write unto
'you, (the Lord being the Author) some
'of those things which are at this time ne-
'cessary to be Known, and which the Lord
'assisting, by the Merits of the Apostles,
'were lately done among us in the Church
'of *Rome*, or are now in Doing. Because
'Charity patronizing, I believe with fa-
'therly Grace, we willingly receive the
'Writings of the Apostolical See, and
'preform the Commandments of the
'same, and rejoyce in the Increases there-
'of. Because whosoever engraffes him-
'self in the root of Charity, neither fails
'of Greatness, (*nec a fructibus inanescis*)

Q 2

'nor

exceeding [...] men, of
[...] endea-
[...] [...] arious.
[...] Graves with
[...] der the *common
[...] [...] is believed;* to
[...] Antiquity, by which
[...] to reprove *Binius* for a
Lyar, who [...] that *it hath hitherto
been received, and without all Controversie maintained.* Nor is he a Lyar onely,
but contradicteth himself, and foolishly
betrayeth his design, while he shuffles
and cuts upon all occasions.

But perhaps you will say his meaning
is, *It is without all Controversie maintained in the Roman Martyrologies and Breviaries.* This reserve he keeps for a *Starting-
hole;* but 'twill not do. He might
say, It was *put in* without all controversie, [...] the *Roman Martyrologies* and
Breviaries were works of Darkness, made
in Secret by the Popes Authority: But is
it *maintained without all controversie,*
when exceeding *many of the most Learned
men endeavour to prove its Acts to be
spurious by strong arguments? Does venerable Antiquity it self sight sharply for
them, compelling a Reverence from the
unwilling by its Majesty;* or is it by the

com-

common Affent of a believed: when exceeding many endeavour to relate it. As for the *Roman Martyrologies,* it is no wonder it should be quiet in them: Some were by but the Actors only, when the Council, as put in, and by dissembling the fraud, is *as retained there,* it is no great breach, that there it is, and that is sufficient.

For my part I could not have believed, that *Binius* or any other sober man, could ever reckon such an horrid piece of Barbarism for a *Council,* had I not seen it with my own eyes in the Author. It is so much against all reason, that a thing so abfurd should be owned, to the disgrace of all Martyrs, Synods, and Councils. And were it not for the *Cause* of the wonder, the *Roman Martyrologies,* whose credit must be saved, it would be my lasting amazement.

Binius is so stiffe in defending this Council, that in the next words he chargeth ignorance on S. *Augustine* for not understanding it.

Love and Hunger will eat through stone walls. His Zeal for the Church of *Rome,* and its Direful necessity, makes him to defend this Council in the *Roman Martyrologies,* against an apparent false-

hood

' nor waxes vain from fruit, neither does
' he by Love lose the Efficacious Work
' of fruitfulness. For Charity it self does
' exercise the Hearts of the faithful, cor-
' roborates their Senses, that nothing
' seemeth Grievous, nothing difficult, but
' all is easy which is done; while its pro-
' perty is to nourish Concord, to keep the
' Commandments, to joyn things disseve-
' red, to correct Evil things, and to con-
' solidate all other vertues by the Bulwark
' of its perfection.

' Wherefore I beseech you to rejoyce
' with us, because by the Entreaty of a
' certain devout Woman, and most no-
' ble Matron *Lucina*, the bodies of *Peter*
' and *Paul* were lifted out of the Cata-
' rumbæ. And first of all, the Body of
' the Blessed *Paul* was carried with Silence
' and put in the Grounds of the foresaid
' Matron, in the Oftienfian Way, neer to
' that Side where he was beheaded. But
' afterwards we received the Body of the
' Blessed *Peter*, the Prince of the Apo-
' stles, and decently placed it neer the
' place where he was crucified, among the
' Bodies of the H. Bishops, in the Temple
' of *Apollo*, in the golden Mountain, in the
' Vatican of *Nero's* palace; the third day
' of the Calend, of *July*: praying God
' and

' and our Lord Jesus Christ, that these his
' holy Apostles interceding, he would
' purge away the Spots of our Sins, and
' keep you in his Will all the dayes of
' your Life, and make you perseverable
' in the Fruit of Good works. But see that
' ye rejoice together for these things : Be-
' cause the Holy Apostles themselves also
' rejoice together for your joy. Praise
' ye God alwaies, and he shall be glorified
' in you. For it is written, What shall I re-
' turn unto the Lord, for all he hath re-
' turned to me? I will take up the Cup of
' Salvation, and call upon the Name of
' the Lord.

In this first part of the Epistle *concern-*
ing the Translation of the Bodies of the B.
Apostles, Peter *and* Paul, the Pope does
you to wit of his wonderful kindness and
charity to the Dead, as also of his devotion and reverence towards the Relicks of such glorious Saints.

Wherein first of all, he would have his
gratitude towards those blessed Foun-
ders of the *Roman See* made conspicuous,
it being a thing meet to be published all
the World over, as it is in most solemn
manner here, by *Decretal Epistle.* 2. He
does intimate the veneration due to Relicks, especially those of such glorious

Q 3   Saints

Saints, as *Peter* and *Paul*. 3. He gives us to know that the Translation of their Bodies from one Grave to another was a matter of such moment, that it was *Quædam ex his quæ nunc temporis necessaria sunt scire*. *A thing, in these dayes, necessary to be known.* 4. That the merits of the Apostles moved God to assist and bless the Church of *Rome* in all her Doings. 5. That God was the Author of those things which he wrote unto them: According to his faith, *Decrevi vobis scribere, Domino authore.* 6. That all the World did, even in *Cornelius* daies, and upward, to the time of S. *Clement* and S. *Peter, Scripta sedis Apostolicæ libenter suscipere, Willingly receive the Writings of the Apostolical See, obey its commands,* and rejoice *in its increases.* For the *Roman* Church is alwaies *increasing* in Tradition, Doctrine, Wealth, &c. 7. That Love is so excellent an ingredient, that like Salt it must season all things, especially this Epistle, Because it covereth a multitude of faults: The Contemplation of it otherwise comes in very boisterously, as little pertaining to the Story of removing the Apostles bones.

The Epistle affords many other Notes even in this little part of it: As that of Saints

Saints are to rejoice for any benefit done to the Church of *Rome* : That the bodies of the moſt bleſſed Apoſtles being too diſhonourably buried before , turned to the greater joy of the Church, which otherwiſe had loſt this occaſion of Feſtivity. If you ask, how it was poſſible they ſhould be *interred ſo gloriouſly* in the days of *Decius* a bloudy Perſecutor ? It was at the intreaty of *Lucina,* a noble Matron, of which kind there are ſome alwayes that have a great influence in the Church of *Rome*. That *Peter* was buried in the *Golden Mountain* as a preſage of his Succeſſors glory. That the Biſhops of *Rome,* were even in the Height of Paganiſme (and Idolatry) buried in *the Temple of Apollo :* That *Peter* was buried in three or four places at once : *among the Biſhops of* Rome, *in the Temple of* Apollo, *in the Golden Mountain, and in the Vatican of* Nero's *Palace* ; a little before *Cornelius* his Martyrdome, on the 3. of the Kalends of *July.*

If you will not believe this, conſider yet further, the holineſs of *Cornelius* affirming it. For while he was ſettling theſe Holy Bodies, he, and the Saints of the Church of *Rome* with him, prayed God and our Lord Jeſus Chriſt, that upon

Q 4 on

on the Interceſſion of thoſe Holy Apoſtles, he would purge away the Sins of all
them to whom he wrote ; the Merits of
the Apoſtles, and eſpecially the Interceſſion of thoſe that ſate in the *Roman Chair*
being eſtabliſhed 1450 years ago, by the
Decretal Epiſtle of *Cornelius* : The Viſi-
on of the Apoſtles, and their knowledge
of things done upon Earth is intimated
ſufficiently, together with the Principality and Piety of the Church of *Rome*, that
was ever a Lover of the Saints, and a
Worſhipper of their Relicks. Way is
made too for Praying to Saints departed :
this Part of the Epiſtle ending with that
notable Paſſage of David, *What ſhall I give
unto the Lord for all his Benefits towards
me ? I will take up the Cup of Salvation,
and call upon the Name of the Lord.* Which
ſhews the honourable uſe they make of
the Scriptures.

　　Now if you enquire, Whether this
Epiſtle be Authentick ? you ſin againſt
the Doctrine of *Implicit faith*, and highly
Scandalize the Church of *Rome*. For
can any man be ſo wicked, as to believe
that *Cornelius*, or any other Pope ſhould
counterfeit GOD to be the Author of
a Counterfeit ; or return ſuch Solemn
praiſes for a feigned Deliverance ; or
write

write Publick Admonitions to all the
Churches in the World concerning a Lie,
or abuse the Holy Scriptures ; and make
nothing of Love, but a pretext to patch
up, and cover Forgery? Yet let us hear
what *Binius* and *Baronius* say concerning
these Matters. For though the Epistle
be never so formally set down, and a Lie
written in the Top, both of the Epistle,
and the Page, *Cornelii Papæ Epistola*
1. And again, *The first Epistle of Pope*
Cornelius : yea, though *Binius* saith in his
Notes on this Epistle, that *S. Jerom wit-*
nesseth Cornelius *to have written many E-*
pistles ; and that this therefore is undeser-
vedly taxed for its faith and authority,
which has gotten so famous a Witness as
Jerom. Yet after all this, (though
(among other Circumstances of Importance) it hath been laid down as a Good
Record by *Binius* his Ancestors) he saith,
That it doth attribute to Cornelius *the*
Translation of the H. Bodies of Peter *and*
Paul *from the Catatumbæ,* (which is, if
I mistake not, from the meaner Graves
of the Common people) *Id ex Libri*
Pontificalis Erroribus in Epistolam irrep-
sisse, probabile, &c. *That that crept in*
into this Epistle, from among the Errours
of the Pontifical, seemeth probable. For
more

more truly that Translation happened in the first Age, a little after their Passion : As by the testimony of S. Gregory the Pope we demonstrated above.

Surely the feet upon which this Peacock stands, are very Black. The pride of *Rome* is founded like that of the great Whore, on the waters at least, if not in the mire.

If you examine What, or Where this Testimony of S. *Gregory* is, that overthroweth this Epistle of *Cornelius*, a Person much more Ancient and Authentick than himself ; and with what Circumstances, or with what form of words *Binius* maketh use of the same? Let your patience turn to *Binius* his Notes on those Words in the Pontifical, *Hic Temporibus*, &c. in the Life of *Cornelius*, and there it shall be satisfied.

CAP.

CAP. XIX.

The ridiculous Forgery of the Council of Si-
nuessa, put into the Roman Martyrolo-
gies. How the City, and the name of it
was consumed, (though when, no man
can tell) by an Earthquake.

MARCELLINUS the Bishop of
Rome entered on his See about the
year 296 in the dayes of *Dioclesian.* The
Pontifical in the Life of *Marcellinus* telleth us, that *he offered incense to an Idol,*
to escape the wrath of the Emperour.

Binius saith, *When* Marcellinus *the*
Roman *Pontifex was therefore accused,*
because in the Temple of Vesta *and* Isis, *he*
burnt incense, and offered Sacrifice to Hea-
then Images and Idols, to wit, that of Ju-
piter *and* Saturn ; *300 Bishops came toge-*
ther in the City Sinuessa, *to pass their Sen-*
tence on the Fall of Marcellinus. *The place*
of meeting was the Crypta Cleopatrensis,
which fifty, one after another could enter, it
not being able to contain them all, by reason
of its straitness. After the discussion of
the Cause, and condemnation of certain
Priests, Marcellinus *the chief Bishop,*
publickly confessing his sin, clouthed with

Sackcloath, sprinckled with ashes, prostrate on the ground, acting Repentance, said, I have sinned before you, and cannot be in the Order of Priests: and so condemned himself by his own Sentence. ¶ *After those* of Magdenburg, *the English Innovators reject this Convention of* 300 *Bishops, as if it were feigned by the Donatists. Because they think it improbable, that in this* 20. *year of* Dioclesian, *wherein the fiercest Flame of Persecution burned, and the Anger of the Emperours did rage more bitterly against the Christians, throughout all the* Roman *world,* 300 *Bishops should be assembled together,* Bin. Not. in Vit. Marcellin.

By the way I must tell you, that the *English* do upon several accounts, besides that of the *Persecution* reject this *Council of Sinuessa,* however it pleaseth *Binius* to ease himself of labour, by mentioning only that. Neither do they fasten it on the *Donatists,* but the *Papists.* For though *Marcellinus* be made a *Donatist* in opinion, his Confession being founded on that Doctrine, that no man guilty of mortal sin, can (though penitent) continue in the Order of Priests : *Binius* himself puts the Doctrine into his mouth : while other *Doctrines* relating to the Popes Supremacy, cy, and other *Perfons* defending this Council, shew plainly enough whose it is, notwithstanding the prefent *Mift* which *Binius* putteth before our eyes. Hear him on.

But if no fear of the Perfecution of De-cius, faith he, *could hinder them, but that about fifty years before this, as we faid in our Notes of the* Roman *Council held in the Interregnum, many Bifhops of the Remoter Provinces, and many others neighbouring on* Italy, *and living in banifhment, came together upon the Letters of the* Roman *Clergy, at* Rome, *and holding a Council there, ordained thofe things, which the pre-fent neceffity of the Church did require: Why fhould it feem more diftant from the truth, that by the moft vigilant care of the* Roman *Clergy, the Bifhops of Forreign Churches fhould be called together by Cir-cular Epiftles, and no fear or Danger of Life deterring them, meet at the time and place appointed, to tranfact and decide that caufe, of all other the moft deplorable, in which not only the* Roman *Church, but the whole Chriftian Religion was brought into the greateft Hazard, wherein the whole Foundation of the Church was fhaken, in the firft Bifhop of the Catholick Faith, and almoft utterly overthrown?*

Binius

Binius you see confesseth the Truth, that *Mercellinus* did offer Incense to an Idol: and that the Gates of Hell had well nigh prevailed against S. *Peters* Chair, in the Idolatry of his Apostate Successor. That therefore they might imitate God, *though the perverse way*, in bringing Good out of Evil: the matter is so neatly ordered, that the Ball reboundeth higher by its Fall; the Weakness of *Marcellinus* increases the Popes power, and his Disgrace is turned to his Greater Glory. His flip is made the establishment of all his Successors. For a Council of 300. Bishops is raised up, by the Invention of the Papists, which do all of them most humbly beseech the *Guilty Pope* to condemn himself, and Decree with one Consent, that the Sovereign Bishop of the City of *Rome* can be condemned by no body. For *out of thine own mouth thou shalt be justified, and out of thine own mouth thou shalt be condemned.* It is an important Point: and no witness fit to be lost, that giveth Testimony thereunto.

Concerning this Council therefore, on the Words *Acta Omnia.* He saith, *Though exceeding many among the most learned of men, have endeavoured to prove those Acts to be Spurious, and of no weight,*
truly

truly by Strong Arguments, and would esteem it as no other than a Device of the Donatists, cunningly contrived that the Name of Marcellinus, well accepted of among all the Ancients, and had in great Esteem, should be defamed: We neverthelesf conceive the same Acts, to be not only not Commentious, or forged, to be ascribed to the Donatists; but rather to be had in great Veneration, both because venerable Antiquity it self fighteth sharply for them, compelling a Reverence even from the unwilling by its majesty : and because by the Common Assent of all, being believed, it hath hitherto been received, and without all Controversy maintained in the Ancient Martyrologies and Breviaries both of the Roman, and other Churches. Baron. *In* Append. Tom. 10. Ad hunc Annum.

Note here, that as *Surius,* and *Binius* and *Baronius,* so even the *Roman Church* hath it self received this Council into her purest Records, her Sacred *Martyrologies*, and *Mass-books*, or *Breviaries.* Which is a reason above all other reasons, compelling *Binius* and his fellowes, *Baronius, Labbe,* and the *Collectio Regia,* to embrace this Council. For it cannot be rejected without Prejudice to the Authority of the *Roman Chair.* Which as it clears

the

the *Donatists* from the pretended imputation, discovers plainly who are the true
Authors of this *Council*.

For though it be more than probable,
that some pitiful barren Head, void of all
Sence and Learning, did at first compose
it, out of the affection he had to the See
of *Rome* : Yet as in Treason all are Prin-
cipals, so here *the Receiver is as bad as
the Thief.* The *Roman* Church by aiding
and abetting this Abomination, hath
made it her own : Be it forged in what
empty Shop it will, she hath magnified
it to the Stars, by fixing it in her *Martyrologies* : The Chair is defiled with the
Forgery it hath adopted : and the Pope
hath made it as much his, as if it had been
the Issue of his own Brain.

Being therefore it cannot now be de-
serted, without discovering the *shamefu*
Secrets of the *Roman Church* ; *Binius* like
a good Son endeavours to maintain it
but with such ill success, that he shame
her more by miscarrying in the enter
prize.

First he saith, *Exceeding many a
mong the most learned of men, have endea
voured to prove those Acts to be spurious.*
By these *most learned of Men* he means the
Papists, not the Protestants : So that ex
ceeding

eeding many of the moſt learned Papiſts have rejected that Council; leſt the Chair ſhould be too much diſgraced with the reproach of *Marcellinus.* 2. He ſaith, *They have endeavoured to prove theſe Acts to be ſpurious, truly by ſtrong Arguments.* He confeſſeth the Arguments to be ſtrong againſt it. And here he varies a little from himſelf: for beſides the Perſecution of *Decius,* there are Arguments and ſtrong ones to, againſt this Council; which he before concealed. Nor do the *Engliſh Innovators* only, but the Papiſts alſo, and the moſt learned among them write againſt it. What Arguments then doth *Binius* bring to defend it? His Opinion, Antiquity, General Conſent, and all reſolved into the *Roman Martyrology.* As for the firſt, his *Nevertheleſs I conceive,* will not do, againſt *ſtrong Arguments.* Antiquity, which is the ſecond, ſtands upon other mens **Legs,** and ſpeaks by other mens Mouths : She may be painted like a **Woman,** but is of neither **Sex:** And though *Binius* would perſwade us, that She fighteth in perſon very *ſharply* for the Council, you can ſee nothing but her *Name,* and his Talk of her Majeſty. She wanted the tongue of the Learned, and is a *dumb Champion.* His *General Conſent* is diſturbed by thoſe

R   ex

exceeding many most Learned men, o
which he had looked before, *that endea
voured to prove these Acts to be spurious.*
They come out of their Graves wit
strong Arguments, to disorder the *commor
Assent of all, by which it is beleived;* t
defile the *Majesty of Antiquity,* by whic
it is asserted, and to reprove *Binius* for *
Lyar,* who saith, that *it hath hithert
been received, and without all Controver
sie maintained.* Nor is he a Lyar onely
but contradicteth himself, and foolishl
betrayeth his design, while he shuffle
and cuts upon all occasions.

But perhaps you will say his meanin
is, *It is without all Controversie maintain
ed in the Roman Martyrologies* and *Brevia
ries.* That reserve he keeps for a *Starting
hole then,* but it will not do. He migh
say, it was *put in* without all controver
sie, because the *Roman Martyrologies* anc
Breviaries were works of Darkness, mad
in Secret by the Popes Authority: But i
it *maintained* without all controversie
when *exceeding many of the most Learne
Men endeavour to prove its Acts to be
spurious by strong Arguments?* Doe ve
nerable *Antiquity* it self fight sharply fo
them, compelling a *Reverence* from th
unwilling by its *Majesty;* or is it by th

common Assent of all believed; when *exceeding many* endeavour to refute it? As for the *Roman Martyrologies*, it is no wonder it should lie quiet in them. None were by but the Actors only, when the Council was put in, and if by dissembling the fraud, it be *maintained there*, it is no great business. But there it is, and that is sufficient.

For my part I could not have believed, that *Binius* or any other Sober man, could ever reckon such an horrid piece of Barbarism for a *Council*, had I not seen it with my own eyes in the Author. It is so much against all reason, that a thing so absurd should be owned, to the disgrace of all Martyrs, Synods, and Councils. And were it not for the *Cause* of the wonder, the *Roman Martyrologies*, whose credit must be saved, it would be my lasting amazement.

Binius is so stiffe in defending this Council, that in the next words he chargeth ignorance on S. *Augustine* for not understanding it.

Love and Hunger will eat through stone walls. His Zeal for the Church of *Rome*, and its Direful necessity, makes him to defend this Council in the *Roman Martyrologies*, against an apparent falsehood

R 2   hood

hood in the bottom of it, againſt very many moſt learned men, againſt all the barbarous and intollerable Nonſence and Tautologies therein, againſt the Killing Circumſtance, that there was no ſuch City or *Crypta* at leaſt in the World, as well as againſt the Impoſſibility of calling it, *on his own Principles*; Beſides all which, the vanity of its Deſign, and the Abſurdity of its meeting on ſuch an occaſion, is ſufficient to detect it.

The Lye in the bottom of it is in thoſe Words, *Cum eſſet in Bello Perſarum.* This Council was convened, as the Title ſheweth, *when* Diocleſian *was in his War with the Perſians.* Upon theſe words *Binius* ſaith, *Hæc niſi emendentur falſa ſunt, &c.* 'Theſe Words be falſe unleſs they be 'mended : for ſince *Euſebius*, and divers 'others witneſs, that *Diocleſian* in this '20. Years of his Reign deveſted himſelf 'of the Empire, and which is more, two 'years before triumphed at Rome with 'his Collegue *Maximianus*, for having 'conquered the Perſians ; how I pray 'you could be this year be going forth 'with his Army againſt the Perſians.

This is one reaſon more, for which the *Writers of Magdenburg*, and the *Engliſh Innovators,* as he is pleaſed to ſtile them, reject

reject that Council. Another is contained in *Binius* his Notes on the word *Sinnessa*, num.] 'So called from the City *Sinnessa* in 'a certain *Crypta* whereof, called *Cleopa-* '*trensis*, they came together secretly to 'shun the Sword of the raging Gentiles. 'For whereas men doubt, whether any 'such City was ever in the World, he pro-'ceedeth to tell us, that it is not to be ad-'mired at al, that there is no mention made 'either of this City, or such a *Crypta*, in any 'other Writers, nor at least the smallest me-'mory of this Place to be found: Since we 'know that by great Earthquakes, not on-'ly mountains and plains have lost their Si-'tuation and Name, but the Desolation of 'some most ample Cities hath bin also made

It is an unlucky Chance that this City should be swallowed up by an *Earth-quake :* As ominous almost as the *Burning of the Nicene Canons* by the *Ar-rians.* That other Places have been lost we know: but no man knoweth that this City was lost, nor is *the least memory of it to be found.* Whereas such Strange Accidents being the fittest Themes for the Trumpet of Famous such a Rarity had made it more remarkable, than if it had continued until this Day: Since *Mar-vels* chiefly busy the Pens of Historians.

That

That they should be Silent, or its Name be shaken out of all Books by an Earthquake, is the greatest *Miracle* Story doth afford.

Inserting the *Notes* of *Peter Crab* and *Surius*, he giveth us another reason for which we reject that Council. Be pleased to look back on *Peter Crab*, and there you shall see his Premonition beginning thus, *Because of the intolerable and too too grievous Depravation of the Copies, &c.* The *Collectio Regia* hath rejected the old ones, and for the smoother Conveyance of that Council hath left them both out, and recorded only the false one that was made in their Stead. So may it come to pass in time, that all the Barbarisms shall be forgotten, and the well-mended but Spurious Copy be taken for the true Record. *They* reject the old one for their *Nonsence*, and we *theirs* for its *Novelty*.

Surius, whose *Premonition to the Reader* Binius reserveth till after the Council, yieldeth us another reason whereupon we refuse it. It is pretty to see the Hypocrisy wherewith he admires *the Care and Diligence* of its first Compilers, notwithstanding the *Depravations* and *Corruptions* of the same. For he telleth us, *It seemed not good to the* * *Collector,*

or, to pass over these things for the fore= *Peter Crab!*
mentioned *Trifles*, which our forefathers
have with so much *Labour* and *Diligence*
left us. That is (when you pull of the
mask, which *Peter Crab* the Collector, out
of some idle Monk or other set on
work by the *Church of Rome*, was pleased
to record, for the interest of that Chair)
though those little *Trifles*, The *intolerable
Difference and Depravation* of the Copies
would otherwise have hindered him.
The reason why he defendeth it, moves
us to reject it. *For they, who being Zealous for the Bishop of Rome, conceit those
things to be feigned by those who rival
the Apostolical See, as if it were unworthy
of the Apostolical Chair, that so great a Bishop should be brought to so strait a Pass,
as to sacrifice unto Idols, seem little to remember how Peter Denial did not hurt
him; or that there is joy among the Angels
over one Sinner that repenteth; or that
this very* Marcellinus *afterwards con-
stantly met his Death for the sake of Christ;
and according to the Proverb, fought man-
fully after he ran away. However it be,
O Reader, we would not have that concealed from thee, which we have found in the
Monuments of the Ancients, leaving the
Truth of this to the Records themselves,*
and

and not prejudicating any mans Sentenc
by our Opinion. His Reaſon why it may b
held for a good and true Record, is th
ſafety of the Roman Chair notwithſtand
ing it ſhould be thought ſo. And one of th
Reaſons why we ſo greatly ſuſpect them
is that very behaviour : The advantag
of the *Roman* See being the only Touch
ſtone among them, of Records and For
geries. By this very example you ſee
that men as wiſe as *Binius* leave the Coun
cil Doubtful ; and by his Teſtimony you
find that many *Romaniſts* renounce it .
So may you diſcern by the Crookedneſ
of their Rule, that they are fit to be ſuſ
pected. It is a very great Secret and warily to be diſcovered, and that to none
but friends ! but *they that are zealous for*
the Biſhop of Rome, ſhape their Opinions
by their Affections. Some that are zealous, *conceit thoſe things to be feigned,*
becauſe they think it unworthy of the Apo-
ſtolical Chair, that ſo great a Biſhop ſhould
ſacrifice to Idols. While ſome of them,
that are *zealous too for the Biſhop of* Rome,
becauſe they remember *how* Peter's *deni-*
al did not hurt him, and know that the
fear of the former might eaſily be removed with pretences enow, think it better
to retain this Council. For *there is joy*
among

Roman Clergy call this Council, before
the Pope was judicially depofed. If
the Roman Clergy take upon them to
condemn him before he is heard, his Condition is worfe than that of other men.
If they prefume to call a Council before
he is condemned, they ufurp his Authority, and act independently to the prejudice of the Chair, in fuch fort as was never heard of; there being no Prefident
or Copy but this, of fuch a Proceeding.
Though the Pope were a Criminal, yet
every one muft not judg him. *I* fuppofe they will Confefs there have been
many wicked Popes, yet while the Pope
is a Pope, no man without his Authority
may call a Council. The thing is
impoffible therefore in it felf. For he
muft Firft be condemned, before a Council could be called to condemn him ; and
before he could be condemned, the
Council muft be called. Which would
feem among Proteftants a Contradiction.

The Abfurditie of the Plot , is another reafon why we reject it. Three
hundred Bifhops in a perfecution adventure their Lives to meet together, upon an unwarrantable Call before the
Pope was convicted as a Criminal, and
without knowing whether he would
come

come to Judgment; though certainly knowing that none could compel him, convene him before them. They produce one Day 14. Witnesses, another Day 44. And care is taken, according to the Decree of the *Epilogus Brevis:* to compleat the number of 72. Witnesses : And when all is done, they confesse they have no Power to condemn him. The Absurdities are not easily fathomed. How gross was it for the Roman Clergy to call a Council for the Deposing of a Pope, whom they before knew nothing could condemn but his own Sentence? How absurd, for them to judg the Pope, whom they continually teach no man can judg? How much more absurd for the Council to meet to depose him, who if he were pleased to declare their Sentence null, all was in vain? It is just as if a *Rebellious* Parliament should meet on their own Heads, to call their King to account, upon pretence of his Crimes. If this be admitted, all must be Disorder and Confusion in Kingdom.

If his Ingenuity had led *him* to depose himself, without giving all these Bishops the trouble, he might have done it at home. That he wanted Ingenuity, his denial,

nial of the Fact (before the Council) teftifieth. Whereupon I wonder what
brought him thither, or what Miracle
made him ftand before the Bar, at his
Tryal? But had he not denied the Fact,
the Ceremony had been loft of *producing
feventy and two Witneffes.* Which relation to the putid Forgery of the *Epilogus Brevis,* as yet unmade, utterly mars
the bufinefs.

The Council it felf is the greateft evidence againft it felf in the World. If you
pleafe to give your felf the trouble of
reading it, either in *Peter Crab,* or *Surius,* or *Nicolinus,* or *Binius,* and compare
it with the Letters of Pope *Sylvefter* and
the *Nicene Council,* recorded afterwards,
you will find reafon to believe the very
fame *Dunce* made them all. Thofe three
being the abfurdeft pieces, that ever
were feen with learned eyes.

For a Tafte of this, take but the beginning of the two old pretended Originals, A. and C. to let go the third, which
being made by latter men, is nothing to
the purpofe.

A.	C.
Dioclefiano & Maxi- miano Auguftis. Cum multi in vita fua afper-	Cum multi in vita fua afperfu mentis fua vacil- litate menticbantur, ori- fi

si mentis suæ vacillitate mentiebantur, ori ine dicentes, quod Deorum Superstitio vanitas super se sentirent, & ad Sacrificandum eo tempore multi inducerentur per pecuniam, ut Sacrificarent Diis. Marcellinus itaque, &c.

gine, dicentes, quod deorum Superstitionem vanis super sentirent, & ad Sacrificandum eodem tempore multi inducerentur per pecuniam ut thurificarent Diis. Marcellinus itaque, &c.

Take which you will, and try to construe it; you will find it impossible: yet in this Dialect he holdeth from end to end. Many things more we might speak, but we study brevity.

CAP. XX.

Divers things premised in order, first to the Establishment, and then to the Refutation of Constantine's *Donation; the first by* Binius, *and the latter by the Author. The Forgeries of* Marcellus, *Pope* Eusebius, *and* Binius *opened.*

An. 304.

MArcellus a Roman sate five years, six moneths, and twenty one days, saith the Pontifical. He succeeded *Marcellinus.* There are two Decretal Epistles ascribed to him, and both counterfeit: The

The one is *concerning the Primacy and Authority of the Roman Church :* the other is written to *Maxentius the Heathen Emperour,* and a Tyrant. Concerning which laſt, *Binius* (in his Notes upon it) ſaith, *Hanc Epiſtolam, Anno* 308. *Scriptam, Additamentum aliquod accepiſſe, Res Scriptæ hic parùm ſibi cohærentes indicant.* He holdeth it for a good Record; but there are ſo many things inconſiſtent in it, that he fears it has *taken a Doſe,* and confeſſeth that ſome things were put in, by way of Forgery.

This is an eaſy way of defending. There was never any Deed forged, wherein the larger half, being *directed purely according to form of Law,* was not Good. But if for that cauſe, when it comes to be Scanned, the forger at every Detection ſhould ſay, *This was forged indeed, but the reſt is good;* the Court would laugh at him : And this is *Binius* his preſent Caſe.

In the time of *Marcellus* there was a Council called at *Eliberis, An.*305. where they forgot *Binius* his *Council of Apoſtles at Antioch ;* and among other Canons decreed this for one, *Placuit Picturas in Ecclesiâ eſſe non debere. Ne quod colitur & adoratur, in Parietibus depingatur.* They
think

think it unlawful to put any Picture of what is adored, in the Church on the Walls. He takes much pains to pick this Thorn out of the Popes foot: but we leave him at his work, and proceed to

THE LIFE, EPISTLES, AND DE-CREES OF *EUSEBIUS* POPE,

Out of the Pontifical of Pope Damasus.

In 309.

Eusebius *a Grecian sate nine years, four moneths, and three days.* Binius proveth, he could sit but *two years,* some *moneths, &c.* And whereas *Eusebius* saith, *the Cross was found in his days,* and Fathers the Invention of it upon one *Judas,* converted thereupon, and called (at his Baptism) *Quiriacus;* though he names the day of the moneth exactly, *the fifth of the Nones of May,* and instituteth an Holy-day thereupon; yet is all this rejected by *Binius* for a Fable. *For by the consent of all Ancient Writers,* saith he, *the Cross was found after the Nicene Council,* by Helena *the Mother of* Constantine *the Great.* Howbeit, there is a very formal Epistle to the Bishops of Tuscia *and* Campania, in the name of *Eusebius,* devoutly abusing H. Scripture, exalting Piety, and the Popes Chair; till at last it decrees an

ly-

Holy-day for this happy Invention, solemnly enjoyn'd by the Authority of this Roman Catholick and Apoftolical Bifhop, though all this be as very a Cheat as any of the former. *Binius* has a cure for this too, but a very courfe one: *This part of the Epiftle we confefs to be counterfeit.* Vid. Bin. in loc.

Melchiades *an African fate three years,* An. 311 *feven moneths, and eight days.* Binius faith. *two years,* &c. And reprehends the Pontificals Confufion, which I fhall not ftand to mention, having greater matters to fhare.

In his time *Conftantine the firft Chriftian Emperour* arofe: Concerning whom the Pontifical is filent in the time of *Melchiades,* having need of him in that of *Sylvefter:* but *Binius* gives us this little Abftract of his Hiftory here.

After an Interval of feven days, Octob. 3. *An.* Chrift. 311. *in the third year of the Emperour* Conftantine, Melchiades *began to fit. In his time, fix moneths from the return of Peace to the Church being fcarcely paft,* Maximinus *in the* Eaft, *being Emperour with* Licinius, *ftirred up a moft grievous Perfecution againft the Chriftians, whom he called the Firebrands, and the Authors of all the Evils in the World.*

S   Eufeb.

Euseb. l. 9. c. 6. Maxentius *in the West oppressed the Empire with a grievous Tyranny:* But Constantine *his Fellow Emperour that Reigned with him in the West, as* Licinius *Reigned with* Maximinus *in the East, being stirred up partly by injuries, and partly by the prayers of the* Romans, *resolved to suppress the Tyrant. When therefore he designed the War, he despised the Aids of the Heathen Gods, and determined in himself to implore only the Creator of Heaven and Earth, whom his Father* Constantius *adored. It happened therefore that while he was praying for Prosperity, he saw at Mid-day the Sign of the Cross, made with Beams of Light, appearing in the Heavens; in which these words were manifestly contained,* IN HOC VINCE. *The Explication whereof when he had learned from our Lord Jesus Christ appearing to him in his sleep, and from his Priests; he undertakes the War against* Maxentius, *and happily conquers him. Which Victory being gloriously gotten, i acknowledgment that it came from tha One Invisible and Immortal God, he erected a Trophy of the Cross in the midst of th City, w. th this Famous Motto :* HOC SA LUTARI SIGNO, VERO FORTITU DINIS INDICIO CIVITATEM VE STRAM

STRAM TYRANNIDIS JUGO LI-
BERAVI. Under this Saving Sign, the
true Mark of Fortitude, I freed your
City from the Yoke of Tyranny. *And
as a manifest Token of his Liberality and
Piety, he gave to* Melchiades *the Publick
House in the* Lateran, *which heretofore was
the Palace of* Fausta *the Empress.* Opt.
Mil. *He restored the Goods of the Church,
gave great Priviledges and Immunities to
the Clergy, and made a Decree, that they
should be maintained at the Publick
Charge.*

In the latter end of this first *Tome*,
Binius has a long Record of *Gelasius Cyzicenus*, in fair Greek and Latine, who
being a very Ancient Author, confirms
all these things, shewing the madness of
Maximinus, and his destruction, the
building of Churches, the evil manners
of *Licinius*, the Victory which the *Religious* Emperour obtained against that
wicked man, the *Peace* of the Churches
after *Licinius* his Death, and the several
ways whereby the good Emperour promoted the Christian Affairs.

Yet as if all this were a Dream, the
Scene is immediately overthrown; *Constantine* a Tyrant, a Murderer, an Op-
pressor, a Persecuter of the Church, and

S 2   smitten

smitten with Leprosie from Heaven! namely for his great abominations. *Licinius* is innocent, and unjustly slain; but *Constantine* is made the Destroyer of peace. For in the Life of *Sylvester* the next Bishop after *Melchiades*, the Pontifical saith, *be was banished into the Mountain* Soracte. Upon which words, *Binius* further saith, that *Sylvester, fearing the cruelty of the Emperour, fled from* the City, *as his own Acts, and* Zozimus, *and* Sozomen *do probably shew.*

As for *Sylvesters Acts* so simply and freely cited here, meerly to cheat the Reader, he afterwards * confesseth them to be a Forgerie. And as for *Zozimus* and *Sozomen* : those Words, [*Do probably shew.*] shew *Binius* to be a *Sophister.* He would fain have father'd the Story upon *Zozimus* and *Sozomen :* but his Courage failed him : for they speak not expresly, but *Probably shew ;* that is, in his conceit, they give him colour enough to side with a Cheat, a Forger, a Lyar, a notorious Counterfeit, *Damasus*, against all the true Antiquities and Histories in the World. The positive Relation of *Eusebius Pamphilus* an holy Father in the *Nicene Council*, that lived in those times, the Records of *Gelasius Cyzicenus* that ancient

* *Bin. Not. in Constant. Edit.*

cient Author, and *Nicolinus*, the late Compiler of the Councils, that commend *Eusebius* as *the most faithful witness among Ecclesiastical Writers*, being palpably contradicted, while *Zozimus the Heathen* is favoured in some dark expression, wherein his Envy tempted him to carp at the Emperour; because he was next under God, the Author of so much Peace and Felicity amongst the Christians. As for *Sozomen* he was a Christian indeed, but too late an Author to contend with *Eusebius* and *Gelasius Cyzicenus*. Neither does *Binius* say he positively avers any such thing, but *probably seems* either a *Fox* or a *Fernbush*: Some frailty perhaps which proves *Constantine* a Man: but *Binius* should have produced clear Testimonies, as found and authentick as the former, if he meant to swim against all Antiquity, in disgracing so glorious an Emperour, positively affirming him to be guilty of Murder, and Parricide, Apostacy, and Idolatry, Persecution, *&c.*

Binius acteth his part too far: for if (as he saith) *Constantine counterfeited* himself to be an *Heathen* only to satisfie the People; *his great munificence, and kindness to the Christians having imbittered*

the

the Multitude, so far, that it almost brake out into a Rebellion : for the appeasing of the sedition therefore, he dissembled his Religion, upon Temporal Considerations, for which God was provoked, Certainly he could never hope to be cured of his Leprosie, by going in earnest to the Heathen Priests and their Idols, as *Binius* pretendeth, when he was so deeply humbled, and in danger of Destruction.

But this whole pretence is overthrown, and the *Genius* of the Man more clearly displayed in the passage following.

In the Life of *Marcellus* with which we began the Chapter, and which was some years before this pretended necessity, he telleth us that *Maxentius, who studied to possess himself of the Tyranny of* Rome, *at his first entrance into the* Roman *Empire, feigned himself craftily to embrace our Faith; thereby to please the* Roman *people, and to take them with his Flatteries, for which cause he remitted the Persecution against the Christians: and put on for a season of Piety, that for a time he shewed a shew of Courtesie, Love, and Humanity.* This he proveth out of *Euseb. l. 8. c. 16.* But for a purpose of which *Eusebius* was not aware: his design being hereby to justifie the Counterfeit *Epistle of*

Mar-

Marcellus, and to palliate the absurdities therein contained, the Popes ranting so foolishly out of the Bible, and threatning *Maxentius the Heathen Emperour*, with the Authority of his Predecessor *Clement*, while he was a Pagan Infidel. Now if *Maxentius* found it necessary to counterfeit himself a *Christian*, to please the People; *Constantine*, who found the minds of men far more inclinable to Religion then *Maxentius* did, was by consequent, more engaged to appear a Christian, than *Maxentius* was; that so he might also please the People. But voluble Wits in *partial* Heads are bended easily to any Cause, they fancy for their advantage: Otherwise the Cross in the Heavens, the Trophies upon Earth, the prevailing glory of *Christianity*, the victories of *Constantine*, the joy and exultation of the people, and the general applause with which he was received throughout the whole World, would have taught *Binius* another Lesson, than *Constantines* necessity to counterfeit himself an *Heathen*, which is the meer *Chymera* of a lying Brain: for which he is not able to produce any one Author in the World, worth the naming.

He produces the Testimony of *Eusebius* con-

concerning the neceffity of *Maxentius*
his counterfeiting himfelf to be a *Chriftian*, but *Eufebius* fpeaketh not one word
of any neceffity lying upon *Conftantine*
to counterfeit himfelf an *Heathen*: but the
contrary, fo far, that *Binius*, who had
quoted *Eufebius* fo gravely before, brand-
eth him with the Reproach of an *Arrian*,
becaufe he croffeth his defign now about
Conftantines Donation.

For the Donation is founded on *Conftantines* Cure, his Cure on his Leprofie, his Leprofie on his Apoftacy, his
Apoftacy upon a Neceffity to comply
with the perverfenefs of the *Heathen*
people, whofe Power was of too great
a fway for his Defign in the Empire : All
which is contradicted by the continual
decaying of *Heathenifm* that then was
day by day, and the growth of *Chriftia-
nity*, which had taken fuch root and poffeffion in the People, that there needed
nothing but the change of the Emperour,
to turn the *Empire* into *Chriftendom*. But
this Neceffity muft be invented : for elfe
it would feem impoffible that he fhould
turn Pagan, after our Saviour had appeared to him in his fleep, after he had
feen the Crofs in the Air, after he had fet
it up in his Standard, after all his Victories

ries gotten under that glorious Banner,
after he had erected its Trophy in the City, and made the World Glorious by his
Munificence to the Churches.

For this Cause, a far off, and so long
before the end could be discovered, to
which it should be applied, does *Einius*
take his Rise from the Fable in the *Dona-*
tion, and shape his Discourse to the Exaltation of the *See*, by rooting the *Dona-*
tion deeper in the Minds of men. For all
he saith is to no other purpose, than to
confirm the *Donation* of the Emperour,
thereby to settle the Empire in the Chair:
for the sake of which, he tramples upon
the Emperour, wryeth Antiquity, wresteth Authority, citeth Forgeries and Heathen Authors, defaceth the History of
the Church, and rewards the greatest of
all Benefactors with the basest ingrati-
tude.

All these Wars are commenced *afar*
off: for the strength of *Rome* is alwaies
at a distance: near at hand she is weak
and feeble; when he comes up close to
the matter, though he makes a great sem-
blance of its evident certainty, writing
over head in Capital Letters, EDICTUM
CONSTANTINI: And putting down
the *Donation* under it at large, commen-
ting

ting on it also very formally, nay and writing in the Margin of his Notes, *Constantini Donatio defenditur*, and near the close of them, *Constantini Donatio confirmatur:* yet after all this, he confesses the Donation to be *Spurious*. His Design being no more, than to make a *Shew*, and cover that *onfession*; which meer necessity, at greatest pinch, wrested from him. His Confession lies in little roome, and his Notes are made for the assistance of *Confederates*; Such mighty Tomes for the Help of a sworn Party. As for the rest of men that are allured perhaps by the Magnificençe of the Books to admire them, and to grace their Studies with them, such as *Lords* and *Princes*, he very well knows, they may feed their Eyes with Great Titles, and Glorious Shews afar off; but they will never penetrate such *Stupendious Volumes*, by reason of other Diversions, Labors, Cares, and Pleasures, which call them to other secular Objects. So that they may easily be deceived with the outward Appearance and splendor of such great and learned Collections, which secret Design is the Mystery of the *Papish* *Councils*.

For in the Body of those Notes, *Bi-*

nius

nius himself by many well studied Arguments sets himself strenuously to overthrow the *Donation* ; and Fathers it on the Knavery of *Balsamon* a Greek, who produced it (as he pretends) with an intent to disgrace the *Roman Chair* ; by making the World believe, that the Popes Supremacy came not by Divine Institution, but the Grant of the Emperour : Which he abhors as fickle, weak, and humane, chusing rather that the Popes Right should rest on the Scriptures.

Labbe, *Cossartius*, and the COLLECTIO REGIA follow *Binius* exactly, even to those Cheats *in the Margin*. But now it is high time to see the Contents of this wonderful *Donation*.

CAP.

CAP. XXI.

The EDICT *of our Lord* CONSTANTINE *the Emperour.*

A Forgery
beginning
in the
Name of
the Father,
Son, and
H. Ghoft.

IN *the Name of the Holy and Individual Trinity, the Father, and the Son, and the H. Ghoft*; Flavius Conftantinus, Cæfar, *and Emperour, in Jefus Chrift, one of the fame H. Trinity,* &c. *To the moft Holy and Bleffed Father of Fathers* Sylvefter, *Bifhop and Pope of the City of* Rome, *and to all his Succeffors about to fit in the Seat of bleffed* Peter, *to the end of the World: And to all our moft Reverend and Catholick Bifhops, amiable in God, made Subject throughout the World to the H. Church of* Rome, *by this our Imperial Conftitution,* &c. It is too long to put it down formally, and at large: We fhall therefore take only the chief Contents, as they lie in the Donation. It firft contains a large account of the Articles of his Faith; Secondly, the ftory of his Leprofie, Cure, and Baptifm: wherein the Font is remarkably called *Pifcina,* (the Popes *Fifhpond* as it were) then he cometh to the Gift it felf.

While

While I learned thefe things by the Preaching of the bleffed Sylvefter, *and by the benefit of the bleffed* Peter, *found my felf perfectly reftored to my health, we judged it profitable, together with* * *all our Nobles, and the whole Senate, my Princes alfo, and the whole People Subject to the Empire of the Roman Glory; that as* S. Peter *upon Earth feemeth to be made the Vicar of the Son of God, the Bifhops alfo that are the Succeffors of him, the Prince of the Apoftles,* **may obtain the Power of Principality given from us and our Empire,** *more than the Earthly Clemency of our Imperial Majefty is feen to have had; chufing the Prince of the Apoftles, and his Succeffors, for our ftedfaft Patrons with God. And we have decreed that this* H. Roman Church *fhall be honoured with Veneration, even as our Terrene Imperial Power is: And that the moft Holy Seat of* B. Peter *be more glorioufly exalted than our Earthly Throne ; giving it Power, and Dignity of Glory, and Vigour, and Honour Imperial. And we decree and ordain, that he fhall hold the Principality, as well over the four Principal Sees of* Antioch, Alexandria, Jerufalem, *and*✝Conftantinople, *as over all the Churches of God in the whole World. And by his Judgment let all things whatfoever, pertaining*

taining

* All the Nobles, and the Senate, converted in a moment.

✝ Not built.

taining to the Worſhip of God, and the Eſtabliſhment of the Chriſtian Faith be ordained.

When *Binius* pleaſes to give Efficacy to a Miracle, all the World ſhall be converted in a moment. Notwithſtanding all the Miracles and Victories before, *Conſtantine* was fain to counterfeit himſelf an Heathen for fear of the people: Now all his Nobles, and the Senate, are changed in an inſtant; and his Leproſie upon Earth has done more than his Croſs in the Heavens. So eaſie it is to blow mens minds with a Breath, when they are dead and gone. *His Princes alſo, and the whole people ſubject to the Empire of the Roman Glory, judged it profitable, together with him, and his Nobles,* to do that which they abhorred before, to give to Baniſhed *Sylveſter*, and his Heirs, the Glory of the *Roman* Empire: As if that one Miracle had in a trice for Virtue outgone all our *Saviours*.

The laſt Clauſe contains ſomething more than the Emperour had power to beſtow. That a Lay-man ſhould by Deed of Gift deviſe, and give away the power of determining all Controverſies in Religion, to whom he fancieth; may be put among the Popes Extravagants (as

ſome

ſome of their Decrees are called:) yet with *Conſtantinople*, (a City yet unmade) this alſo is given to the Pope in the preſent *Donation*. But upon good reaſon: *For it is juſt that the Holy Law ſhould retain the Head of Principality there, where our Saviour, the Inſtituter of Holy Laws, commanded the B.* Peter *to undertake the Chair of his Apoſtleſhip.*

A merrier accident follows, *he bequeaths his Goods to the Lead*! It is true indeed he was allied to them, for he was dead when the Deed was made, as well as they. S *Peter*'s Truſtees having the management of his Pen, knew very well, that whatever he *gave to his moſt bleſſed Lords,* Peter *and* Paul, (ſince dead men never want Heirs) would fall to their ſhare: and like our late Long Parliament, conſpired to give large Boons to themſelves, in form following.

'WE Exhort and admoniſh all, that *Ibid.* 'with us they would pay abundant 'thanks to our God and Saviour Jeſus 'Chriſt, becauſe being God in Heaven 'above, and in Earth beneath, he hath vi-'ſited us by his H. Apoſtles, and made us 'worthy to receive the H. Sacrament of 'Baptiſme, and the health of our Body. 'FOR WHICH we grant to the H. Apo-
'ſtles

Constantine the Great gives his Cloaths to S. Peter and S. Paul in heaven.

'itles themselves, my most Blessed Lords,
'Peter and Paul, and by them also to
'B. Sylvester our Father, the chief Bishop
'and Pope of our Universal City of
'Rome, and to all Bishops his Successors
'that shall ever sit in the Chair of B. Pe-
'ter, to the end of the World, Our Dia-
'dem, to wit, the Crown of our Head,
'together with our Mitre, as also the
'Cloak on our Shoulders; viz. the
'Breast-plate which is wont to compass
'our Imperial Neck, as also our Purple
'Clamys, and Violet Cloak, and all the
'Imperial Attires. The Dignity more-
'over of our Imperial *Horsemen*: Giving
'him also the Imperial Scepters, with all
'other Signs, Badges, Banners, and other
'Imperial Ornaments, with the whole
'manner of the Procession of our Impe-
'rial Highness, and the Glory of our
'Power.

The Popes Guard.

'WE Decree also and Ordain to the
'most Reverend Clergy-men serving that
'H. Roman Church, in their divers Or-
'ders, the Height in Singularity, Power
'and Excellency, with the Glory where-
'of our most ample Senate seemeth to be
'adored; that is, that they shall be made
'*Patricii*, and *Consuls*. As also we pro-
'mulgate it for a Law, that they be beau-
'tified

Secular Power.

' tified with the other Imperial Dignities.

' AND as the Imperial Army is adorned,
' so do we Decree the Clergy of the
' Roman Church to be adorned : And as
' the Imperial Power is adorned with di-
' vers Offices, as that of Chamberlains,
' Porters, and all Guards; so we will have
' the Roman Church to be adorned.

The Popes Army.

' AND that the Pontifical Glory may
' shine most amply, we Decree this also ;
' That the Horses of the Clergy of the
' said Roman Church, be beautified with
' Caparisons, and Linnen Vestures of the
' whiteft colour, and so to ride. And
' as our Senate useth Shoes, *cum Udoni-*
' *bus*, made bright and illustrious with
' fine white Linnen, so let the Clergy al-
' so do : And let the Heavenly, as the
' Earth'y things are, be made comely to
' the praise of God.

The Popes Horses.

' BUT above all, we give Licenfe to
' our most H. Father *Sylvefter*, Bishop
' and Pope of the City of *Rome* himfelf,
' and to all that shall fucceed him for
' ever, for the Honour and Glory of
' Chrift our God, in the fame Great, Ca-
' tholick, and Apoftolick Church of God,
' by our Edict, *Ut quem placatus proprio*
' *Confilio clericali voluerit, & in numero*
' *religioforum Clericorum connumerare,*

Falfe La- tine, and Nonfenfe.

T   ' *nullum*

‘ *nullum ex omnibus præsumentum superbè*
‘ *agere.*

Binius for *Clericali* will have it *Cleri-care*, which he puts over against it in the Margin. Here are more Barbarismes than one: but I think the drift is, *that no man but he whom the Bishop of* Rome *pleaseth, shall be made a Priest: and that no man so made, shall behave himself proudly against the Bishop of* Rome.

WE have Decreed this also, That the same Venerable Sylvester *our Father, the High-Priest, and all his Successors, ought to use the Diadem, to wit, the Crown which we gave him from off our Head, of pure Gold and Precious Stones, and to wear it on his Head, to the praise of God, and honour of S.* Peter. * *BUT because the most Holy Pope himself will not endure a Crown altogether of Gold on the Crown of his Priesthood, which he bears to the Glory of the B.* Peter, *we have with our own hands put the Mitre of Resplendent White, signifying the most Glorious Resurrection of our Lord, on his Head:* * *And holding the Bridle of his Horse, for the Reverence we owe to S.* Peter, *we served him in the Office of a Stirrup-holder: Ordaining, that all his Successors shall in single and peculiar manner use the same Mitre in their Proces-*

sions.

Did

The Popes modesty.

Constantine the Great the Popes Groom or stirrup-holder.

sions, in imitation of our Empire.

The Popes Modesty comes off purely: Because he would not have his Shaven Crown profaned with a Crown of Gold; therefore the Emperour must give him the Mitre too: because it was unlawful for him to wear the one without the other; that is, his Conscience made a scruple at the one, unless he might have both: being so made exactly like the Heathen Monarchs at *Rome*, *Pontifex Maximus*, and *Emperour* together.

The Regalities were affected, not for themselves; Alas, Ornaments are but shadows, the Body and Substance is the thing desired.

WHEREFORE that the Pontifical Crown Ibid. *may never wax vile, but be more exalted also than the Dignity of the Terrene Empire, and the Glory of Power: Behold, we* The Popes *give and leave as well our Palace, as was* Dominions. *before said, as the City of* Rome, *all* Italy, *and all the Provinces, places, and Cities of the Western Empire, to our foresaid most B. High Priest and Universal Pope, and to the Power and Tenure of the Popes his successors, by firm Imperial Censure,* Per hanc The Pope *Divalem & Pragmaticum Constitutum;* Latine *By this our Divine and Pragmatical Constitution, we Decree them to be disposed,*

and

*and grant them to remain under the Right
and Tenure of the H. Roman Church.*

Poor Priests are fain to cheat the people by witty Miracles, and small Devices, at *Shrines* and *Images*, for a little Silver and Gold. The best of them can attain no more than Lordships, and the Territories of *Subjects*: As the Manours evidence, which are given to *our Lady of Loretto*, and those Lands which *Jesuites* squeeze out of dying men with the fear of *Purgatory*. But the Pope and his Cardinals find it not suitable to their State and Dignity, to juggle for less than Empires and Kingdoms; and therefore soar high, you see, in the present *Donation*.

Ibid.

'Wherefore, *saith the Emperour*, we
'have thought it convenient to change
'and remove our Empire, and the power
'of our Kingdom into the Eastern Coun-
'tries, and in the best place of the Pro-
'vince *Byzantium*, to build a City after
'our Name, and there to found our Em-
'pire. Because where the * Head of the
'Principality of Priests, and of the Chri-
'stian * Religion is ordained to be by the
'Cœlestial Emperour, it is not just that
'the Earthly Emperour should there have
'any Power.

The Pope the Head of Religion.

Here is a high Career of notorious He
resie

refie and Blafphemy together. S. *Peter*
was called the Prince of the Apoftles, but
the Pope is the *Head of the Principality*;
nor Head of the Priefts only, but *of the*
Chriftian Religion: which I think none
but our Saviour can poffibly be. It fmells
rank of Blafphemy; but that the Prieft-
ly and Imperial Power fhould be incompatible, is Rebellion and Herefie. It fhews
how incompatible *Popifh* and *Imperial*
Power is: Yet all thefe things are ratified by other *Dival Sanctions*, made by
the Emperor, though recorded no where;
as you may fee in the words following.

BUT all thefe things we alfo have de-
creed, and ratified by other Dival Sancti-
ons, and we decree them to ftand unble-
mifhed, and unfhaken, to the end of the
World. WHEREFORE we proteft before
the Living God who commanded us to
Reign, and before his Terrible Judgment
by this our Imperial Conftitution, that it
fhall not be lawful for any the Emperours
our Succeffors, nor for any of our Nobles and
Peers, or for the moft Ample Senate, or
for all the people of the whole World, now,
or hereafter, from hence in all Ages, lying
under our Empire, by any means to con-
tradict, or break, or in the leaft to dimi-
nifh thefe things; which by this our Im-

The Sanc-
tion of
the Decree

T 3 *perial*

perial Sanction are granted to the Holy Roman Church, or to all the Bishops of the same. But if any Breaker or Contemner of these shall arise (which we do not believe) let him be knotted and ensnared in eternal Damnation, and find the Saints of God, and the Princes of the Apostles Peter and Paul, Enemies unto him, both in the Life present, and in that which is to come : and being burnt in the lower Hell, let him perish with the Devil and all the wicked.

The great Council of *Chalcedon* consisting of 630 Fathers, lies under this Sentence ; because they made the Patriarch of *Constantinople* equal with the Bishop of *Rome* : If *Constantine* the Great did make it, *with the consent of all his Nobles and the whole Senate, before all the Princes and People of* Rome, as is pretended in the Donation. It was too publick a thing not to be heard of, and too remarkable to be let pass in silence. Since therefore it is incredible, that so many Fathers should wilfully fall under the Curse, it is certain the whole Donation is a Counterfeit. Howbeit as the Substance of the Act, so the Ceremony is worth the observation.

But ratifying the Page of this our Im-
perial

perial Decree, we laid it with our own hands on the venerable Body of the blessed Peter *Prince of the Apostles*, and there *promising to that Apostle of God, that we would inviolably keep all these things, and leave them in charge to be kept by the Emperours our Successors, we delivered them to our blessed Father* Sylvester, High-Priest, and *Universal Pope, and to all the Popes his Successors, the Lord God, and our Saviour Jesus Christ allowing it, for ever, and happily to be enjoyed. And the Imperial subscription. The Divinity keep you many years, most holy and blessed Fathers. Dated in* Rome, *on the third day of the Kalends of* April. *Our Lord* Flavius Constantinus Augustus *the fourth time, and* Gallicanus *being Consuls.*

* Gregory the Great's Blasphemous Title

A NOTE.

No Emperour being ever accustomed, to stile himself *Our Lord*, &c. Those words *Our Lord* Flavius Constantinus, coming out of *Constantine*'s own Mouth bewray the Donation, as made by some other, unless he were at the same time both his own Subject, and his own Emperour.

CAP.

CAP. XXII.

The Donation of Constantine *proved to be a Forgery by* Binius *himself. He confesseth the Acts of* Sylvester, *which he before had cited as good Records, to be Counterfeit.*

THose things (faith *Binius* in his Notes) *which are told concerning the Dominion and Temporal Kingdom, given to the See of* Rome, *are manifestly enough proved to be likely, by what we said in our Notes upon the former Epistle; as well as by the Munificence of the Emperour himself, never enough to be praised.*

Observe here the modesty of the man! He ought to prove the Instrument it self; but that he throws by, and talks of the *Dominion,* and *Temporal Kingdom.*

2. Neither will he undertake to prove it *certain*, but *likely*, that the Dominion and Temporal Kingdom was given to the See of *Rome.*

3. He cites his Notes on a counterfeit Epistle, to make it *likely:* For the Epistle going before was the *Epistle of Melchiades,* which he confesseth to be a Forgery.

4. *The*

4. *The Munificence of the Emperour makes it probable, that he gave away the Empire to the See of* Rome. If you will not believe this, you are an hard-hearted man; for *Binius* fays it.

His Notes upon the *former Epistle*, to which he refers you, are these : ' That the ' things which are written in this Epistle ' concerning the Donation of *Constantine* ' to *Melchiades* and *Sylvester*, are true, is ' proved not only from hence, but most ' firmly also by the Authority of *Optatus* ' *Milevitanus* , a most approved Writer. ' For he writeth , *lib. 1. cont. Parm.* that ' *Constantine* and *Licinius* being the third ' time Confuls, to wit, in the year of ' Chrift 313. a Council of 19 Bifhops was ' held at *Rome* , in the Caufe of *Cæcilia=* ' *nus* and the *Donatifts*, in the *Lateran*, in ' the Houfe of *Faufta*, which was the Seat ' of the Roman Bifhop. Truly he doth ' not exprefly write, that the Houfe was ' given to *Melchiades* by the Emperour : ' but fince no reafon doth appear for ' which it is neceffary, that the Conven- ' tion of 19 Bifhops fhould require larger ' Rooms out of the Houfe of *Melchia-* ' *des*, that wherein the forefaid Synod ' was affembled, to wit, the *Lateran*, or ' Houfe of *Faufta*, can by no prudent ' perfon

' person any more be doubted, to be gi-
' ven by the Emperour to *Melchiades* the
' Bishop of *Rome*.

The *Lateran* is not so much as named
in the Epistle of *Melchiades*; but that *he
left the Imperial Seat, which the Roman
Princes had possest, and granted it to the
profit of the blessed Peter, and his Bishops.*
Which considering what follows, is far
more fit to be understood of the Emperours *leaving Rome*, and granting it to
the Bishop : whence they pretend, he did
go on purpose. So that the agreement between *Optatus Milevitanus*, and the Epistle of *Melchiades*, is very small, or none
at all.

But admit that *Melchiades* and *Optatus
Milevitanus* had said, both of them, that
the *Lateran* was given to *Melchiades* ;
what is that to the *Dominion and Temporal Kingdom?* A single House, instead of
an Empire ! Though, that the House was
given, *Optatus Milevitanus* doth not affirm, even by *Binius* his own confession.

How *the things in this Epistle* should be
concerning the Donation of Constantine
to Melchiades *and* Sylvester, is difficult
to conceive; because *Melchiades* was
dead before the Donation was made to
Sylvester. It is very unlikely therefore
that

that *Melchiades* fhould make mention of that *Donation.*

His Epiftle talking of *Conftantine his being Prefident in the H. Synod that was called at* Nice, is a manifeft Impofture, *Melchiades* being dead before the *Nicene* Council; as is before obferved: Yet hence it is proved, that *Conftantine* made a *Donation* to *Melchiades* and *Sylvefter.*

Binius holdeth faft the *Donation,* though he lets go the *Epiftle.* Like a Logician, who lets go the premifes, but keeps the conclufion.

For it is moft firmly proved by *Optatus Milevitanus.* What is proved by him? *That* Conftantine *the Great gave the La- teran to* Melchiades. How is it proved? Why *he* teftifieth, *that a Council of* 19 *Bifhops met in* Faufta's *houfe in the* Late- ran. *Truly he doth not exprefly write, that the houfe was given to* Melchiades. But it feemeth probable to *Binius* his imagi- nation: And fo it is *moft firmly proved by* Optatus Milevitanus, *a moft approved Writer.* Thus *thofe things that are told concerning the Dominion and Temporal Kingdom given to the See of* Rome, *are manifeftly enough proved to be likely by what we faid in our Notes upon the former Epiftle. But it is better proved, by the*
continual

*continual poſſeſſion of thoſe houſes , by the
ſpace of thirteen Ages , until now;* as he
afterwards obſerveth. Though the length
of an unjuſt Tenure increaſeth the Tranſ-
greſſion.

Having firſt proved the *Donation* , he
proceedeth thus. *Hoc Edictum à Græcis
perfidâ Donatione (quâ, juxta illud.* Virg.
2. Æneid. *Timeo Danaos & Dona feren-
tes ; donare ſolent acceptum) mutilum
eſſe, ac doloſè depravatum, hæ rationes evi-
denter demonſtrant. Theſe following reaſons evidently ſhew this Edict of* Conſtantine, *by the perfidious Donation of the*
Greeks, *to be maimed, and treacherouſly
depraved.*

He enters upon the buſineſs gently,
pretending at firſt (as if the Donation
were true) that it was *depraved* by the
Greeks. But afterwards, when he is a
little warm in the Argument, and ſomewhat further off from his Sophiſtical Defences, he falls foul upon it as a *Counterfeit*, and rejects it altogether; as in the
cloſe will appear to the conſiderate Reader. But here let us ſee what Arguments
he produceth, to prove it *maimed, and
treacherouſly depraved.*

Bin. Not in
Conſtan-
tin. Edit. ' 1. Becauſe it pretendeth the Primacy
' of the Church to be granted by a Lay-
'man,

'man, which was immediately given to
' *Peter*, by God himfelf, and by our Lord
' Jefus Chrift; as is manifeft by thofe
' words, *Thou art* Peter, *and upon this*
' *Rock will I build my Church.*

'2. The Emperour, by this Edict, is
'made to give a Patriarchal Dignity to
' the Church of *Conftantinople*: Which
' if it be true, how then could *Anatolius*,
' the Bifhop of *Conftantinople*, be faid to
' take the Patriarchal Dignity to himfelf
' long after; even after the Council of
' *Chalcedon* was ended, *Leo*, *Gelafius*, and
' other Roman Bifhops refifting him?

'How could the Church of *Conftanti-*
' *nople* be a Patriarchal See at this time,
' wherein even the name of *Conftantino-*
' *ple* was not yet given to *Byzantium.*

'3. This Edict was firft publifhed by
' *Theodorus Balfamon*, out of the Acts of
' *Sylvefter* the Pope, falfly written in
' Greek under the name of *Eufebius*, Bi- Forgeries in the Name of *Eufebius*.
' fhop of *Cæfarea*: not that he might do
' any fervice to the Church of *Rome*, but
' that he might fhew the Patriarchate of
' *Conftantinople* to be the eldeft. Which
' Acts of *Sylvefter* were not known till a The Acts of *Sylvefter* forged.
' thoufand years after Chrift, coming then
' forth in *Eufebius* his name, out of a cer-
' tain Book of Martyrs; but were now
      ' increafed

' increafed by the Addition of this Edict
' of *Conftantine*.

His defign is, if it be poffible, to clear
the Church of *Rome* of this too palpable
and notorious Counterfeit : And for that
end he would fain caft it on the *Treacherous Greeks*, that he might thereby acquit the more Treacherous *Romans :*
Which he further purfues in the claufe
following.

*The new found Hereticks that oppofe
this Edict of* Conftantine, *tranflated out
of* Greek *into* Latine, *with fuch great endeavour, and impertinent ftudy; let them
know, that in this they rather further our
Caufe, than fight againft us : Who do our
felves, with* Irenæus, Cyprian, *and other
Holy Fathers, as well* Greek *as* Latine,
profefs the Priviledges of the Church of
Rome, *not to be conferred and given of
men, but from Chrift to* Peter, *and from*
Peter *to his Succeffors.*

Where the fau ts are fo great, we need
not make a Remark on the common
Cheat, *his vain Brag of the Fathers.* But
this we may obferve, that whereas the
Popes Claim is fomewhat blind to the
Prerogative, which is pretended to be given to S. *Peter*, *Binius* hints at a proper
Expedient to make it clear. For fuppofe
our

our Saviour made S. *Peter* the Rock on which he built his Church: How comes the Pope to be that Rock? Since S. *Peter* being an Apostle immediately inspired, and able to pen *Canonical Scripture*, some of his Prerogatives were *Personal*, and died with him? He tells you, that the Priviledge was granted *from Christ to* Peter, *and from* Peter *to his Successors.* So that it was not *Christ*, but *Peter* that gave it to the Bishops of *Rome.* Now it would extremely puzzle him to shew, where *Peter* gave that power to the Bishops of *Rome*; in what place, at what time, by what Act, before what Witnesses. All he can produce, is S. *Clement's* counterfeit Letter, and that miscarries.

But *in opposing the Edict of* Constantine, *the Protestants further their Cause, rather than fight against them.* Is not this a bold Assertion? Their Popes have laid Claim to the whole Empire of the Western World, even by this very *Edict*, or *Donation of Constantine :* And yet the Protestants did nothing, when they proved it to be a Forgery. This *Donation* is n old Evidence, proving the Divine ight of *Peter's Primacy*, and the *Popes Supremacy :* Did they promote their ause, that proved it to be a Cheat? Certainly

Certainly they that have Fingers so long as to grasp at an Empire, and Foreheads so hard as to claim it by *Frauds*, will stick at nothing they can conceive for their advantage. Is it impertinent to discover Knavery in the Holy Roman Catholick Church; or Imposture in the Infallible Chair? And together with the Credit of *Rome*, to take away an Empire? Besides the *Spiritual Right* of being the *Rock*, there are ample *Territories* and *Cities* claimed, with a Temporal Kingdom.

Let him therefore pretend what he will, the Authority of such Instruments is very convenient: And because he knows it well enough, he produces the *Diplomata*, or the *Patents of other Kings and Emperours*, to confirm the Churches Secular Right, *extant*, as he saith, *in the Original, with their Imperial Seals; as particularly those of the Most Christian Princes of* France, *restoring those things which the* Longobards *took away*. But he does not tell you, by what Arts they got possession of those Territories at first, nor by what Ancient Evidences, Seals, or Patents, they held them before the *Longobards* touched them.

And because a Kingdom is of much moment

Moment in the Church of *Rome*, he further faith, *As for the Dominion of things temporal given to the Church, herself proves them by the Broad Seals of the very Emperours giving them, yet extant in the Originals, and she quietly enjoyeth them.* How quiet her injoyment is, you may fee by that ftir and oppofition fhe meeteth, and by all the clamour throughout the Chriftian World, that followeth her Ufurpations. Which fhe defendeth here by the *Seals of Emperours* in general Terms, but what Seals they are, fhe fcorneth as it were, to mention in particular. Which argueth her caufe to be as *Bad*, as her pretence is *Bold*.

But as for the Rights granted to the fame Roman *Church*, S. Leo, Fælix, Romanus, Gelafius, Hormifda, Gregorius, *and other their Succeffors, that flourifhed famoufly from the times of* Conftantine, *have defended them*, faith he, *not by the Authority of this Conftantinian Edict, but rather by Divine and Evangelical Authority, againft all the Impugners of them.* The man is warily to be underftood ; for fome of thefe, whom he pronounceth as Defenders, violently oppofe their claim, as *Gregory* in particular : who for himfelf and all his Predeceffors, renounceth that *Blaf-*

V

phe-

Greg. lib.
Ep.
phemous *Title*, which *John* of *Conftanti*
nople firft arrogated, but the Bifhops o
Rome acquired afterwards, by the Gift o
Phocas, the bloody Emperour. So tha
all thefe are *Mummers*, brought in, as i
were in a Mafque, to fhew their vizars
and fay nothing. For of all thefe Roma
Bifhops mentioned by *Binius*, *Gregor*
was the laft : who teftifieth, that *none o*
Greg. lib.
4. Epift. *his Predeceffors ever claimed fuch a Ti*
tle.

We may further note, that he fpeak
here with much Confufion, becaufe h
fpeaks *of the Rights granted to the Roma*
Church ; but does not diftinguifh be
tween the *Divine* and *Humane* Rights o
which he is treating. For the Bufinefs h
is now upon, is the *Temporal Kingdom*; i
defending of which thefe Popes down t
Gregory did forbear to ufe the Authorit
of this *Conftantinian Edict*, as he calletl
it (by way of fcorn) not becaufe the
had it not, but rather (as he pretends)be
caufe they had no need of it , havin
enough to fhew by *Divine and Evangeli*
cal Authority for the fame. Which i
another pretence as bold and impuden
as the former. For, I think, none of hi
own Party will aver, that the Bifhop o
Rome can claim *a Temporal Kingdom* b
the Holy Scripture.

As for any other Claim by this *Conftan-tinian Edict*, or any *Donation* elfe of *Em-perours*, before the *Longobards*, he flight-eth all: efpecially the Authority of this *Conftantinian Edict*, conceruing which, he faith, 'None of all thofe, who fate 'over the Church before the year 1000. 'many of which faw the genuine Acts of 'Sylvefter recited, concerning which we 'fpake above, is read to have made 'any mention of this Edict. For as much 'as the *Counterfeit Edict* was not yet ad-'ded to the Acts by the Greek Impo-'ftors.

He does not tell us how he came to know, that many of the *Roman* Bifhops faw *the genuine Acts of* Sylvefter, before the year 1000. that being an Artifice or Color only, as if there were two divers Books of *Sylvefters Acts*, and the one a true one. He tells us not a word of the Contents that were in them: but he be-fore told us plainly, that *the Acts of* Syl-vefter *the Pope, were falfly written in Greek under the name of* Eufebius *Bifhop of* Cæ-farea, *that they were not known till* 1000. *years after Chrift, coming then forth in* Eufebius *his Name*. And now he telleth us as plainly, that *the Counterfeit Edict was not yet added to the Acts by the Greek Impoftors*.

The

The poor *Greeks* on whom he layes al
the Load of Impofture, never injoyed th
benefit of thefe Acts, nor ever pleade
the Impofture as the *Latines* did.   An
in all likelyhood they made it, that lai
Claim and Title to the Supremacy by it
Since therefore the Queftion is come t
this, *Who were the Impoftors?* we mu
define againft him, that *the Counterfei
Edict was added to the forged Acts, not b
the Greek, but Latine Impoftors.*

For how Counterfeit fo ever he wil
have it, *Pope* Adrian *in his Epiftle to* Con
ftantine *and* Irene, *which remains infe
ted in the* Nicene Council, *recites th
whole Hiftory almoft in the fame manne
and fo confirmes it by the Truth of th
Edict.* As *Binius* himfelf telleth us o
the words *Ipfe enim.*] So that the *Edi*
was pleaded long before the *Greeks* a
ded it to the Acts of *Sylvefter.* F
Pope Adrian died in the year 79
and the Acts of *Sylvefter* were unknov
till the year 1500. Yet this *Adri*
founded his Epiftle to the Empero
and Emprefs, in the fecond *Nicene Counc*
upon the truth of this Edict. And in ve
truth, the Story he telleth is the fame
Conftantine's Leprofie, &c. contained
the *Donation.* Which if *Binius* had be

pleaf

pleafed to remember, was publifhed by the *Latines* in *Ifidore Mercator's Collecti-on of the Councils*, about the year 8oo. Where the *Greeks* in all probability firft found it, and were cheated, (as many Wifer men have fince been) with the appearance of it there. So that fearching it up to the Fountain Head, it refts ftill among the *Romans*.

By the way, to fhew you that *Binius* is his Crafts-Mafter, over againft thefe words concerning *Adrian* before mentioned, he putteth down that Famous Marginal Note; *Donatio* Conftantini *confirmatur*, *The Donation of* Conftantine *is confirmed*: not by *Binius*, as the fimple Reader would fuppofe, but by *Adrian's Epiftle*, recorded in the 2 *Nicene Council*, and exprelly containing the whole Fable of *Conftantine's* Leprofie, Vifion, and Baptifm. So that the firft that ever knew it in the World, for ought I can yet perceive, was this *Adrian*, of whom we have fpoken fomewhat before.

Now he comes to fhew, how greedily the Popes received this Cheat of the Greeks. *Among thofe who received the* *Acts of Sylvefter in good footh, corrupted thus with the addition of this counterfeit Edict, by an evil Art, and by the forg faith of the Grecians carried out of the East into the West , and that earnestly defended them as Legitimate and Genuine, and pure from all fraud and Imposture, the first is found,* saith he , *to be Pope*

* Pope Leo 9. citer the Donat on.

* Leo *the Nineth:* Who in an Epistle to Michael *of* Constantinople *, and* Leo *of* Acridanum *,* Bishops, *in the year of our Redemption,* 1054. *makes mention of the Donation of this* Constantinian Edict, *made to* Sylvester. *From whence , I believe, it was, that much Faith and Authority being hereby added unto it , very many*

* The Gravest and most Learned Doctors among the Papists use it without any suspition.

of the * Gravest *and most Learned Doctors, without any suspition of Fraud or Imposture, with good Faith did read and receive it.*

He makes a large Confession here ; wherein three things are fit to be noted. *The first that ever used this Edict was a Pope:* Pope Leo 9. 2. *He used it immediately after it came forth:* For *Sylvesters* Acts came forth about the year 1060. *being afterwards increased with the Addition of this Edict of* Constantine ; and some 54 years after, the Pope made use of the Donation in it. Wherein *he is followed by many , very many of the Gravest and most Learned Popish Doctors;* which is the third thing to be noted. This fault of the Popish

Popish Doctors, who did *read and receive* this Donation of *Constantine, without any suspition of Fraud and Imposture*, being by *Binius* charged upon the Pope. The Shepherd went out of the way, and the Sheep followed him. The Captain, and the Herd, did all stray and miscarry : *Leo* 9. being somewhat like the Dragon in the *Revelation*, that threw down the third part of the Stars with his Tail.

Binius his Cure is but the shift of a *Mountebank*, to save his Credit. There are Errours and Heresies in the *Donation of Constantine*, which whosoever receiveth the *Donation*, he receiveth them in like manner : And to say, that the Head and its Members in the Church of *Rome* were deceived *by the Evil Art and sorry Faith of the Grecians*, while they licked up this Vomit of *Balsamon*, for the Popes advantage; is but a sorry shift, a Corrosive that eats like a Canker. For it shews how the Holy Catholick Roman Church may be *deceived*; Head and Members, Pope and Doctors, Priests and People. They were imposed on by an *Evil Art* it seems, and swallowed down *Heresie* in *Constantine's Donation*.

But that *Binius* lyes in his prevarication about the *Greeks*, and that the *Greeks*

V 4   were

were not the Authors of the Donation, and that it did not intend to hurt the Popes Chair, is evident by this. The Donation was made not to overthrow, but confirm the *Divine Right* of the Popes Supremacy, point blank against what *Binius* pretends. He that made it had an eye both to the *Temporal* and *Spiritual* Priviledges of the *Roman* Chair. For the *Donation* applieth those Scriptures, on which the Popes build their Right, to S. *Peter's* Successors, and makes the Emperour to note, that the Will of our Saviour was the Root of all his Kindness to the Chair: nay it expressly throws all on our Saviours Institution. *For it is just,*

Constantin. *that the Holy Law should retain the Head*
Donat. *of the Principality there, where our Saviour, the Instituter of H. Laws, commanded the blessed* Peter *to undertake the Chair of the Apostleship.* Where you may note another fetch of the Papists: Lest what our Saviour did to S. *Peter* should seem too remote to concern *Rome;* that they might make the Channel of Conveyance clear, these old Counterfeits record, that S. *Peter* did not come to *Rome* by chance, but being invested in so great an Hereditary power, our Saviour chose the place where it should rest: and that *Peter* came

to

to *Rome*, and there undertook the Chair of his Apoſtleſhip, *by our Saviours Commandment*. Which if they could make the World believe, their work would be half done. So that it utterly deſtroys the Intereſt of the *Greeks*, and the Donation is Root and Branch altogether *Roman*. Neither did the *Greeks* ever uſe it to diſgrace the Roman Church, for ought I can find, though the Romans uſed it, to magnifie their Church above all other Churches.

CAP. XXIII.

Melchiades counterfeited. *Iſidore Mercator confeſſed to be a Forgery. The Council of* Laodicea *corrupted, both by a Fraud in the Text, and by the Falſe Gloſſes of the Papiſts.*

THe Forgery put out at firſt in the name of Melchiades, *concerning the Primitive Church, and the Munificence of the Emperour* Conſtantine, hath now gotten a clauſe added to the Title, *viz. Falſly aſcribed to* Melchiades: In *Binius, Labbé,* and the *Collectio Regia.* Upon thoſe words, *Falſly aſcribed to Melchiades,* Binius

nius speaketh thus. 'That this Epiftle
'was afcribed to *Melchiades*, appeareth
'*Can. Futuram* 12.*q*.1. *& Can. Decrevit.*
'*Dift.* 88. which bearing the name of
'*Melchiades*, contain for the moft part
'the things which are written here. It
'appeareth from hence alfo, that hitherto
'it was commonly put in the former Edi-
'tion of the Councils, juft after the De-
'crees of *Melchiades* the Pope. Thus
was this counterfeit Epiftle placed a-
mong their Laws and Councils. 'But
'that it was noted with the falfe Title and
'name of *Melchiades*, appeareth from
'hence; (faith he) becaufe it maketh
'mention of the *Nicene* Council: which
'by the confent of all men happened af-
'ter the death of *Melchiades*, and after
'the Baptifm of the Emperour: not un-
'der *Melchiades*, but under *Sylvefter*, in
'the year of Chrift 325. being the 20
'year of *Conftantine*, as almoft all Hifto-
'rians unanimoufly do teftifie. Perhaps
'therefore it is more true, that *Ifidore*
'himfelf, being a Compiler, rather than a
'Collector, was the Author of this Epi-
'ftle: Which it is certain was made out
'of the third Canon of the Council of
'*Chalcedon*, and a certain fragment of the
'24 Epiftle in the 1. Book of Pope *Gre-*
gory,

'*gory*, and the History of the *Nicene*
'Council. *Baron. An.* 312. *Nu.* 80.

Here we come to know the manner
how Decretal Epistles were made : Good
passages stoln out of the *Fathers*, are
clapt Artificially together, and a Grain
or two of *Interest*, thrust neatly in, makes
up an *Epistle*. This of *Binius* is plain
dealing. *Isidore* is confessed to be a *Compiler*, that is, a Forger, rather than a *Collector*, or Recorder of the Councils.

* Note this well : because *Isidore* is
the Fountain (a muddy dirty one) out of
which they drink their waters.

This acknowledgment is the more considerable, because *Baronius*, *Labbè*, and
Cossartius, and the *Collectio Regia*, herein
do keep *Binius* Company.

Confessing it to be stoln out of S. *Gregory*, he acknowledgeth it to be made
almost 300 years after it was pretended :
Which draws near to the time of *Hadrian*
the *First*, and sheds another Ray of Light
on the Original of these Impostures.

In the time of *Sylvester* there happened
many Councils. One Feather is finely
thrust in, into that at *Arles*, to adorn the
Papacy : The Pope is set before the Emperour. In that of *Ancyra*, the *Marriage of Deacons is permitted.* Can. 1. *Priests*
also

also were not compelled to leave their Wives, unless they were taken in Adultery. Can. 8. *The Cup and the Bread were both given to the People.* Can. 13. In the Council of *Laodicea* it is determined, that *the Scriptures should be read on the Sabbath days.* Can. 16. And *that we ought not to leave the Church of God, and go and call upon Angels, and make Congregations which are known to be forbidden. If any one therefore be found observing this hidden Idolatry, let him be accursed; because he leaves our Lord Jesus Christ the Son of God, and gives himself over to Idolatry.* Can. 35.

The Invocation of Angels, though they were known to be Angels, is by the Council of *Laodicea* called *Idolatry*: Which vindicates Dr. *Stillingfleet*, in his acceptation of the word *Idolatry*, from the cavils of his Adversary. The Council esteemeth the very *calling upon Angels a forsaking of Christ, and an hidden Idolatry.*

Many attempts have been made to overthrow the *Canon*: I should be tedious, should I give you all their several ways to evade it. That which lies under my Cognizance, is their corrupting of the place.

Angelus

Angelus and *Angulus*, being two words in the Latine, near of Kin, though in the fenfe they differ much, the one fignifying an *Angel*, the other a *Corner*; fome have been fo bold, as to turn *Angelos* into *Angulos*, *Angels* into *Corners:* making the Canon to run thus; *We ought not to leave the Church of God, and to go and call upon Corners.* Though neither the fenfe of the place, nor the word in the Greek Tongue, nor the occafion of the Canon will bear it.

Binius indeed is not fo bold as to put it into the *Text*, but as a *various Reading* he puts it over againft the Text in the Margin; to ftumble the Reader, or make him obdurate.

Theodoret, an Ancient Father, living near the times of this Council, obferves that by this Canon *thofe Hereticks were condemned, who taught that Angels were to be worfhipped:* As *Binius* himfelf upon the place confeffeth.

Theod. in Colof. 2.

Epiphanius, among other Hereticks, mentions the *Angelici*; againft whom, in all probability, this Canon was made.

Epiphan. Haref. 60.

Bellarmine defends *Theodoret*, and approves of his Expofition. *For there is no doubt* (faith he) *but* Theodoret *was found and Orthodox in his Opinion, concerning*

Lib. 1. de SS. Beat. cap. 20.

the

the Worship of Angels. But then he has a fetch to clear the Church of Rome : *Not every pious Veneration of Angels is forbidden, but that only which is due to God.* Doubtlefs *Theodoret* was willing to give a *pious Veneration to Angels*; but neither he, nor the Council of *Laodicea*, knew of any *pious Invocation of them.*

But we leave thefe to come unto *Binius.* In his Notes upon *Pius his Epiftle* before mentioned, he faith, ‘ The words of ‘ S. *Paul*, Colof. 2. are written, not as ‘ *Hierom* fuppofeth againft the *Jews*, who ‘ believed the Stars of Heaven to be Angels ; nor againft the *Simonaici*, as *Bellarmine* fuppofed ; but rather againft ‘ the pernicious Doctrine of *Cerinthus*: ‘ who holding Chrift to be a naked man, ‘ extolled all the Angels , as the Makers of the World, above him. Yet a little after he faith the clean contrary : ‘ That *Cerinthus* did not only not teach, ‘ that Angels were as Makers of the ‘ World to be adored ; but rather they ‘ were to be had in hatred , as the Authors of evil. For the one he citeth *Irenæus, Epiphanius*, and *Tertullian*: *Baronius* for the other : And (which is very ftrange) himfelf fideth with all. Which you muft conceive to be a *neat* effect of

clean

clean conveyance : For by how much the more impoffible the Operation is, the *Juglers* flight is the more to be admired. In very truth, his behaviour is fuch, that it makes me too juftly to fear, they fay any thing in every place, that will ferve their turn, make Cyphers of the Fathers, and care not a farthing how much they contradict themfelves, fo they be not difcerned in doing it : Nay, his contradictions are fo palpable, as if long cuftom had made him carelefs of being feen too, and deprived him of his feeling: For Lyars, fpeaking truth and falfhood indifferently, for a long time, at laft note not themfelves, nor well apprehend which of the two they are fpeaking. And they that make a *Trade* of contradictions, inure themfelves, by long habit, till they become infenfible : Which (if need be) we fhall more fully and clearly fhew, out of *Binius* himfelf, upon this occafion.

C A P.

CAP. XXIV.

Threescore Canons put into the Nicene *Council after* Finis, *by the care and Learning of* Alphonsus Pisanus. *The counterfeit Epistles of* Sylvester, *and that Council. A* Roman *Council wholly counterfeited. Letters counterfeited in the Name of Pope* Mark, *and* Athanasius, *and the Bishops of* Egypt, *to defend the Forgeries that were lately added to the* Nicene *Council.*

B*Inius* hath the Code of the *Nicene* Council, fairly written in Greek, and at the end of it ΤΕΛΟΣ : or in Latine, FINIS.

After this, in another place, (by it self) under the name of *Alphonsus Pisanus,* with the Patronage of *Francis Turrian,* he bringeth in a whole Legend of Canons, to the number of fourscore, Fathered all upon the *Nicene* Council.

In the *Code* it self there are the Epistles of *Alexander Alexandrinus, Constantine the Emperour,* and the whole *Synod,* the *Emperours Oration,* the *Recantation o* Theognis *and* Eusebius *Bishop of* Nicomedia, the *Nicene Creed,* and the 20 Ca-

nons of the Nicene *Council.* All curiously written in fair Greek.

Out of the *Code*, after ΤέλΘ, there is a counterfeit Lift of the Bishops *Subscripti-ons* (but miserably depraved) to put the better face on the reft of the Forgeries: and like many other of the *Frauds*, written only in Latine. Then there is an humble Letter, whereby the Council submitteth it self to the Popes Censure; but in the Column on the other fide (for there are 2 Columns in the Leaf) it is defaced with an empty Blank, for want of a Greek Copy.

For fear this Letter fhould not be feen often enough, he hath it again, with the Anfwer of Pope *Sylvefter* thereunto; both recorded in another place, near to the *Arabick* Canons; detected by thefe marks: They are without any Greek Copy, are not among the Acts of the Council, are full of miftakes and Barbarifmes, and clearly refelled by the Genuine Acts of the Council it felf.

The Epiftles are thefe.

SYNODI NICÆNÆ

Epiftola

AD *SYLVESTRVM* PAPAM.

‘ Beatiffimo Papæ Urbis *Romæ*, cum om-
‘ ni Reverentiâ colendo, *Sylvefiro*; Hofius
‘ Epifcopus

X

'Epifcopus Provinciæ *Hifpaniæ*, Civita-
'tis *Cordubæ*; *Macarius* Epifcopus Eccle-
'fiæ Hierofolymitanæ, *Victor* & *Vincenti-*
'*us* ex Urbe *Romæ*, Ordinati ex directio-
'ne tuâ.

'QUONIAM omnia corroborata de
'Divinis Myfteriis Ecclefiafticæ utilita-
'tis, quæ ad robur pertinent Sanctæ Ec-
'clefiæ Catholicæ & Apoftolicæ, ad fe-
'dem tuam Romanam explanata, & de
'Græco redacta funt, fcribere confite-
'mur, nunc itaque ad veftræ Sedis argu-
'mentum accurrimus roborari. Itaque
'cenfeat veftra Apoftolica Doctrina, E-
'pifcopos totius veftræ Apoftolicæ Ur-
'bis in unum convenire, veftrumque ha-
'bere Concilium, ficut docet myftica Ve-
'ritas, ut firmetur noftra Sanctimonia,
'gradufque fixos, vel textus Ordinatio-
'nis tuæ Sanctimoniæ noftra poffit habere
'Regula. Quoniàm decet numerum di-
'ctorum tuorum Coepifcoporum à te
'difcere gradus vel ordinis conftituere
'Urbis. Quicquid autem conftituimus
'in Concilio Nicæno, precamur veftri
'oris confortio confirmetur. Oret Beati-
'tudo tua pro univerfo Concilio. Data
'2. Kalend. *Julias.* Accepta 13. Kalen-
'das *Novembris*, *Paulino* & *Juliano* fum-
'mis Confulibus.

There

There are a great many faults in it, which *Binius* mendeth; but he did not consider how accurate they were in Dating *the time wherein the Letter was received :* nor how much the Council condescended to the *Bishop of Rome*, while they wrote in Greek to the *common people* of *Alexandria*; but translated their Acts into *Latine*, for the *Popes* understanding. *Ad sedem tuam Romanam explanata, & de Græco redacta.* As if the Pope and his Clergy were unacquainted with the Greek Tongue.

RESCRIPTUM SYLVESTRI
ad Synodum Nicænam.

SYLVESTER Episcopus Sedis Apostolicæ & Sanctæ Catholicæ Ecclesiæ Reverendæ Religionis Urbis Romæ, *fratribus & Coepiscopis, qui in* Nicænum *Concilium convenerunt in Domino Salutem.*

GAUDEO *promptam vos Benignitatem servare. Nam & confirmo sigoque ad vestræ Doctrinæ reclamantes de Mysterio vel unitate Trinitatis Chrysmatis vos secundùm Dicta & Doctrinam Evangelicam Sanctam accepisse Gratiam. De quo Examinationis probo vera fuisse & esse mansura, quæ in vestrum nostrumque manavere Mysterium. Meum Chirographum & Discipulorum meorum offero in vestro Sancto Concilio,*

X 2   *quic·*

quicquid constituistis unà parem dare consensum. Atque in gremio vestræ Synodi parva propter Disciplinam Ecclesiæ alligabo præcepta, propter Victorinum qui arbitrio suo quicquid vellet affirmabat, & Cyclos Paschæ pronunciabat fallaces, & cum Episcopis totius Vrbis Italiæ examinatam universitatis vestri Sancti Concilii dignetur accipere veritatem. Et aliâ manu, Oret pro nobis Beatitudo vestri Sancti Concilii Trecentorum Decem & Octo: ut Charitatis quæ vobis data est Domini nostri Jesu Christi servetur Augmentum. Data 5. Kalendas Novembr. Accepta 4. Idùs Februarii, Constantino Septiès & Constantio Cæsare Quarto Consulibus.

Though the Nonsense be the most horrible that ever was seen, the exactness is great: For in token of the Spirit of Prophecy, the Bishop of *Rome* telleth them at *Nice*, that they were *three hundred and eighteen*, and dateth the day on which his Letter was received: which I think was extraordinary.

But there is a contradiction in thes Dull Letters, that mars all. They a *Nice* inform the Pope, that *all the Bishop of the Apostolical City were assembled in one* and held his Council for him there: Th Pope on the other side tells them of Counc

Council at *Rome* of the Bishops *of all the City of* Italy (*assembled*) *whence* he sent the Truth examined by his Disciples there (as he calls them) for them at *Nice*, to receive: which he prayes them to accept, &c. I confess the nonsence so terrible, that it is difficult to construe it to any sense at all: but divers circumstances interpret the words so, that *Præcepta* signifie *Canons*, and *Episcopi totius urbis* Italiæ, the Roman Synod under *Sylvester*: As those other words, *Meum Chirographum & Discipulorum meorum offero*; his own Subscription, and the Subscription of the Bishops under him, whereby he confirmed the *Nicene* Council.

For the Legend goes, that while the Council was sitting at *Nice* of 318 Bishops, *Sylvester* called a Council at *Rome* of 267 Bishops; where they made Canons as they did at *Nice*, and as good luck was, confirmed the Council there: Else all at *Nice* had not been worth a Rush And to this *Roman* Council *Sylvester* relateth, when he saith, *I send you mine, and my Disciples hands to give our joynt consent to all that you have ordained.* This is that Council which made the *Epilogus Brevis*, the commending of which to the *Nicene* Council, (were there nothing in

X 3   the

the Letter befide) would difgrace it for Cofin-German to that putid Forgery, fo often touched in the *Epilogus Brevis.*

This Council is fet by *Binius* (I know not why) before the *Nicene* Council; though it profefleth it felf to be held *at the fame time.* Perhaps the reafon is, that they cou'd not be fet down both together, and Priority was to be given to the Synod at *Rome.*

The Title of this Council is,
CONCILIUM ROMANUM
Aliud, fub Sylveftro *Papa Primo.*

It immediately follows *Conftantines Donation,* and dependeth on the truth of the fame.

The Popes *See* is magnified therein above the Skies; and for that reafon it fhineth among the Councils, as a Direful Comet among the Stars of Heaven.

The Proem fet before it bears the name of the *Epilogue,* Epilogus brevis, &c. *A fhort Epilogue of the following Roman Council.* A Trip in the Threfhold bewraying the Author. A Learned Council it was, no doubt, that began with the conclufion : For the *Epilogue* is the clofe of any difcourfe, the *Prologue* is the beginning.

But

But this First is a small Indecency, we proceed to the matter. The *Nicene Council* has the good fortune of being full of smoothness, clarity and Majesty: But *Binius* finds this so rude and rough, that he is fain to clear the way by a *Premonition to the Reader*.

The following Canons were written verbatim, saith he, *out of two Ancient Copies, which in many places, by reason of the depravation of the Exemplars, can scarcely, or indeed not at all, be understood. Let the Reader censure favourably, and communicate, if he hath, something more certain.*

Bin. in Concil. Rom. sub Sylvest.

You must touch it gingerly you see, or it will fall to pieces. *Solecismes* and *Nonsense* are like Rust and Cobwebs, signs of *Antiquity* in the *Roman Church*: Else certainly they would never have dared to present such *Mouldy* Instruments to the Face of the World. * But such Councils are fit to support the *Mystery of Iniquity*, which is made a *Mystery*, by making and supporting such Councils.

Since the *Canons* are so rude, we will let them go, and come to the *Epilogus*, which beareth the force of the most Authentick Canon.

Therein it is recorded, that *in the time*

of

of Sylvester *and* Constantine *the most holy Emperour, while* 318 *Bishops sat in Council at* Nice, *by the Command of* Sylvester; *on the thirteenth of the Kalends of* July, *there was a Council of* 267 *Bishops convered at* Rome, *by the Canonical Call of the* Pope: *That again condemned* Callistus, Arrius, Photius, *and* Sabellius, *before condemned in the* Nicene *Council, and ordained, that no* Arrian *Bishop returning, should be received by any but the Bishop of the place. In which also, by the consent and Subscription of all, it was ordained, That no Lay-man should accuse a Clergyman, and that no Priest should accuse a Bishop, no Deacon a Priest, no Sub-Deacon a Deacon, no Acolythite a Sub-Deacon, no Exorcist an Acolythite, no Reader an Exorcist, no Door-keeper a Reader. It was further ordained, that no Bishop should be condemned but by the Testimony of at least threescore and twelve Witnesses, nor shall the Highest Priest be judged by any,* &c.

This Decree is put among the Popes Laws by *Ivo Cartonensis,* &c. Doubtless to the very great ease and satisfaction of the *Roman Clergy:* For it reaches down, you know, to the lowest Orders of *Readers* and *Door-keepers.* So that they may write as many Forgeries as they will: If

it

it be a Pope, no man can condemn him : If it be a Bishop, no less than threescore and twelve Bishops, must on their Corporal Oath prove the Fact against him : forty four *Equals*, against a Cardinal-Priest, twenty six must depose against a Cardinal-Deacon of the City of *Rome*, and seven against a Door-keeper ; all which must be at least his Equals. A Marvellous Priviledge for *the City of Rome*! Which word *Rome*, though annexed only to *Cardinal-Deacons*, yet, for ought I know, the Judge will interpret its Extent, to all the other Orders ; or use it *Equivocally*, as himself listeth, or as his Superiour pleaseth. So that in Causes pertaining to the Interest of the *Roman Church*, other Priests perhaps, beside them in the City of *Rome*, shall enjoy the benefit of this Law ; but in Causes displeasing the Pope, and his Accomplices, none shall enjoy it, but the Priests of *Rome*. Many such *Trap-doors* are prepared in Laws, where Rulers are perverse and Tyrannical ; and whether this be not one of those, I leave to the Readers further Examination.

Mark succeeded *Sylvester* in the See of *Rome :* Between whom, and *Athanasius*, there were certain Letters framed, that

stand

stand upon Record to this day, to prove the Canons of the *Nicene* Council to be *Threescore and ten.* Heretofore they were good *old* Records magnificently cited : but now they are worn out : for *Baronius* and *Bellarmine* have lately rejected them; who are followed by *Binius,* as he is by *Labbe* and *Coßartius* and the *Collectio Regia,* all concluding the Letters to be Forged. The three last have this Note upon that of *Athanasius. Hanc surreptitiam & ab aliquo confictam fuisse quinque rationibus ostenditur, &c.*

Bin. in Ep: Athan. ad Marc: 'That this Epistle is a Counterfeit de-'vised by some body, appeareth evident-'ly by five reasons. Whereof the first 'is this, In the Controversie between the 'African Churches, and the Roman Bi-'shops, (*Zozimus* and *Boniface*) concer-'ning the number of the *Nicene* Canons, 'this Epistle was unknown. 2. *Athana-*'*sius,* as is manifest by what went before, 'was at this time fled into *France,* and so 'it could not be written from *Alexandria* 'and from the Bishops in *Egypt.* 3. That 'Divastation fell upon the Church of 'Alexandria many years after these times 'in theReign of *Constantius,*&c. As *Atha-*'*nasius* himself witnesseth in his Epistle 'ad omnes Orthodoxos. 4. *Mark* died in 'the

' the Nones of *October* this prefent year:
' *Constantine* himfelf being yet alive.
' 5. If Pope *Mark* had fent a Copy of the
' *Nicene* Council out of the Roman Ar-
' chives, to them at *Alexandria*, furely
' the Roman Copy and that of *Alexan-*
' *dria* would have agreed thenceforth as
' the fame : How then were thofe three
' Canons wanting in the Copy, which S.
' *Cyril* fent from *Alexandria* to the Afri-
' cans, which were found in the Roman
' Copy?

He pointeth to the *Commonitorium*
fent from *Rome* to the Sixth Council of
Carthage; and verifies all the Story we
have related; by rejecting thefe Letters
of *Mark* and *Athanafius*, made on purpofe to defend the Forgeries there detected. For which he cites *Baron. An.*336.
nu. 59,60. and *Bellarm. de Rom. Pont. lib.*
2. *cap.* 25.

This Epiftle was alledged by *Harding*
againft *Jewel*, and by *Hart* againft *Rai-*
nolds for a good Record. How formally it was laid down by the Elder Collectors you may fee with your eyes: and
may find it frequently cited by the moft
learned Papifts. Such as thefe being their
beft and only Evidences.

After *Mark Julius* fucceeded. *The Epi-*
ftle

ftle *sent by* the *Bishops of the Eaft to Pope*
Julius 1. is now confeſſed to be a Forgery. *Veram & germanam non extare præ-*
ter authoritatem Baronii *illud aſſerentis,ea*
quæ ſupra in principio Epiſtolarum Julii
annotavi confirmant : Saith *Binius.* Again
he ſaith, ' This Epiſtle which is put in the
' ſecond place, bearing the Names of the
' Biſhops of the Eaſt, ſeems to be compi-
' led by ſome uncertain Author, both by
' the concurrent Teſtimony of *Sozomen,*
' and *Socrates,* and becauſe thou mayeſt
' obſerve many things to be wanting, and
' ſome in the words and things expreſſed
' to be changed,

Reſcriptum Julii] The Epiſtle which
Julius returned in anſwer hath the like
Note upon it. *Hanc mendoſam,corruptam,*
& a quodam ex diverſis compilatam, &c.
' That this Epiſtle is counterfeit, corrupt,
' and compiled by ſome body out of di-
' vers Authors, the Conſulſhips of *Felici-*
' *anus* and *Maximianus* evidently ſhew,
' &c.

The matter in theſe Epiſtles is *the Popes*
ſupremacy : the unlawfulneſs of calling
Councils, but by his Authority ; his Right
of receiving Appeals ; with other Themes,
which Ambition and ſelf Intereſt ſuggeſt,
and of which genuine Antiquity is totally
ſilent. Hav-

Pin. in Epiſt.
Julii.

Having so fortunately glanced upon that Sixth Council, I shall not trouble the Reader with any more : but bewailing what I observe, beseech him earnestly to weigh this *Business walking in the Dark*, and take heed of a *Pope* and a *Church*, that hath exceeded all the World in Forgerie. For let the Earth be searched from East to West, from Pole to Pole, Jews, Turks, Barbarians, Hereticks, none of them have soared so high, or so often made the Father of Lies their Patron, in things of so great Nature and Importance. Since therefore the Mother of Lyes hath espoused the Father of Lies for her assistance, and the accursed production of this adulterate brood is so numerous; I leave it to the Judgement of every Christian, what *Antiquity* or *Tradition* she can have, that is guilty of such a Crime, and defiled with so great an Off-spring of notorious *Impostures*.

A N

AN
APPENDIX.

Cardinal Baronius *his Grave Censure and Reproof of the Forgeries: His fear that they will prove destructive and pernicious to the See of* Rome.

A *Piarius*, a Priest of the Church of *Africa*, being Excommunicated by his *Ordinary*, for several notorious crimes, flies to *Rome* for Sanctuary; *Zozimus* the Bishop receives him kindly, gives him the Communion, and sends Orders to see him restored. Hereupon the *African* Churches convene a Council, namely, the *sixth Council of Carthage*, whence they send a modest Letter, but as Sincere as Powerful, shewing how after all shifts and Evasions, *Apiarius* had confessed his Enormities; and that both the *Nicene Council*, and clear *Reason*, was against the disorder of such *Appeals*: All Causes being to be determined in the Province where they arose, by a Bishop, Patriarch, or Council, upon the place. *Otherwise,*

lay

say they, *how can this Beyond-Sea Judg-* *Epiſt. Con-*
ment be firm, where the neceſſary appea- *cil. Carth.*
rance of Witneſſes cannot be made, either *6. ad Cale-*
by reaſon of weakneſs of Nature, or Old *ſtin.*
Age, or many other Impediments? They
decry the Innovation of the Biſhop of
Rome in arrogating that Authority, *leſt*
the ſmoakie Puff of the pride of this World *Ibid.*
ſhould be brought into the Church of Chriſt.
This Epiſtle is on all ſides owned and
confeſſed to be a good Record. It was
ſent to *Celeſtine* the Succeſſor of *Zozimus*
and *Boniface.*

About 100 years after, *Eulabius* ſate in
the Chair at *Alexandria,* (ſome call him
Eulalius:) Between him and *Boniface* 2.
there are two Epiſtles extant, out of
which it is gathered, that after the ſixth
Council of *Carthage,* the African Churches were Excommunicated by the Roman for 100 years, and reconciled at laſt
upon the Submiſſion of *Eulalius,* Arch-
biſhop of *Carthage,* accurſing S. *Auguſtine,*
and his own Predeceſſors.

Concerning theſe two Epiſtles, Cardi-
nal *Bellarmine* giveth his Opinion thus : *Bel. de*
Valdè mihi eas Epiſtolas eſſe ſuſpectas, &c. *Sum. Pont.*
' I have a mighty ſuſpition of theſe Epi- *lib.2, cap.*
' ſtles : For firſt they ſeem to be repug- *25.*
' nant to thoſe things which we have ſpo-
' ken

'ken concerning the Union of S. *Augu-*
'*stine*, *Eugenius*, *Fulgentius*, and other
'Africans with the Roman Church : And
'again, either there was no *Eulabius* of
'*Alexandria*, to whom *Boniface* seemeth
'to write; or at least there was none at
'that time : as is evident out of the Chro-
'nology of *Nicephorus* of *Constantino-*
'*ple.* Besides, *Boniface* intimates in his
'Epistle, that he wrote at the Command-
'ment of *Justinus* the Emperour. But
'*Justinus* was dead before *Boniface* began
'to sit; as is manifest out of all Histories.
'Moreover, the Epistle which is ascribed
'to *Boniface*, consists all of it almost of
'two fragments, of which the one is ta-
'ken out of the Epistle of Pope *Hormis-*
'*da* to *John*, the other out of the Epistle
'of S. *Gregory* to the Bishops of *France* :
'even the 52 Epistle of his fourth Book.
'Now S. *Gregory* was not born at that
'time : nor is it credible that *Gregory*
'took those words out of *Boniface*, since
'the Stile is altogether *Gregorian.*

'In the Epistle also which is Fathered
'upon *Eulabius* the *Carthaginian*, there is
'a Sentence of S. *Gregories* inserted, out
'of the 36 Epistle of his fourth Book :
'and the rest of that Epistle is nothing
'but a fragment of an Epistle of *John*,
'the

' the Bishop of *Constantinople*, to Pope
' *Hormisda*.

Notwithstanding all these reasons, *Bellarmine* is afraid to *damn* the Epistles: but Cardinal *Baronius* is a little more bold. He judges it inconvenient for the Church of *Rome*, that any such Forgeries were ever made: And upon the occasion of these *two Epistles*, utterly disgraces *Isidore Mercator* for a meer *Impostor*.

Whether in so doing he salves the Sores of the *Roman* Church, that hath been guilty of *vending* them, the experience of Ages yet to come, will hereafter evidence. In the mean time let us see what he saith.

In Not. Martyrol. ad 16. *Octobr.* he layeth down these words: *Scias falsam & adulterinam Epistolam illam, quæ fertur nomine* Bonifacii 2. *&c. Know, that the Epistle which is carried abroad in the name of* Boniface 2. *to* Eulalius *Bishop of* Alexandria, *which is extant, and published in the second Tome of the Councils of the latter Edition, is false and adulterate.*

And speaking concerning the Schism, Excommunication, and Re-union of the *African* Churches, he saith, *Si hæc vera sunt, &c. If these things are true, certainly then all the Martyrs and Confessors,*

Y *which*

which were at that very time crowned with Martyrdom in the African *Church, or otherwise waxed famous by the Merits of their Eminent Sanctity, must be blotted out of the List of Saints, which* THE HOYL ROMAN CHURCH *it self hath, in its Martyrology, numbred among the Martyrs, or reckoned among the Confessors. Since it is most manifest by a thousand Sentences of* Cyprian, Augustine, *and all the Fathers, that out of the Church there can be no Martyrdom, nor any kind of Sanctity.*

If Lyes were always consistent, *Truth* would be amazed. God doth infatuate the Counsels of his Enemies, and turn their Wisdom into Foolishness. They run into inconveniences, sometimes so great, that they cannot be remedied. Could a Lye shun all inconvenience, and see to its Interest on every side, it would be as wise and perfect as Truth it self.

Quin amplius ex Collegis Aurelii, *&c.* 'But yet further, among other Companions of *Aurelius,* the most holy Father 'S. *Augustine,* the most glorious Beam of 'the Catholick Church, was accused in 'that Epistle. Who being clouded with 'the same Myst of Schism, must (if thos 'Epistles be true) be blotted out of the 'Class of the Doctors of Holy Church

‘ out of the number of Saints, nay out
‘ of the Martyrology; nor only so, but
‘ out of the Kalender of the HOLY RO-
‘ MAN CHURCH. For it is most cer-
‘ tain, that after the aforesaid *Aurelius*,
‘ he departed this life, within the space
‘ of the time before-mentioned. What
‘ should I reckon the *Fulgentiuses*, the *Eu-*
‘ *geniuses*, and others, almost innumerable
‘ men, most Famous for Holiness and
‘ Learning, to be accounted in the same
‘ condition *?*

It is a common Artifice in the *Church
of Rome*, to propagate these Forgeries as
far as they are able, by them to possess the
minds of men with great apprehensions
of the Popes high and Infallible Power;
and if at at any time they are detected, to
cast the blame on *private* persons: while
the Church is free (they pretend) from
such Abominations. I desire you to note
therefore, that the HOLY ROMAN
CHURCH it self is the Author of Her
Martyrologies and *Kalendars*, and that the
HOLY ROMAN CHURCH *her self*
hath Canonized her *Saints*, and made
Holy-days, and put them into her *Breviaries:* And it was this very HOLY RO-
MAN CHUCH, that put the *counterfeit
Council of Sinuessa* into her *Martyrologies*,

Y 2 the

the Lying Legend of *Sylvester* into the *Roman Breviary*, Authorized by three Popes, and the Council of *Trent*; and her counterfeit *Decretals* among her Laws, in all her *Consistories*, and Ecclesiastical Courts of *Highest Judicature.* So that if *Baronius* do not err, the ROMAN CHURCH is liable to the Charge of these Bastard-Antiquities: For which cause he might well break out into that angry Extasie, *Ecce in quod Discrimen Unus* Isidorus Mercator, *illarum Epistolarum Collector, res nostras adduxit! ut ex eâ parte periclitari videatur Ecclesia, &c.* ‘Behold into what peril, one *Isidore Mer-* ‘*cator*, the Collector of those Epistles, ‘hath brought our Affairs! So that the ‘CHURCH seemeth on that side to be ‘endangered, if we shall say, those things ‘which he hath collected, or rather feign= ‘ed, be firm and certain. If the Roman ‘Church be found guilty of Forgery, in *Baronius* his judgment, she is utterly ruin= ed.

It is of no small Importance, did he on-ly confess the things to be feigned (ra-ther than collected) which their great Masters of the Councils find in *Isidore,* their first Author. But his acknowledg-ment of the hazard which the *Roman Church*

Church runneth, is more. For they have so many Subterfuges about the *Roman Church*, that it is more difficult to find it, than to vanquish it. It was not the Pope in a *formal Council*, that Excommunicated the Church of *Africa*, or that put her Saints first into the *Roman Martyrologies*, yet it was the *Holy Roman Church*. And indeed, if the *Holy Roman Church*, and her Authority, be not to be found in her *Mass books* and *Breviaries*, her *Courts* and *Consistories*, her *Laws* and *Decrees*, her *Martyrologies* and *Kalenders*, her *Popes* and *Doctors*. I know not where to meet with Her: And if nothing else be the *Roman Church* but a Pope and Council United, the *Roman Church* is but a blinking business. There is no *Roman Church* (upon this account) sometimes for two or three Ages together: for she always vanishes upon the dissolution of the Council.

The *Roman Church* is in a great strait; but she may thank her self. She threw her self into this *Peril*, by making her self a Schismatick, an Usurper, a Forger. She first breaks the *Rules*; and if the Pope and his Doctors about him be the *Roman Church*, as they certainly must needs be; (for all that depart from them, shall be

Schism-

Schifmaticks:)if the Head of the Church, and all the Members that cleave unto it, be the *Roman Church*, fhe firft brake the *Rule*, and then forged *Ancient Canons* in the Name of the *Nicene Council*, to defend her Exorbitancy: fhe cut her felf off from the true Church in the fixth Council of *Carthage*, by a perverfe inveterate obftinacy; and to acquit her felf afterwards, laid the Curfe and Scandal upon others. She pretends, at leaft, that the moft Holy Churches were Excommunic:ted; that 217 Bifhops in a Sacred Council, *Alypius. S. Auguftine, Aurelius*, and all his Collegues, were *puffed up with pride by the Inftigation of the Devil*, and accurfed by a *Dreadful Excommunication*: for fo it is in the *Epiftle* of *Boniface* 2. to *Eulalius*. And now fhe hath nothing left to fupport her Enormity, but that *Greatnefs* alone, which by thefe Forgeries fhe hath acquired and maintained. Thefe *Thorns* are never to be pulled out, but the *Veins* and *Sinews* will follow after: For in rejecting thefe (Thorns in her fides) all her *Authority, Infallibility, Antiquity, Tradition, Unity, Succeffion, Credit* and *Veracity* is gone.

As for *Baronius*, and the way he takes, a man may fafely throw away the Sword, when

when he has killed the Enemy : but the
Church of *Rome* is not arrived to such an
happiness. Politicians pull down the
Ladder by which they have gotten up to
the *Top* of their desires. But the case is
altered here : They are undone, if the
Ladder be removed. To acknowledge
these *Helps* to be Forgeries, is their apparent *Ruine*.

Some Papists use these Counterfeits, by
vertue of which their Predecessors acquired, and established their Empire, as
Usurpers do *Traytors*, by whose villanous
help they are seated in the Throne. But
they can never wash off the Guilt they
have contracted ; nor make the Act, or
the Crime (committed once) to be again
undone. After 700 years enjoyment of
the Benefit, they begin to slight the means
of acquiring it : But it is, because they
cannot help it. The Cheat is detected,
and they wou'd fain perswade the World
they are Innocent of it. All of them either hold these things to be no *Forgeries*,
or (if *Forgeries*) to be *none of theirs*.
The Confession is not Genuine, like that
of *S. Peter* ; rather it is awkward and un-
toward, like that of *Apiarius* ; which
Confession the sixth Council of *Carthage*
observes to be *forced*. For after he had

obftinately perfifted, as long as poffible, in an impudent denial, reviled his Judges, abufed the *Roman* Chair, difordered the Church, and inflamed the World, when God had brought him into fo vaft a ftrait, that he could do no otherwife: then the *Fraudulent Diſſembler*, as they call him, fled to Confeſſion; but the Root of his Malevolence he retained in him.

Some Papifts confefs thefe Forgeries, but deny them to be theirs: They confefs the things, but juftifie themfelves. The things they fay are *Forgeries*, but themfelves no *Forgers*: And whether of the two be the greater Impudence, is hard to define: They confefs the *Fraud*, but make no *Reſtitution*. All their Drift is to fave their *Skin*: when one pretence is broken, they fly to another: nay, they go on to quote thefe things, even now they confefs them: where they are not detected they ftill do quote them; and with ftill, they were as able to conceal and defend them, as ever: For for one that knows them, they meet with a thoufand that are ignorant of thofe devices. There they diffemble their Conviction, and hide their Confeſſion with the Ignorant, and before fuch make fhew of thefe Frauds, as of great and glorious

Anti-

Antiquities; though, like *Proteus*, they transform themselves into other shapes before the more Learned. They find it meet and necessary to sail with every Wind, and to adapt themselves fitly in their discourses, both to them that know them, and to them that know them not; with them that know them they seem to decry the Impostures.

These things I speak, not to the poor simple *seduced* Papists, who did they believe and know these things, would abhor them to the Death; but to the *Seducers* themselves, who so delude the Ignorant, and are by all *Methods* ever busie in carrying on the Cause of the *Temporal Kingdom of the Church of* Rome: as by their obstinate practises is most apparent.

Baronius himself bewrayeth his Confession to be without any purpose of amendment; even by the Defence he maketh, for his good Old Friend, the Bastard *Isidore.*

A *Jerom of Prague*, or a *John Huss*, a *Latimer*, or a *Ridley*, though never so holy and pure in other things, were to be cursed with *Bell, Book and Candle*, if the least Errour appeared in them, that reflected on the Popes *Security:* Though never so Innocent, they were with all
violent

violent fury purfued to the Fire. But if a man have this one Vertue, of maintaining the Popes *Interest*, he may lye, and cog, and cheat, and forge; abufe Apoftles, Councils, Fathers, and be followed by an Army of Popes and Doctors : becoming a *Zealous* and Venerable Saint notwithftanding. *Hincmarus* of *Rhemes* could hardly efcape, for offering to mutter againft *Isidore*. But *Isidore* himfelf, becaufe he did the Pope Service, though he be a *Sacrilegious* perfon, and deferves all that can be called *Bad*, for the incomparable height and depth of his *Villany*; yet he is received to fair Quarters, and well efteemed of by Cardinal *Baronius : Testimonium illi perhibeo (utar verbis Apostoli) (* faith he *) quòd Zelum habuit, fed non fecundùm Scientiam,* &c.

I will give him this Testimony, (and here I will ufe the words of the Apostle) He had a Zeal, but not according to knowledge. For becaufe the contention of Aurelius, *Bifhop of* Carthage, Auguftine, *and other African Bifhops, feemed to him a little more hot than it fhould be, with* Boniface *and* Celeftine *the Roman Popes, in the Caufe of* Apiarius *the Prieft : he fuppofed it expedient, in that Epiftle which he feigned in the name of* Boniface, *to patch*

up

up what was cut away. But away with these things! The Church of God is not founded, nor does it lean upon Chaff, it self being the Pillar and Ground of Truth. Baron. Martyrol. Octob. 16.

I will not note, how he abuseth the *Scriptures*, nor how he wresteth the words of the H. Apostle, to cover a filthy piece of Knavery : nor yet in what sense he maketh the last words, which he uttereth, to sound ; concerning the *Roman* Churches being *her self the Pillar and Ground of Truth.* Though matters are so carried, as if she were great enough to be her own *Support*, and without being founded on any other, were her own *Foundation.* All I shall observe, is, that *Hadrian* 1. and *Leo* 9. have been very zealous and tender of these Records : that *Benedictus Levita* got them confirmed by the *Roman Chair :* that several Popes, since *Leo* 9. have imbraced, countenanced, and furthered them, as Pope *Paul* V. and *Sixtus* V. in particular : that *Isidore Mercator*, whom *Baronius* confesseth to be a Cheat, is the common Father of the *Popish Compilers :* That the Codes, or *Tomes* of the *Councils*, at this day received in the *Roman Church*, for good and Sacred *Records*, are by these *Collectors*,

James

James Merlin, Peter *Crab*, *Laurentius Su-rius*, *Carranza*, *Nicolinus*, *Severinus Bi-nius*, *Labbe*, the *Collectio Regia*, old *Ivo*, *Gratian*, &c. have digested thefe Impo-ftures, and recorded them as the *Sacred Authenticks* of the *H. Catholick Church*: that whole Armies of *Cardinals*, *Arch-bifhops*, *Bifhops*, *Doctors*, *Schoolmen*, *Je-fuites*, *Monks*, *Fryars*, *Canonifts*, &c. have cited them for many Ages as true Re-cords: that *Turrian* in particular (with divers others) have fet themfelves ftre-nuoufly to defend them: that they have impofed the Cheat upon *Kings* and *Em-perours*: that the Forgeries are backed with the Authorities of *Popes*, *Empe-rours*, *Kings*, &c. All, no doubt, *having a zeal*, *but not according to knowledge*; that is, being exceeding regardful of the Intereft of the Chair, and ftudioufly maintaining the *Temporal Kingdom of the Church*, as they call it; but erring in the *manner*. While they thought this the way to advance her, which is now become her apparent fhame, and a pro-bable means (without fudden amend-ment) to bring her to Confufion.

That

That Princes may a little more clearly see into the Myſtery of theſe counterfeit *Decretals*, it is meet, in the cloſe of all, to expoſe to the view of the World one *Paſſage*, out of many other, which we have paſſed over in ſilence. The Deſign of it touches Kings and Emperours to the *Quick*, though (for greater ſecurity to the Chair) it be covertly expreſſed. It is in the Oration of S. *Peter* to the people of *Rome*, in S. *Clements* Letter to S. *James*, and it is commended to the conſideration of the World by all the *Popiſh* Compilers of the Decrees and Councils, from — downwards.

— revived in the firſt Epiſtle of *Anicetus*, as *Binius* * obſerves: And expreſly repeated (becauſe they will make much of it) in the counterfeit Letter of * *Fabianus*, a Roman Biſhop and Martyr, that lived about 1400 * years ago, to this purpoſe.

> *When he had ſaid theſe things, and many more like unto theſe, looking upon the people, again, he ſaid, And you my deareſt Brethren, and Fellow-Servants, obey this * Man that preſideth over you to teach you the Truth, IN ALL THINGS: Knowing, that if any one grieveth him, he receiveth not* Chriſt, *who intruſted to him the*

* *Bin. Marg in Clement. Epiſt. 1.*

* *Fab Epiſt. 1.*
* *An. Chriſt 258.*

S. Peters Forged Oration.

* *The Roman Biſhop.*

the

the Chair of Teaching: *and he that receiveth not* Christ, *shall be judged not to have received* God *the* Father: *and therefore neither shall himself be received into the Kingdom of Heaven,* &c. *But ever coming together to* Clement, *Date omnes operam pro ipso sentire,* (it is an Emphatical expreſſion) *make it your buſineſs to be of his Opinion; and with your utmoſt ſtudy to ſhew your favour towards him: Knowing, that for every one of your ſakes, the Enemy is more inraged againſt him alone, and ſtirs up greater Wars againſt him. Ye ought therefore to endeavour with your utmoſt ſtudy, that being all knit together in the Bond of love towards him, ye may cleave unto him with a moſt perfect affection. But you alſo be ſure to continue unanimous in all Concord, that you may ſo much the more eaſily obey him with one Conſent and Unanimity. For which, both you may attain Salvation, and he, while ye obey him, may more readily bear the weight of the Burden laid upon him.* They muſt with their *utmoſt ſtudy* favour him, and bend all their Charity to each other, [for this very end] that they may cleave the faſter unto him; for doing which, they ſhall attain *Salvation.* This environs the Popes Chair with Armies of

Well-

Well-wishers and *Servants.* But the *Dangerous Passage* follows, which shakes all the Thrones and Kingdomes in the World! Lest they should be an Army of silly *sheep*, and simple *Doves*, wanting the *serpents* Fraud and *sting.* He admonisheth them further, that they all must be Enemies to their Popes Enemies, and hate all that he hateth. I leave Kings and Princes to judge of the words.

Quædam etiam ex vobis ipsis intelligere debetis, &c. *Some things also ye ought to understand of your selves ;* If there be any thing which he dares not evidently and manifestly speak out, for fear of the Treacheries of evil men. As for Instance : If he be an Enemy to any one for his Deeds, do not ye expect that he should tell you, Be ye not Friends with such an one : but ye ought prudently to observe, and to do his Will without any Admonition, and to turn from him, against whom ye perceive he is an Enemy ; nor so much as to speak to him, with whom he speaketh not, &c. That every one in fault, while he covets to regain all your Friendships, may the sooner make haste to be reconciled to him who is over all ; and by this return to Salvation, while he begins to obey the Admonitions of his Superiour. But if any one shall be a Friend

to thofe to whom he is not a Friend, o
fpeak to thofe to whom he fpeaketh not, h
is one of them, &c.

This dangerous Intimation is a fufficient hint for *Jefuitical* Souls : He declares
his Principle, that he is an *Enemy* to fome
contrary to our Saviours Order : an
gives order to his Difciples to guefs a
his meaning, and without any public
notice to execute the fame. *Hatred* re
moves its Object; he hates, *and the*
muft do his Will without Admonition. I
they miftake his meaning, provide
they do it out of Zeal, he can eafily con
nive at it : which fuits with their Practi
fes, of Poyfoning Emperours, Murdei
ing Kings, attempting on Queens, the
Maffacre at *Paris,* the Gunpowder-Trea
fon, & c. The *Inftruments* of which Act
are by fuch Records rather favoure
than difcouraged; and fome of the
Canonized, rather than punifhed in th
See of *Rome.*

F I N I S.

CPSIA information can be obtained at www.ICGtesting.com
Printed in the USA
LVOW121925090712

289368LV00012B/58/P